M000113563

Imitation Democracy

Imitation Democracy

The Development of Russia's
Post-Soviet Political System

Dmitrii Furman

Translated by Ian Dreiblatt

Foreword by Keith Gessen
Afterword by Tony Wood

VERSO

London • New York

This publication was effected under the auspices of the Mikhail Prokhorov Foundation Transcript Programme to Support Translations of Russian Literature

 transcript

This English-language edition published by Verso 2022
First published in Russian as *Dvizhenie po spirali* (Spiral Motion), Moscow 2010

1 3 5 7 9 10 8 6 4 2

Verso
UK: 6 Meard Street, London W1F 0EG
US: 388 Atlantic Avenue,, Brooklyn, NY 11217
versobooks.com

Verso is the imprint of New Left Books

ISBN-13: 978-1-78873-353-3
ISBN-13: 978-1-78873-356-4 (US EBK)
ISBN-13: 978-1-78873-355-7 (UK EBK)

British Library Cataloguing in Publication Data
A catalogue record for this book is available from the British Library

Library of Congress Cataloging-in-Publication Data
A catalog record for this book is available from the Library of Congress

Typeset by Biblichor Ltd, Scotland
Printed and bound by CPI Group (UK) Ltd, Croydon, CR0 4YY

Contents

Foreword by Keith Gessen   vii
Introduction   xv

1. **The Fall of the Soviet State and the Emergence of
   New Political Systems**   1
   1.1 The Path of Transformation   5
   1.2 The Unwalkable Path to Democracy   10
   1.3 For Russia, a Means of Direct Transition to
        Democracy in 1991 'Could Not Be Found'   14
   1.4 The Strengths and Weaknesses of the
        Democratic Movement   23
   1.5 One Liquidation for All, with Different
        Consequences for Each   41

2. **The Development of Russia's Political System**   45
   2.1 Conflict with the Parliament and Ratification of the
        Constitution   46
   2.2 The First Post-Soviet Presidential Elections   66
   2.3 The Succession Crisis   76
   2.4 Suppressing Separatism and Subordinating
        Regional Power   88
   2.5 The Submission of the 'Oligarchs' and the Media   92

2.6 The Creation of United Russia, the Movement toward a
Quasi-One-Party System, and the Establishment of
Control over Parliament   98
2.7 Politics as a Series of 'Special Operations' and the
Increasingly Strong Role of the Special Services   101
2.8 Ideological Quests   104
2.9 Russia 'Rises from Its Knees' and Faces Increasing
Confrontations with the West   108

3. 'The Golden Age': A Developed System   118
3.1 Putin's Second Term   120
3.2 Achieving Power's Greatest Possible Control over
Society and the 'Limits of the System's Growth'   126
3.3 What Could Have Frightened the President?   130

4. The Growth of Contradictions and the Movement toward
a Crisis of the Political System   134
4.1 Atrophy of Feedback Mechanisms   137
4.2 Social Mobility 'in the Bureaucratic Style'   139
4.3 The Only Ideology Is Guaranteeing Loyalty   143
4.4 The Crisis Is Sure to Come as a Surprise   146

5. In Place of a Conclusion: Possible Outcomes of the
Coming Crisis   151
5.1 The First Alternative: A Successful Transition to
Democracy   152
5.2 The Second Alternative: A Return to No-Alternative
Power and the Start of a New Cycle   156

Afterword by Tony Wood   159
Index   171

Foreword

Keith Gessen

I first started reading Dmitrii Furman while living in Moscow in 2008, after seeing a discussion of his work in an essay on Russia by Perry Anderson. I was immediately charmed and amazed. Furman, born in 1943, was part of the generation of intellectuals who had cheered on the fall of Communism and then watched as much of the former Soviet Union descended into anarchy and despair. Many in his generation of Russian liberals had thrown in their lot with the 1990s reforms, and in the aftermath of their failure had become crabby and defensive, blaming everyone but themselves. Others had retreated into their academic disciplines, focusing on Tolstoy or Byzantium; still others had taken up academic posts in the West. Furman moved in the exact opposite direction. During the Soviet era, he had been a comparativist scholar of religions, had written books on highly obscure topics, but perestroika pulled him into his country's present. In the post-Soviet era, he started producing a series of books and articles on the political development of the states of what had once been the Soviet Union. He was funny, shrewd, and morally unforgiving. He cleared away a vast edifice of selective memory and self-justification. He was unlike any Russian political observer that I had read.

The thing that Furman did, which others of his time and place for various reasons failed to do, was look at the other post-Soviet states: at Kyrgyzstan, Moldova, Kazakhstan, the Baltics. From this vantage, one could see that Russia, for all its uniqueness, was far from unique.

Somehow or other, while some of the post-Soviet states had established stable democracies, and others had established unstable ones, a select few (Kazakhstan, Uzbekistan, Turkmenistan, and Russia) had established what Furman called 'imitation democracies'. To varying degrees, the imitation democracies carried out the rituals of democracy and paid lip service to the will of the people, but actually gave the voters no real choice. Furman was not alone in defining a number of states in this way – the same period gave us the concept of 'competitive authoritarianism', and one theorist inside the Kremlin had even come up with the clunky term 'sovereign democracy' – but Furman's insight was about the instability of these regimes. This instability came to the fore during elections. It was alleged electoral fraud in Georgia, Ukraine, and Kyrgyzstan that brought about the Rose and Orange and Tulip Revolutions in those countries in 2003 and 2004 and 2005, and in the coming years, disputed elections would cause massive protests in a number of post-Soviet states, including Russia in 2011 and, much later, Belarus in 2020–1. Though the authorities knew that elections were fake, and though voters basically knew the same, somehow the simple act of going through with the ritual could sometimes infuse elections with meaning. Like many of Furman's observations, this one was both shrewd and useful.

Furman was unique among his liberal contemporaries for the absolute moral clarity with which he saw 1990s Russian liberalism. The story as it was told at the time (and even now, to some extent) was that the reforms were never given a chance, that Russian democracy was strangled in its cradle by Vladimir Putin and the resurgent KGB. Yeltsin, to many, remained a romantic figure, flawed but heroic, the man who stood on a tank to put the final nail into the Soviet Union; the real villain was Putin, whom Yeltsin had mistakenly entrusted with power, when he should have chosen someone else.

Furman saw through this. For one thing, he writes, Yeltsin, in comparative perspective, was hardly the dissident that he came to seem in the last few years of Soviet power. Looking at the other post-Soviet states, Furman notes that some, like Kazakhstan and Uzbekistan, simply transitioned their first secretaries into the presidency. But others, including Poland, Czechoslovakia, and Georgia, elected actual former anti-Communist dissidents, people who had spent time in prison under the Communists. Russia did something in between: Yeltsin was a member of the Politburo who had fallen out of favour and rebelled against the leadership. A kind of rebel angel of Communism, he seemed to many Russian anti-Communists like the best of both worlds; as it turned out, this was not the case.

The problem, for Furman, was that the 'democratic' movement which came to power in Russia in 1991 was always a minority inside the country. Yeltsin himself was briefly very popular, but the programmes of reforms and the dismantling of the USSR never had majority support. That did not mean it could not win; it could win, and it did. 'A vigorous, powerful minority', Furman writes, 'with a fortuitous leader', Yeltsin, 'could well rise to power, as it had in 1917 and as indeed it would again in 1991. What it by definition could not do was rise to power – let alone entrench itself firmly in power – through democratic means.' The Yeltsin government, elected during the Soviet period but ruling past it, lacked democratic legitimacy. Yet it had a great deal of moral certitude. Russia needed to be transformed, the liberal economists who accompanied Yeltsin to power believed, and fast. If that meant holding on to power through means that were not entirely legitimate – as Yeltsin, cheered on by the Moscow intelligentsia and the Clinton administration, held on to power through the 1996 election – so be it. 'Russia's democrats came to regard their own victory as utterly inseparable from that of democracy', Furman writes. 'There was simply no awareness of the straightforward and obvious notion that democracy is affirmed not through the victory of any one party – not even the most democratic – but rather through the cycle in which one party is defeated and an opposition . . . rises to replace it.'

This concept of a rotation in power was crucial to Furman. It was the ultimate test of a democracy. Many countries in the post-Soviet space had managed to do it – to hold an election in which the opposition actually won. Some, like Belarus and Azerbaijan, had managed to do it only once; others, like Ukraine and Georgia, a few times. But Russia had not ever managed to do it.

There was an important reason, according to Furman, that Yeltsin refused to give up the presidency. Yeltsin himself felt personally implicated in some of the actions he had undertaken as the head of a minority government, specifically the signing of the Belovezh Accords that dissolved the Soviet Union. Their legality was uncertain, and in their aftermath, Yeltsin could never give up power to the opposition for fear of what would happen to him. When he could no longer function as president, he had to hand power to a successor who could guarantee his legal and personal safety. It was not an anomaly or a terrible mistake that Yeltsin chose a former KGB agent to succeed him. In fact, it was perfectly logical. Writes Furman: 'The transfer of power from Yeltsin – a leader among "democrats", an associate of Sakharov's and in certain ways his successor, a man who had once had ample reason to fear the KGB – to a "KGB man" presents an "irony of history".' Sadly, it was not. The seeds for the rise of Putin were sown by the democrats of the early 1990s. That is what Furman saw.

Imitation Democracy: The Development of Russia's Post-Soviet Political System, in Ian Dreiblatt's deft and witty translation, is the first of Furman's books, and almost the first of any of his texts, to appear in English. (In 1981 the Soviet propaganda house Progress Publishers did issue his *Religion and Social Conflicts in the USA*, but it is hard to track down a copy.) Written in 2009 and published in 2010 as *Dvizhenie po spirali* (Spiral Motion), it is a remarkable account, step by step, detail by detail, of Russia's gradual descent into perdition. Furman begins by stating that, in effect, time is up for the 'transitionological' narrative. 'It has now been eighteen years since the fall of the USSR and the Communist system', he writes. 'That is a very long interval. All the countries that were actually transitioning to democracy over this period have managed to do so.' Russia has not. The question is why.

The fundamental reason, as we have said, is that the Yeltsin regime began as a minority regime in 1991. But still there would be many ironies, and even some potential off-ramps, in the years to come. Furman recounts the key events in the decade after Yeltsin came to power in 1991. He describes the dramatic stand-off with the Supreme Soviet in the fall of 1993 (a stand-off in which the red-brown alliance in parliament became a defender of Russia's constitutional order); the rise of Chechen separatism and its tragic aftermath; and the dramatic reelection of Yeltsin in 1996. Furman points out, as few others do, the commonality with other imitation democracies across the post-Soviet space, which also saw parliaments disbanded when they crossed the president. And he is alive to other possibilities, such as the brief period of hope, during the premiership and then presidential candidacy of Yevgeny Primakov, when it looked like Russia might actually see a transfer of power. But it was not the path that Yeltsin took. Anyone still nostalgic for the Yeltsin years will be well cured of that nostalgia by reading this book.

Throughout *Imitation Democracy*, you can see the traces of Furman's background as a scholar of religions. He places great emphasis on the cultural and historical background of the peoples he writes about. In a remarkable passage, he describes the many 'more or less plausible' stories various countries, from Ukraine to Kazakhstan to the Baltic states, tell about their pre-Soviet democratic histories. Russia lacks this history; it was, since the sixteenth century, the imperial oppressor, not the colonized oppressed. In the words of the historian Stephen Kotkin, 'It's been a long time since the Kingdom of Novgorod.' The formation of a viable democracy was always going to be a challenge.

Furman can sometimes seem either naïve or absolutist about democracy. For him, in these pages, a country either is or is not democratic, according to whether it allows for the consistent transfer of power to an opposition. And whether it is able to do this is largely determined by whether it has been democratic in the past. Democracy comes to seem a bit of a closed circle. There is less room in this view than one would want for the idea that a nominally democratic country can backslide. From the vantage point of 2022, given the state of Viktor Orbán's Hungary, for example, Furman's confidence in the Central European states seems premature. The same might be said of the state of democracy in the United States. Furman, writing still in the long wake of the Soviet collapse, believed that all countries were moving, inevitably, in the same direction, that is, toward democracy. In 2022, that belief seems less self-evident than it did ten years ago.

Furman, in his emphasis on electoral democracy, leaves some things out – chiefly, as his most eloquent English-language expositor Perry Anderson has written, economics and geopolitics. While Furman is keenly aware of what he calls the 'market romanticism' of the Russian reformers, he does not spend much time on the nature of the Soviet and post-Soviet economies and how these affected the prospects for democratic transition. He is also not that interested, again as Anderson points out, in Russia's position as a geopolitical subject – in its relations, for example, with NATO – or in its actual and imagined interests in the post-Soviet space.

Furman died of cancer at the age of seventy, in 2011. He did not live to see the large (but not large enough) Russian protests over the fraudulent Duma elections of 2011. He also did not live to see the much larger and more determined protests in Ukraine in 2013 and 2014, that brought down the government of Viktor Yanukovych and triggered the first Russian invasion of Ukraine. In Russia, the aftermath of both the 2011–12 protests and then the Ukraine invasion has been dramatically heightened repression against the tiny political opposition, non-governmental organizations, and journalists. These culminated in the attempted assassination, by poisoning, of the political activist Alexei Navalny in the summer of 2020. As I write, Russia has again, at much greater scale, invaded Ukraine.

I do not think Furman would have been surprised by these developments. Even while writing at the height of the relatively 'vegetarian' period of the tandemocracy, when Dmitrii Medvedev was temporarily president while Putin served as prime minister, he predicted that the system would not be able to reform itself. If Yeltsin could not safely transfer power to the opposition, then the likelihood of Putin being able to do so was that much less. The only way out was an acute crisis. 'We paid for the stability enjoyed by Russia's nineteenth-century autocracy, contrasting so starkly with the turbulent history of Western Europe, with the catastrophic events of 1917', Furman writes. 'It is very likely that the cost of the Putin era's stability and manageability will similarly be repaid through a coming period of chaos and collapse.'

For Furman this was a tragic possibility, but not one without hope. His image of a spiral, which gave the original Russian edition of this book its name, was one in which history advanced, but slowly, and with frequent retreats. One moved along the spiral toward freedom, often backsliding into authoritarianism and unfreedom, but then moved on again. The reason to read this wise and intelligent book and to think more deeply, and again, about what went wrong with Russia after 1991, is that there will likely someday be another chance to get it right.

Introduction

During the emergence and formation of the post-Soviet Russian state, a view of the new Russia as a society transitioning from the Soviet system to democracy and the market, 'from Communism to capitalism', prevailed uncontroversially over official rhetoric, opinion writing, and scholarship in both Russia and the West.[1] This understanding was only natural, considering that the dismantling of the Soviet system, as in all countries then emerging from Communism, was carried out under slogans of democracy and the free market. But if people had rejected Communism and proclaimed the goal of democracy, the question remains of what else besides democracy they might have transitioned to. Perhaps this transition proved slower and more laborious for countries like Russia and Kazakhstan than for the Czech Republic and Poland, but that all countries liberating themselves from Communism and declaring the goal of democracy were following a similar trajectory seemed beyond dispute.

This view of the Transitional character of society in post-Soviet Russia, as well as in other post-Communist countries, was, however, not just the simplest. It was also the most expedient, politically and psychologically. Post-Soviet rulers unendingly repeated the same idea: the period of transition cannot but be difficult, we cannot demand everything at once, a full-fledged democracy and market cannot be built in a year, we must be patient.[2] This idea of a difficult

---

1 See, e.g., Juan J. Linz and Alfred Stepan, *Problems of Democratic Transition and Consolidation* (Baltimore: John Hopkins University Press, 1996). For a critique of 'transitionology', *see* Stephen F. Cohen, *Failed Crusade* (New York: W. W. Norton, 2000).

2 Islam Karimov: 'We will arrive at the democracy you dream of. Additionally, we'll get there a little later than you do' (*Obshchaya Gazeta*, 10–17

transition to democracy and the market presented a kind of actual-
ization of the ancient archetype of an exodus from Egyptian bondage
to the promised land. In the early Soviet era, authorities had justified
their actions (and the masses, in turn, had justified the authorities'
actions) by arguing that struggle and deprivation were combatting
the burdensome legacies of tsarism and capitalism, that it would be
necessary to live first for a period in anticipation of socialism, and
then later, when it was announced that socialism had been built, with
happiness still yet to arrive, of Communism. In exactly the same way,
the legacy of Communism had to be defeated early in the post-Soviet
era, and hardships had to once again be endured until our arrival in a
new promised land. The idea that a difficult transitional period was
inevitable provided authorities and elites with a perfect excuse for
what they had done – an excuse they could present to themselves, to
the international community, and to their own people. There was
practically nothing that could not be explained in terms of the Transition: usual norms were suspended, and the well-known injunction
not to change horses in midstream was widely applied.

This view was convenient not only for post-Soviet leaders, but also
for the leaders and societies of the West. It supported the general
mood of optimism that had been created by perestroika and the fall of
Communism, enabling them to turn a blind eye to the obviously
undemocratic tendencies of post-Soviet states, which they chalked up
to the challenges of transition, thus easing their headaches. When

---

March 1994). Nursultan Nazarbayev: 'We can't simply leapfrog from where we
were yesterday into French- or American-style democracy; that's not how it
works' (*Nezavisimaya Gazeta*, 21 April 1994). And also: 'It took them 150, 200
years to achieve democracy. They want us to do it overnight?' (*Nezavisimaya
Gazeta*, 15 November 1995). Saparmurat Niyazov (Türkmenbaşy): 'We want
to create a secular, democratic state with a diversified, efficient economy, in
which all basic human rights are guaranteed: freedom of speech, of
conscience, of movement, freedom to choose one's place of residence, and
more. All of these freedoms observed. Right now, it is quite another matter
that during the transitional period the state must regulate activities in these
areas for the protection of our society itself' ('We Must Set the Rhythm of
Reforms for Ourselves: An interview with S. Niyazov' [in Russian], *Nezavisimaya Gazeta*, 20 October 1992).

post-Soviet leaders declared that the Transition would necessarily be difficult, Western leaders concurred in relief and gladness.[3] The West's broad support for Yeltsin and other 'pro-democratic' Russian leaders through many acts that were brazenly illegal and undemocratic was psychologically and morally possible only through a logic of 'the challenges of transition'. Clearly, the expediency and comfort this perspective offered to both post-Soviet and Western elites allowed its obvious conflict with reality to go unnoticed for a long time.

It has now been eighteen years since the fall of the USSR and the Communist system. That is a very long interval. All the countries that were actually transitioning to democracy over this period have managed to do so. Samuel P. Huntington wrote that democracy – a system in which winners alternate with losers, based on the free choice of an electorate operating under uniformly applied rules of the game – can establish itself as a norm only after two or three such rotations. But if we accept Huntington's perspective (which seems indisputable), we will have to acknowledge that the majority of post-Soviet countries, after nearly two decades, have failed to take even their first decisive steps down this path. Excluding the Baltics, in the rest of the post-Soviet space, there have been only five cases since 1991 of an opposition peacefully coming to power. Three of these did it in 1994 – Moldova[4] (a very peculiar development) once, Belarus once, and Ukraine twice (though the second Ukrainian rotation, marked by the Orange Revolution, can hardly be called 'peaceful and constitutional'). At the same time, the Belarusian rotation, which hypothetically might have marked the start of a transition to

---

3   Here is a perfectly grotesque example of such compromise. US senator Alan Cranston reportedly said, after a visit to Turkmenistan, sounding like Türkmenbaşy himself, 'Of course, you don't build a democratic state in a day. In America, we've been at it 200 years, and even here it isn't perfect. In my opinion, Turkmenistan is slowly but surely walking a path toward a democratic society and economic transition' (N. Zhukov, 'The Path toward Democracy Inspires Optimism' [in Russian], *Nezavisimaya Gazeta,* 10 September 1992).

4   On the development of Moldova, *see* Dmitrii Furman, 'Moldavian Moldavians and Moldavian Romanians', *Scientific Notebooks of the Institute of Eastern Europe* [in Russian] 2 (Moscow, 2008).

democracy, instead marked the electoral victory of Alexander Lukashenko and the creation of a rigid, change-resistant regime of 'no-alternative'[5] power that resembles Russia's. The Ukrainian one represented an attempt to create the same kind of regime, promptly washed away in the Orange Revolution. In no other countries, and certainly not in Russia, was there any peaceful, constitutional rotation at all. No opposition has ever come to power through peaceful, legal means.[6]

Nor is that all. If we could at least see in the development of these countries the approach of a first rotation – for example, if in the early 1990s, it had seemed out of the question for an opposition party here in Russia to come to power through constitutional means, yet it now seemed a more proximate possibility – then we might say that Russia and countries like it were moving in the same direction as those countries that have successfully made the transition to democracy, albeit more slowly, lagging in their development, which would still only be in its preliminary phase. But this is not the case. Over the course of our political evolution, the possibility of a peaceful, constitutional rotation of power has not only failed to grow more likely, it has grown less likely and, at present, has shrunk to zero. The logic by which the political systems of Russia and similar countries are developing is by no means one of gradually eliminating the figures inherited from Communism and moving toward a democratic model.

---

5   Throughout the text, Furman frequently uses the words *bezal'ternativnyj* and *bezal'ternativnost'*, which refer to elections incapable of producing actual rotations of power and are hard to render very precisely in English. 'Alternativeless' and 'alternativelessness' somewhat capture the flavour, as do 'uncontested' and 'uncontestedness'. For ease of reading, I have generally rendered them 'no-alternative' and 'no-alternative system'. —Trans.

6   There were, however, coups: in Georgia, a bloody one (to overthrow Zviad Gamsakhurdia) in 1991, and a bloodless one (the Rose Revolution) in 2003; in Azerbaijan in 1992 (the revolution of the Popular Front Party) and 1993 (the overthrow of Abulfaz Elchibey); the civil war in Tajikistan from 1992 to 1995; the coup in Kyrgyzstan in 2005 (the Tulip Revolution); a bloodless coup in Armenia in 1998 (the president's resignation in the face of an ultimatum from the *siloviks*); and a number of attempted others, both violent and bloodless.

On the contrary, we can rather say that as these systems have evolved, it is the emergent traces of democracy present during the brief period of actual transition from the late 1980s to the early 1990s that have been eliminated. We have, so to speak, 'moved along a spiral', with many characteristics of the Soviet system recapitulated in a gentler form. In its political orientation, Russia today (like Belarus, Kazakhstan, and comparable post-Soviet countries) is indisputably closer to late Soviet society than to Russia (or Belarus) at the end of perestroika and the start of the post-Soviet era.

Of course, in the longer view, all societies are in transition from one thing to another. For example, the USSR, viewed in the context of the history of the Russian people, could be considered the transitional phase between an autocratic and a post-Soviet Russia. Within certain limits, such an approach may even bear fruit – it could productively reveal how certain elements of the post-Soviet system were formed within the Soviet one. Still, its total inadequacy is apparent. Russians, and other peoples who 'joined' the USSR, in fact 'passed' the Soviet period, and then 'left' it (different than they'd entered), continuing to live and evolve. But the USSR itself was destroyed. The USSR had been a living organism, functioning and developing according to its own natural patterns, completing its own life cycle. We cannot understand Soviet history and its logic purely through a model of transition; the same is true for post-Soviet Russian history. In the broader historical perspective, of course, this is a transitional society. The people of Russia have 'joined' the post-Soviet system just as they once 'joined' the Soviet system, and they will exit it substantively changed. But at the same time, post-Soviet Russia is an entire living organism, functioning and developing according to its own logic, advancing through its own unfinished life cycle. In one sense, Russia has already long since transitioned: it has developed its own comparatively stable political and social system, albeit one strikingly different from those found in democratic countries (even in Europe's post-Communist countries, with the sole exception of Belarus).

This is not a system based on uniform rules of the game by which various political forces can prevail and rise to power, but one in which those already in power always win, and the rules of the game can be changed at the whim of these constant winners. Democratic and legal norms and institutions here play the role of decoration, the camouflage that conceals a different, authoritarian configuration of power. But unlike under other forms of authoritarianism, here power finds its basis neither in the physical force of the army as in military dictatorships, nor in ancient tradition as in absolute monarchies, and the democratic camouflage is a requisite, immanent element of the system.

In fundamental distinction to democratic systems,[7] the Russian system is clearly of a type with a number of others that emerged in the post-Soviet space after the collapse of the USSR, in which a façade of democracy and constitutionality coexists with personal power held by no-alternative presidents who rule for as long as they like (most often, they like to rule for life) and hand power to whomever they wish. In the following study, we will see many features shared by the Russian and other post-Soviet systems, and the presence within them of a shared structure and logic of development, which speaks to their belonging to a shared 'species'.[8] But this

---

7   I do not say 'to *Western* democratic institutions'. Democracy has long since broken the confines of the West. The democracies of South Korea, Japan, and India are of similar structure to those in Western countries. And the systems of Syria, Egypt, and Uzbekistan are not some kind of 'Eastern democracy'; rather, they are simply systems of a totally different kind.

8   Among Russian political scientists, there is a tendency to exaggerate the peculiarities of Russia's post-Soviet development. We have practically no comparisons of the Russian system and its evolution with the systems of other post-Soviet countries and their evolutions. Such a study would undoubtedly reveal the common 'species' represented by most of them. This shortcoming haunts even the otherwise exemplary work of Lilia Shevtsova, in which Russia is compared with various other countries (Brazil, South Africa); it seems to me we need comparisons with more kindred regimes, like Kazakhstan or Belarus. (See also Lilia Shevtsova, *The Regime of Boris Yeltsin* [in Russian] [Moscow, 1999], 502–9.) In *Putin: Russia's Choice*, Richard Sakwa compares Vladimir Putin's policies with those of a huge range of figures, from Deng Xiaoping to Charles de Gaulle, but not with those who have faced similar problems and chosen similar solutions to Putin's, like Nazarbayev or Aliyev. This is hard to explain. If it were found only among

'species' is distributed across an area much wider than the post-Soviet sphere. Analogous systems have existed, and continue to exist, in many countries of the erstwhile 'third world'.[9] Just as it is impossible to show any fundamental, 'species'-level distinctions between post-Soviet Russia and post-Soviet Kazakhstan or Belarus, it is equally impossible to show such differences between Russia (or Kazakhstan) and Algeria, Tunisia, Egypt, or the regime Hugo Chávez is building in Venezuela.[10] These systems, which have, in my view, been vastly undertheorized, share no self-designation (indeed, they are all simply 'democracies'; in Russia, the closest thing to a self-designation is 'sovereign democracy', a term that bubbled up from the depths of the Putin administration but has never been

---

Russian authors, it might be explained as some kind of natural 'Russo-centrism' or an 'imperial complex' ('How can we compare great Russia with an outfit like Uzbekistan!'); but how can we explain its prevalence among Western authors?

I attempt a systematic comparison of the political development of various post-Soviet countries in my article 'The General and the Particular in the Political Development of Russia and Other CIS Countries', in *Paths of Russian Post-Communism: Essays* [in Russian], ed. Marian Lipman and Andrey Ryabov (Moscow: Carnegie Moscow Center, 2007).

9   Such regimes acquire a relatively 'mass' character only after decolonization. Thus the collapse of the USSR broadened their range of distribution. Earlier analogues, of course, can be found in the history of Latin America, where we see, far earlier than in other countries, a combination of the absence or extreme weakness of ideological alternatives to democracy and the inability of societies to live under conditions of democracy.

10   The very leaders of these regimes have observed their close kinship with Russia's. In one interview, Hosni Mubarak said, 'Western-style democracy is hardly a single standard applicable to every time and place. Every individual society has its own distinctive and inherent characteristics growing out of the conditions under which its own people live. Ongoing chatter about the urgency of spreading Western democracy turns a blind eye to this . . . I remember hearing President Putin speak of "Russian democracy", meaning exactly what I'm discussing here. Every society has its own experience building democracy. The foundations of this experience should be laid in the specific conditions under which that society exists and operates' (Hosni Mubarak, 'Friends Should Always Be Candid' [in Russian], *Rossiyskaya Gazeta*, 23 March 2008).

officially adopted); they have no clear name in political science. They are often called 'managed democracies' or 'imitation democracies'. (I will use the latter term, but I do not do so insistently. What matters is not the terminology, but the clarity with which we understand this kind of system.)

If Russia's post-Soviet system belongs to a species alongside its Kazakh and Belarusian – not to mention Algerian, Tunisian, and so on – counterparts, it is certainly a markedly different species from its Soviet predecessor. The Soviet system, too, was marked by elements of 'imitation democracy' – legal and democratic camouflage for the actual mechanisms of governance: the USSR was 'socialist', but a democracy; 'bound forever to the great Rus'', yet a federated republic; run by elections, but by no-alternative elections confined to such matters as would not disturb the absolute power of the CPSU, under a constitution enumerating all rights and freedoms. In 'people's democracies' there was even more such democratic camouflage – many of them were even quasi-multiparty systems! But these elements played some limited role in all Communist systems. The Soviet and other Communist systems were based in an ideology of totalitarian dogma that conceptualized its differences from democratic systems in terms of the distinction between true, socialist democracy and bourgeois pseudo-democracy. The maintenance of stability in such systems therefore required total ideological control by the state.

As I will attempt to demonstrate, however, while the Soviet and post-Soviet systems share much in the logic by which they function and develop (notwithstanding many additional ideological and other differences), in the logic by which the post-Soviet Russian system and the democratic systems of post-Communist countries in Central Europe and the Baltics have developed, little or nothing is shared, despite the absence of clear ideological distinctions. If we may expand the analogy to biological classifications (which I find apt), Russia's Soviet and post-Soviet systems share not a species but a genus.

The similarities between our system and others do not, of course, make them identical. Every system of imitation democracy is in its own way unique, and the Russian system has many idiosyncrasies (it should suffice for now to point to Medvedev and Putin's present 'tandemocracy', which is completely atypical of post-Soviet imitation democracies) deriving from the particular character of Russian culture, the historical circumstances under which the post-Soviet Russian state emerged and developed, and a slew of other factors. Its whole development reflects not the mere unfolding in time of immutable, permanent characteristics, but a living history. Membership in a genus and species, and the shared patterns of function and life cycle that implies, can hardly negate the uniqueness of an individual specimen with its own fate and narrative.

The aim of this work is to demonstrate the logic by which the post-Soviet Russian system emerged, developed, and, in the end, will decline, noting features it holds in common with both the Soviet system that preceded it and with other, comparable systems, as well as those features peculiar and distinctive to it alone. Accordingly, the work is divided into five sections: (1) the origins of the system, (2) the development of the system, (3) the characteristics of the developed system, (4) the emergence of contradictions within the system and its progression toward a 'final crisis', and (5) the possible outcomes of this crisis.

1

The Fall of the Soviet State and the Emergence of New Political Systems

All the post-Soviet states (and their political systems) rose from the ashes of the unified Soviet state (and its unified Communist system) at practically the same moment and under very comparable circumstances. (This makes the post-Soviet space an ideal subject for researchers in political science, who nonetheless have largely ignored it.) When we compare it with the fall of the Russian Empire, and the 'all-against-all' civil war that filled the vacuum left by the autocracy, the fall of the Soviet state, once so indestructible a monolith, seems light, bloodless. This owes mainly to two factors.

First, by the time the USSR fell, the age of forceful, utopian, and even quasi-religious ideologies evoking fanatical allegiance had become a thing of the past.

Over the years of its total domination, Communist ideology had lost nearly all of its vitality and force; in its 'reformist' iteration, it was almost wholly incapable of anchoring Gorbachev's perestroika (despite being the only ideology that could possibly have done so), nor could it meaningfully oppose the rising tide of anti-Communism. Totalitarian ideologies are in constant struggle with visible dangers: external enemies, protest movements, revisionists, dissidents. But when conformist behaviour conceals a loss of faith in them, there is nothing they can do. The USSR housed several Soviet missiles for every potential enemy missile. For every dissident, a thousand KGB and tens of thousands of CPSU members. But the Communists themselves had long since abandoned their faith in Communist ideology, by this point formalized into dogma. Gorbachev's injunctions to go 'back to Lenin', to 'socialism with a human face', his yearning to uncover some constitutive humanism in the origins of Communist ideology, elicited no response except insofar as they offered a convenient form of protest, and then only so long as people feared and believed in the durability of Communism, and remained afraid to express themselves openly. In order to implement his plan to democratize the Soviet state while preserving its ideological herit-age, Gorbachev needed a certain number of people who understood his calls not as mere rhetoric, but as literal and sincere. These people never appeared.[1]

No sooner had fear of the regime subsided than the system, already weakened from within, began to collapse. The expression 'clay-footed colossus' could hardly be more applicable. The middle-class intelligentsia, dreaming of free and secure lives ('as in the West'), quickly became revolutionized, compensating for their former conformism and opportunism with a radicalism that the conditions of perestroika had made safe as they turned on Gorbachev, now seen as insufficiently radical and decisive. With an ease for which it is difficult to find any historical parallel, those atop the party and state made the pivot from the ideology of Communism to one of democracy and markets (which did allow them largely to

---

1   The question arises: What would 'the success of perestroika' have looked like? Clearly, it could not have meant the actual, full democratization of the USSR, with rotations into power of different political forces. The best fate perestroika might have hoped for was to see the CPSU transformed into a party ideologically based on a 'Marxist-Leninist reformation', the democratic and humanistic reading of Marxism-Leninism that Gorbachev espoused at the start of perestroika (and which had been earlier the ideology of the Prague Spring). Such a party could operate under democratic (or relatively demo-cratic) conditions, remaining the no-alternative party of power for a long time, with the opposition of a handful of small, radical parties – something between Mexico before Vicente Fox and the Indian National Congress. Such a situation could, in theory, have provided a certain measure of stability, though in the end it should still produce a crisis. I think this would have offered a far better course to the post-Soviet republics than those they actually followed, enabling them to avoid 'decompression sickness' and sidestep emergent forms of authoritarianism. But to implement this would have required a significantly more forceful presence by Marxist-Leninist ideology – something like what existed in the 1960s.

preserve their social position). When, after the dismantling and outlawing of the Communist Party of the Soviet Union, the Communist Party of the Russian Federation[2] was created, practically none of the former Soviet leadership joined. Many party leaders even became harsh anti-Communists (perhaps the most grotesque example being the transformation into a virulent anti-Communist and anti-Marxist of Aleksandr Yakovlev, erstwhile ideological director of the CPSU's Central Committee). No real equivalent of the White movement emerged; practically no one remained who was willing to fight for the CPSU and USSR. As Tatyana and Valery Solovei write, 'Russia's marshals and generals surrendered the country exactly as a sergeant surrenders his guard.'[3]

On the other hand, no new ideologies of anti-Communism or anti-Communist totalitarian utopianism emerged – they were essentially absent from the de-ideologized culture then prevailing. The goal of revolutionary anti-Communist movements was not the achievement of some ideal society, some heaven on earth in whose name to give one's life and shed rivers of strangers' blood. Rather, it was the attainment of a global 'norm'. No longer was there any group analogous to the Bolsheviks, the Social Democrats, or the anarchists, those who had strived to make Russia a beacon to all humanity, the world's first truly liberated territory. Now there were only 'democrats', striving to make Russia part of 'the civilized world'. There were elements of utopianism in the ideology of the anti-Communist movements, since the 'civilized world' was taking on utopian resonances in people's minds, and fanatics for democracy and anti-Communism emerged, perhaps best explained with the ironic label *demshiza* – that

---

2   The CPRF's ideology is by no means comparable to Gorbachev's 'socialism with a human face'. The Marxist component is negligible. Its ideology is rather one of populist nostalgia for the 'good old days'. On the ideology of the CPRF and other post-Soviet Communist parties, *see* D. B. Urban, 'Communist Parties of Russia, Ukraine, and Belarus (The Unsuccessful Quest for Unity in Diversity)', in *Belarus and Russia: Societies and States* [in Russian], ed. Dmitrii Furman (Moscow, 1998).

3   Tatyana Solovei and Valery Solovei, *A Failed Revolution* [in Russian] (Moscow, 2009), 279.

is, 'democracy schizophrenia'. Still, the utopianism and fanaticism on display paled in comparison to those of the early twentieth century. The ultimate powerlessness of Communist ideology and the weakness of the new revolutionary utopianism made this conflict practically bloodless.

The second reason for the relative ease with which the Communist system and the unified country collapsed was the federative character of the USSR. At first, this had been a fictitious federativity, albeit one with a dogmatized ideological significance. But it gradually began to accumulate real meaning. In the republics, systems of power began to take shape that were capable of functioning without the Union centre, and the borders between the various republics were crisply defined. Under perestroika, which sought to load the forms of Soviet rule with democratic content, the republics began to swiftly increase in independence, ultimately leading to the collapse of the larger Union.

The impotence of Communist ideology, the mass exodus from it of the Communist elite, and the weakness of the utopian, quasi-religious elements in anti-Communist ideology spared the USSR any real bloodshed between Communists and their opponents. But primitive, elemental nationalism remains a force that can push people to heroism or to atrocity. During the collapse of Yugoslavia, it was not between Communists and anti-Communists that wars raged, but rather between various ethnic groups. Similarly, during the fall of the USSR, blood was spilled primarily not in ideological conflicts but in ethnic ones (the Nagorno-Karabakh war; skirmishes with separatists in Russia, Moldova, and Georgia; the Ossetian-Ingush conflict), as well as the Kyrgyz-Tajik conflict, which was regional and subethnic but only mildly tinged with ideological concerns.

Nonetheless, the existence of Soviet republics with their systems of power and borders facilitated the downfall of the USSR. The most devastating conflicts would have been between Russia and neighbouring republics over territories with sizable Russian populations; these were largely avoided. The ethnic bloodshed that accompanied the fall of the Soviet Union was on a completely different scale from the war of all against all that sprang up in 1917 and ended only with the establishment of the Communist government. 'The greatest geo-political catastrophe of the century', as Vladimir Putin called the fall of the USSR, was surprisingly swift and easy.

1.1 The Path of Transformation

While the USSR was collapsing, processes of socio-political trans-formation, revolutionary in their significance but relatively bloodless in their execution, took place differently in different republics. In some (Turkmenistan, Kazakhstan, Uzbekistan), former party bosses and the old elite of the nomenklatura continued to rule, changing their ideological clothing without any particular issue and success-fully guiding their countries from Communism to imitation democracy and clan capitalism. The role of spontaneous anti-Communist movements was minimal. In other republics, affairs developed more violently and national-democratic movements rose to power, leading to significant vertical mobility in the political sphere. The models for transition from Communism to post-Communism varied widely. Nonetheless, all fifteen of these newly minted countries proclaimed the same goal: the creation of democratic societies with market economies.

It was the only goal they could have proclaimed. The contempo-rary world simply no longer houses any other viable, 'serious' ideologies that can offer a socio-political alternative to democracy or advance an alternative mode of political legitimization (with the highly dubious exception of Islamic fundamentalism). Here lies a primary difference between the situations of 1991 and 1917, when there were a range of ideological alternatives to democracy, from proto-fascism to anarchism. Today, democracy has come to be seen as a modern global norm, the appeal to its principles universal and even 'compulsory'.[4] This appeal to democratic principle became even

---

4 Undemocratic regimes positioning themselves as alternatives to demo-cracy are rudimentary formations in the contemporary world. These are either traditionalist regimes preserved under particularly favourable circumstances,

more unavoidable under the conditions of struggle against, and the overthrow of, any existing undemocratic system.

With the collapse of the USSR, slogans about democracy and 'human rights' became the only language viable for any, or practically any, political actors to use anywhere in the post-Soviet space. They have continued using it through the present. In the principles and goals they proclaimed, or even constitutionally enshrined, we see only minor (if any) differences between true democracies and obvious nondemocracies.[5] An identical democratic lexicon is deployed by

---

like Saudi Arabia and certain other Arab monarchies, as well as Swaziland and Bhutan, or Nepal until quite recently, or equally rudimentary Communist regimes, like Cuba and North Korea, not to mention, for all their economic achievements, Vietnam and the People's Republic of China. Both these and others may persist for some time, but they are not models to be emulated (the PRC has seen impressive economic development, but its political system could not function elsewhere) and are unable to enlarge their areas of dispersion, which in fact are shrinking. The overwhelming majority of modern systems are either actual or imitation democracies. Open military dictatorships appear as (and actually are) temporary regimes, created by extraordinary circumstances and transitioning either to actual democracy (the army retreats, elections are held) or to imitation democracies (a military dictator organizes 'managed' elections and emerges as a 'democratically elected president').

5 Note how post-Soviet states define themselves constitutionally (see *The Constitutions of CIS and Baltic States* [in Russian] [Moscow, 1999]): 'The Azerbaijani state is a lawful, democratic, secular, unitary republic' (p. 26); 'The Republic of Armenia is a sovereign, democratic, lawful, social state' (p. 25); 'The Republic of Belarus is a unitary, democratic, social, lawful state' (p. 118); 'The political structure of the state of Georgia shall take the form of a democratic republic' (p. 164); 'The Republic of Kazakhstan avows itself a democratic, secular, lawful, and social state whose highest values are the human being, his life, his rights, and his freedoms' (p. 102); 'The Kyrgyz Republic is a sovereign, unitary, democratic republic' (p. 246); 'The Republic of Moldova is a democratic, lawful state' (p. 290); 'The Russian Federation – Russia – is a democratic, federal, lawful state with a republican form of government' (p. 338); 'The Republic of Tajikistan is a sovereign, democratic, legal, secular, and unitary state' (p. 384); 'Turkmenistan is a democratic, legal, and secular state' (p. 412); 'Uzbekistan is a sovereign democratic republic' (p. 440); 'Ukraine is a sovereign democratic social lawful state' (p. 474); 'Latvia is an independent democratic republic' (p. 534); 'The Lithuanian state is

Nazarbayev,[6] Lukashenko,[7] Azerbaijan's Aliyev dynasty,[8] Islam Karimov,[9] Emomali Rahmon,[10] and even the late and grotesquely authoritarian Saparmurat Niyazov, the 'Türkmenbaşy' who erected golden statues of himself and renamed the months of the calendar after himself and his parents.[11] Not a single leader of any CIS state has ever disavowed democracy or tried to pass something off as an alternative model.[12] With even Turkmenistan proclaiming democracy

---

an independent democratic republic' (p. 554); 'Estonia is a self-governing and independent democratic republic' (p. 600).

6   'Our goal is to establish Kazakhstan as a democratic, secular, lawful, and social state whose highest values are the human being, his life, his rights, and his freedoms.' 'Democracy cannot just be declared – it must be won through suffering' (*Kazakhstanskaya Pravda*, 1 February 2003).

7   'Today it is precisely in Belarus that the most democratic process in the world has been started' ('A. Z. Lukashenko to Address the Upper Chamber of the National Assembly' [in Russian], 10 June 1997).

8   'The leader of our republic, having spelled out in considerable detail the successful reforms carried out in Azerbaijan based on the experience of European transitions, emphasized that human rights have been established in our country, freedom of speech and the press guaranteed, a multiparty system created. He stressed that democratic reforms will continue into the future' (lib.aliyev-heritage.org).

9   Islam Karimov: 'Our goal is to build an open, lawful, democratic state' (*Nezavisimaya Gazeta*, 3 June 2002).

10   Emomali Rahmon: 'For Tajikistan, the answer is clear: the future belongs to democracy within sovereign state borders, and to the democratization of international political and economic relations . . . Our own experience confirms that today, all nations are ready for democracy, and all peoples accept it. The values of Asian peoples are the same as those of Europeans, Americans, and Africans' (un.org/russian/ga).

11   'We want to create a secular, democratic state with a diversified, efficient economy, in which all basic human rights are guaranteed: freedom of speech, of conscience, of movement, freedom to choose one's place of residence, and more' (' "We Must Determine the Pace of Reform for Ourselves": An Interview with S. Niyazov' [in Russian], *Nezavisimaya Gazeta*, 20 October 1992).

12   Naturally, oppositions in these countries (to whatever degree they exist) are oppositions to presidential authoritarianism, advancing slogans in favour of democracy (with the possible exception of the most radical Islamists in the opposition factions in Muslim states). Thus, in countries where presidents have

during the collapse of Soviet power, one can hardly imagine Russia, a more developed country with a more European orientation, over-throwing Communism under any slogans besides those of democracy, nor proclaiming anything but democracy on completing that overthrow. And for all the embitterment of political struggle in Russia, practically everyone engaged in that struggle appealed to democracy,[13] deploying (as indeed they still do) 'democratic language' – the orchestrators of the 1991 coup;[14] the leaders of the parliamentary party during the constitutional crisis of 1993; Aleksandr Rutskoy[15] (who called for the creation of a 'Communists for Democracy' faction) and Ruslan Khasbulatov,[16] both Communists;[17]

---

ruled from 1990 to the present and where there is either no opposition or only underground and 'semiunderground' opposition, we find no ideological opponents of democracy, either in power or among those seeking it.

13   Of all Russia's major political figures, only Zhirinovsky allows himself to speak in direct opposition to democracy. Still, it is difficult to understand what Zhirinovsky stands for; he labelled his own party 'Liberal Democratic', and at its March 1990 constituent assembly proclaimed, 'The primary goal of the Liberal Democratic Party of the Soviet Union is the construction of a de-ideologized, lawful state' ('An Experience Researching Recent History' [in Russian] *UFO* 84, no. 2 [1990]: 116). Authentic 'antidemocrats' of the fascist persuasion, like Aleksandr Barkashov's Russian National Unity, occupy a highly marginal position.

14   From the State Committee on the State of Emergency's 'Appeal to the Soviet People': 'Stomping the tender shoots of democracy, extremist forces have emerged . . . Before our very eyes, all the democratic institutions the people's will has created are being robbed of their weight and efficacy . . . We stand for truly democratic processes, for the consistent implementation of reforms' (og.com.ua).

15   'Today, the strength of Russia's young democracy, of Russian parliamentarianism, is being tested.' Statement by acting president of the Russian Federation Aleksandr Rutskoy, 23 September 1993 (Aleksandr Rutskoy, *Bloody Autumn* [in Russian] [Moscow, 1995], 62).

16   From Khasbulatov's last speech to the deputies, with the building already under siege: 'I would like to emphasize our firm commitment to genuine democratic reforms in both the political reorganization of the state and the sphere of economic life' (Ruslan Khasbulatov, *The Great Russian Tragedy* [in Russian] [Moscow, 1994], 335).

17   Zyuganov: 'What interests everyone today is a triumph of civilized democracy, reliable and accountable. The right and the left, the Westernists

of course, Boris Yeltsin, along with his supporters; and the self-proclaimed 'only real democrat' Vladimir Putin[18] and his successor, the even greater democrat Dmitry Medvedev.[19] Public opinion polling routinely shows a significant majority of the country in favour of democracy, and only a visible minority – which has no discernible alternative to offer – against it.[20]

---

and the *pochvenniks*, the conservatives and the liberals' (Gennady Zyuganov, *Lessons from My Life* [in Russian] [Moscow, 1997], 370). Also Zyuganov: 'I want you to know our true condition and to understand that among you are the last defenders of free speech and thought, of human rights. There is no one else in Russia to defend these democratic values' (utro.ru).

18   Vladimir Putin, when asked whether 'we will seek a distinctive path forward for Russia', replied, 'There's no need to look for any path forward. We already have the path. It's the path of democratic development' (Vladimir Putin, *From the First Person* [in Russian] [Moscow, 2000], 155). Speaking in the mid-aughts at the Valdai Discussion Club, Putin said, 'The foundations of Russia's political and economic system are in full compliance with international standards. If we accept that political system, it means electoralism, a real multiparty system' (rg.ru).

19   In his article 'Forward, Russia!' [in Russian] Medvedev even avers that, in some undetermined Russian future, 'parties and their coalitions will form the federal and regional executive bodies, and not vice versa, making nominations for the head of state, regional directors, local government' (gazeta.ru).

20   Thus, according to data from the Levada Center, in 2008, 62% of Russians believed Russia needed democracy, while only 20% opposed it. But this number may be misleading – within that 62%, 13% supported democracy of the precise kind practiced by the USSR, and another 45% supported democracy 'suited to the national qualities and peculiarities of Russia'. Of course, 'democracy suited to the national qualities and peculiarities of Russia' may mean something as far from actual democracy as 'socialist democracy'. And 60% understood 'democracy' to mean, more than anything else, 'a high standard of living across the population'; meanwhile, only 31% understood it to mean control over the application of power; 12% the separation of powers; 8% the absence of state control over mass media. In 2008, answering the question, 'What is democracy?' the answer most frequently chosen (47%) was: 'Economic prosperity for the country'. It is not surprising that 54% believed democracy was developing in Russia (see *Public Opinion – 2008 Yearbook* [in Russian] [Moscow, 2008], 22–4). But although these data do not demonstrate real support for democratic values, they do indicate the absence of concrete alternatives to democracy and the ubiquity of 'democratic language'.

But with such near-unanimous support for democracy, one cannot help asking why, of all the post-Soviet nations proclaiming identical democratic principles and goals, only the Baltic states have, from the beginning, actually pursued the path of democracy. Why have Russia and the other post-Soviet countries taken off in so markedly nondemocratic a direction?

1.2 The Unwalkable Path to Democracy

I do not think words like 'demagoguery', 'hypocrisy', 'lies', and so forth describe those who proclaimed democracy while in fact creating systems of imitation democracy. It would, of course, be naïve to take their assurances of a commitment to democracy at face value, to suppose that the use of such language by Türkmenbaşy, Karimov, Nazarbayev, Zyuganov, the conspirators of 1991, Yeltsin, and Putin reflects a deep faith in democracy and the resolve to build it up. But it would be no less naïve to believe that they knowingly lied, privately thinking the opposite of everything they were saying in public. It is rare to find either deliberate mendacity or deep conviction in anyone, and between these poles there exists a vast continuum of more or less unthinking utterances that have become widely accepted and expedient. Without exactly lying, a person might easily fail to consider the precise meaning of these phrases and the direction they must eventually lead in – especially a person with many more pressing matters to consider.[21]

---

21 Likewise, we cannot straightforwardly write off the official rhetoric of the late Soviet Union as, simply, so much 'lying'. After the fall of the CPSU and the USSR, those who had changed their ideological attire faced the dilemma of how to explain this change in appearance to themselves and others. Their explanations were of two kinds. The first follows an 'insight' model. The person simply claims that he absolutely believed what he said before the period of 1989–91 and somewhere along the line had a sudden 'insight'. The second might be called the 'Stierlitz' model – a person claims he has been playing the long game, so to speak, pretending to be a Communist for cover while weakening the Communist system from within. Obviously,

In life, as in history, we are constantly confronted by the realization that the acceptance of norms and principles – and not just unthinking, passing acceptance, but even sincere, knowing acceptance – has little to do with whether one adheres to them. An official who accepts a bribe is by no means a 'principled supporter of bribery'. Such a person may in fact harbour dreams of a society wholly free of such corruption. He just needs money, and the bribe is hard to refuse. (All the more so if he lives in a society where bribes are commonly paid and received, where if he staunchly refuses the bribe, he will come across as some sort of curiosity, while accepting the bribe leads to no unpleasantness at all.) For that matter, the entrepreneur paying the bribe may well be a firm believer in legally regulated free markets, one who simply in the present moment needs to achieve some concrete goal. And in precisely the same way, the creation of a regime of no-alternative power, under which the opposition cannot rise to high office – or possibly even exist at all – does not in the least require leadership ideologically opposed to democracy.

The process of transition to democracy contains a paradox: such a transition is inseparable from the possibility of the electoral defeat and removal from office of those who rose to power under the banner of democracy. The most important tool for the establishment of

---

both of these grotesquely exaggerate and rationalize a dynamic process that is mostly unconscious or semiconscious. [Max Otto von Stierlitz was the name adopted by Maksim Isayev, a fictional Soviet superspy, while operating undercover in Nazi Germany in a series of popular Soviet novels written by Yulian Semyonov beginning in the early sixties. —Trans.]

Communist figures who had spoken of the advantages of socialism, socialist democracy, the struggle for peace, etc., had not been 'lying' – that is, they had not privately believed what they were saying to be untrue. Only very few realized that what they were saying was false, and that they were, therefore, lying. But we can see that this was not an article of deep faith for them in the very ease with which they abandoned Communist ideology and transitioned to an ideology of democracy and the market. Their remarks seem to exist somewhere in the middle of a continuum running from outright lies to total candour. The same can be said of the democratic remarks made by leaders in the post-Soviet era. To put it simply, Yeltsin, Putin, Nazarbayev, and the others became democrats in exactly the same way they had once been Communists.

democracy is not the ability to triumph in the struggle for power, but the ability to admit defeat and relinquish power. But it is never desirable to fall from power, and if doing so can be avoided by violating constitutional norms 'just a little', the opportunity proves very hard to resist.

Moreover, such a ruler may not only support democracy but be sincerely convinced (to convince himself) that everything he undertakes is precisely in the name of democracy, lest 'irresponsible demagogues' rise to power and destroy it. Here is how Boris Yeltsin framed his own decision to dissolve the parliament: 'The president is formally violating the Constitution, even taking anti-democratic measures, in dissolving the parliament – to assure the preservation of democracy and legality in the country. The parliament is defending the Constitution in order to overthrow the legally elected president and establish a Soviet system throughout. How entangled we are in all these contradictions!'[22] I am certain Yeltsin truly believed what he said – that he was dissolving the parliament to preserve democracy – just as Putin believed that he was the 'real democrat', and even as Türkmenbaşy believed he was building a nation of laws. Authoritarian post-Soviet systems were built not by lying, power-mad villains, nor by secret 'supporters of authoritarianism', but by the most ordinary people.

Just as a ruler's acceptance of democratic ideology and use of democratic rhetoric do not in themselves constrain him, given the opportunity, from flaunting democratic norms to tighten his grip on power, so too does the absence of any ideological alternatives to democracy in a given society, and the universal quality of democratic rhetoric, mean nothing about whether those in that society live under an actual system of democracy, as we can see in a great many examples. Democracy requires more than the acceptance of democratic platitudes, however sincere, and more too than an abstract desire to 'live as those in the civilized world do'. It requires a certain psychological and moral basis, a general readiness to follow constitutionally

---

22   Boris Yeltsin, *Notes of a President* [in Russian] (Moscow, 1994), 361. Published in English as *The Struggle for Russia* (New York: Crown, 1994).

enshrined rules of the game, not only when one wins (which is fairly easy) but also when one loses (which can be far more difficult). This presupposes a high level of morality, respect for the law, and tolerance – primarily, of course, among those in power, but by no means exclusively so. If the opposition lacks these qualities, the ruler will naturally tend to tighten his grip on power, and his own justifications for violating the 'rules of the game' will grow stronger and more elaborate. (It is clear, for example, that Yeltsin would have had a much harder time justifying himself in 1993 had Barkashov and Makashov's followers not been among the defenders of the parliament.)[23] The rules must be accepted by all players of the game and by society as a whole, which must 'encourage' adherence to them and 'punish' deviations from them.

A society's development contributes to the gradual formation of the cultural, psychological, and moral base that democracy requires, a process that in various countries can be either facilitated or hampered by the peculiarities of local cultural traditions. But notwithstanding a very few Western countries – the first to come to democracy thanks to the special character of their cultures – this is everywhere a slow and painful process. It is almost unheard of for democracy to be established and take root on the first try. Suffice it to recall how long was the path leading from the first 'demands' for democracy to its ultimately taking root even in Western European countries like France, Germany, and Italy, now prime examples of stable democracies. There were many bumps in the roads they travelled.

The general climate of the world today is vastly more favourable to the establishment of democracies than it was during the nineteenth or early twentieth centuries. And certain of the elements that a democratic base requires were present in the republics of the USSR. Clearly, though, they did not suffice. Of the fifteen former Soviet republics that declared democracy during the fall of the USSR, the

---

23   Aleksandr Barkashov and Albert Makashov are well-known Russian nationalist politicians of the far right, both involved in the defence of the White House in 1993. —Trans.

only ones in which political forces rotated into power and transitioned to actual democracy were those most like Western Europe:
protestant Estonia and Latvia and Catholic Lithuania, places that had
some experience of independent and democratic development. And
even then, it happened only after the removal from political life in
Estonia and Latvia of post-war foreign interlopers. For the majority
of post-Soviet states, which lacked this culture and this experience,
such a transition simply proved too difficult. Indeed, it proved too
difficult for Russia.

1.3 For Russia, a Means of Direct Transition to Democracy in 1991 'Could Not Be Found'

We may point to two factors that were to some extent favourable for
Russian democracy.

The first is a general cultural orientation toward the West, toward
Europe. The very physical type of ethnic Russians, their Christian
religion (albeit of an Eastern character), and Russia's participation
since the time of Peter I in the politics and culture of Europe have
forced representatives of other cultures to regard Russia as a part of
the European world, if an idiosyncratic and marginal one. As
Vladimir Putin has put it, 'We are part of Western European culture.
Herein, in fact, lies our value. No matter where Russians live, whether
in the Far East or the South, we're Europeans.'[24]

Russia's European orientation can be distinguished from the
powerful feeling of being an inalienable and organic part of the
Western world that characterizes the Baltic countries; it includes a
powerful ambivalence, and can easily give way to the drawing of
strong contrasts with the West.[25] There were no culturally similar

---

24   Vladimir Putin, *From the First Person* [in Russian] (Moscow: 2000),
156. Medvedev told Angela Merkel, 'We, too, are Europeans' (pskov.kp.ru).

25   Most Russians would not agree with Putin's assertion that 'we are
Europeans'. Asked, 'Do you consider yourself European? Do you feel you
are a part of European society's culture and history?' 30% said yes in
1999 and 32% in 2008, compared with 54% and 59% answering no in the

peoples for the Russians to use as models in their attempted transition to democracy, in the way the Estonians had the Finns, or the
Estonians and Latvians the Swedes, or the Lithuanians all the Catholic countries of Europe. Nonetheless, the West served as such a model
for Russia significantly more than it did for the Muslim post-Soviet
states.[26]

The second factor conducive to Russia's democratic transition
was the relatively high degree of cultural development achieved
during the Soviet period. In 1989, 13 per cent of Russians had
completed some or all of the work for an advanced degree. In 2004,
21 per cent of the population between the ages of twenty-five and
sixty-five held advanced degrees, placing Russia on a par with Britain
and Sweden, ahead of not only all developing countries, but many
developed ones.[27] The cultural advancement of a country undoubtedly affects its capacity to embrace democracy.

This generically European cultural orientation and comparatively
high level of cultural development could not but influence Russia's
political process. There can be no doubt that they explain the force
(relative to the USSR's Asian republics) of the Western-democratic
movement among the intelligentsia in the late eighties and nineties.
From this derive a number of 'stylistic' peculiarities of the regime
that has taken hold in Russia (most of all its far greater emphasis on
formal constitutionality than is found in the Asian republics). But
there was also a range of stronger cultural and psychological factors
that pushed in the opposite direction and made the establishment

---

same years (*2008 Yearbook*, 150). But in Kazakhstan or Uzbekistan, the
question would itself be meaningless, and 30% is, at any rate, a sizable
minority.

26   The West as a model is to some degree present in the thinking of all
peoples. But for non-European peoples, it is an abstract, distant one. In fair-
ness, the Muslim post-Soviet countries have a far more proximate model of
democracy in Turkey. But democracy in Turkey is not as developed as in
Europe, and Muslims have the Arab and Iranian models as alternatives to
Turkey's democratic model.

27   *See* E. M. Shcherbakova, 'Educational Trends in Russia', *Sociological
Research* [in Russian], no. 11 (2006): 109. *See also* demoscope.ru/weekly/2009/
0375/analit02.php.

of democracy difficult, at times seemingly impossible, for Russia
in 1991.

Like most of the peoples of the USSR, Russians had no historical
experience of choosing their own government through elections
offering true alternatives, and almost no experience of democracy at
all. In any first (or nearly first) attempt at a transition to democracy,
certain elements of anarchy and chaos are only natural, indeed inevitable – just as emerging fears of this chaos, nostalgia for order, and
the temptation to calmly watch the retreat or rejection of democracy
in the name of 'order' are natural. To one extent or another, this can
be found in the post-Soviet history of every former republic of the
USSR.[28] But the Russian historical experience engendered a particular striving to 'escape from freedom', one that outpaced other Soviet
peoples', including those with non-European cultures.

The Tatar-Mongol conquest marked the last time the Russian
people were ruled by outsiders (indeed, they have imposed their own
rule on a number of other peoples), and they experienced the despotic political systems (first autocratic and then Soviet) under which
their history unfolded as autochthonous, rather than imposed from
without. The Baltic peoples could appeal to an authentic democratic
past (conveniently 'forgetting' that the democracies of the interwar period fell not to Soviet conquest but to internal weaknesses and
the attempt to overcome them under the protection of dictatorship).
The Ukrainians could lean on the mythically enhanced memory of
a late-medieval, semi-anarchist (and, arguably, protodemocratic)
Cossack state eventually demolished by Russia, and also on the
Ukrainian People's Republic during the civil war, likewise destroyed
by the Bolsheviks. The people of Azerbaijan, Armenia, and Georgia

---

28   A poll conducted in Kazakhstan in 1998 beautifully illustrates the
state of the post-Soviet mind, by no means limited to Russia. Respondents
were asked to choose from a list the one socio-political system capable of solv-
ing the problems facing Kazakh society: 4.4% chose 'Communism', 7.3%
'socialism', 5.9% 'capitalism', 2.3% 'Islam', 8.8% 'Western-style democracy',
and 59.6% 'any system so long as it brings order' (*see* V. Dunayev, 'Conflicting
Structures in the Kazakh Model of Interethnic Integration', *Central Asia and
the Caucasus* [in Russian], no. 5 [6] [1999]: 14–15).

could claim that during the period of the civil war, they were successfully building democracy, and that they, too, were impeded only by
the intrusion of Bolshevik troops. Even the Kazakhs and the Kyrgyz
could point to the memory of a 'nomadic democracy' and claim that
'our khans were always elected'. All these peoples were able to create
mythologized, but more or less plausible, versions of their own histories in which they had been the bearers of protodemocratic and
democratic traditions until Russian conquest interceded to bring
despotism into their lives. And while the presence of such mythologized versions of history clearly did not suffice for the transition to
democracy, they all had real psychological and political meaning,
instilling in these peoples some confidence in their own power, in the
possibility and naturalness of the path of democratic development.
The Russians, on the other hand, not only had practically no real
experience of democracy (the 'people's rule' of medieval Novgorod
and Pskov is confined to the distant past and persists in popular
awareness – to the degree that it persists at all – mostly as an example
of an unviable political order, an obstacle overcome on the path to
Russia's more familiar forms of autocratic statehood), they were
unable even to construct a framework comparable to other people's
democratic mythologies; the autocracy and the Bolshevik revolution
were both of Russian origin.

In Russia, as the eighties turned into the nineties, it was difficult
for supporters of the Western model to find any historical basis for
democracy, or some glorious hero in the mass imagination available
to be included in the democratic pantheon; the best that could be
found were 'authoritarian modernizers' like Peter I and Pyotr Stolypin.
More than other peoples, Russians tended to view democracy as an
anomaly without familiar historic precedents (even semi-mythical
ones), 'alien' and novel. More to the point, they tended to look on
it more fearfully than other peoples, worrying it would carry with it
threats and dangers.

It is true that Russian history is dotted with gaps in autocratic
power, but these have taken on a traumatic character in the mass
imagination. The period between the Rurik and Romanov dynasties,
without a strong authority, lives on in popular memory as the Time

of Troubles, an era of chaos and anarchy, when Russia was pulled
from the jaws of catastrophe only by the return of autocracy under a
new dynasty. Russia's brief and unsuccessful attempt at a transition
to democracy in 1917 likewise became a 'time of troubles' – and one
even more terrifying. The traumas inflicted by these events are of a
different, deeper character than those inflicted in other states by the
collapse of various proto- or quasi-democratic configurations of
government under the pressure of Russian conquest. Democracy
destroyed by outside forces is one thing; democracy turned to anarchy from which the people themselves rush to the arms of an
authoritarian regime to be saved is quite another.

The traumatic experience of 1917 (and, to some extent, of the
Time of Troubles) hung over the Russian conception of the period of
perestroika and the early nineties. The desire to dismantle the
Communist system and establish democracy mingled with the fear
of a replay of the 1917 transition from democracy into anarchy and
then to bloody dictatorship – a fear that created the psychological
backdrop against which the anti-Communist revolution of 1990–1
unfolded. This period represents the acme of democratic ideation.
But even then, according to a 1991 poll, 57 per cent of the population
named 'order' as the key goal of society, while 24 per cent answered
'offering the populace greater opportunities to impact the decisions
of authorities', 14 per cent listed the stabilization of prices, and 2 per
cent named freedom of speech. In 1989, 44 per cent agreed with the
assertion that 'under no circumstances should all the power of
the state be concentrated in the hands of a single person'. But in the
same year, 25 per cent agreed that 'our people always need a "strong
hand"', and another 16 per cent that 'we need one in certain circumstances – for example, the present'. The year 1989 was but the dawning
of freedom; by 2008, having experienced post-Soviet developments,
only 18 per cent agreed with the first statement, 29 per cent with the
second, 20 per cent with the third.[29]

---

29   *2008 Yearbook*, 28. Polls show a wide stratum of Russia's population
who believe that in Russia, the people should not control power at all. Thus,
67% of respondents agreed that Russia's citizenry absolutely cannot, or can

Insofar as the Communist system in Russia sprang from revolution by Russians, rather than arriving with foreign bayonets as in most other Communist countries, and as it was under this system that Russia attained unprecedented power as the core of the largest empire in world history, the paths of nationalism and democratic anti-Communism diverged. If in other countries the struggle against Communism entailed resistance to subordination by foreigners based in Moscow and the fight to raise the status of one's own nationality and government (which inevitably served as a boon to a democratic anti-Communism that took on a nationwide character), in Russia it had, objectively speaking, the opposite effect: the collapse first of the socialist camp united around Moscow, then of the USSR itself (a country in which Russians had long considered themselves the 'older brother' of other peoples), and finally, threats of secession by ethnic minority border territories – nearly, that is, the collapse of the Russian state itself.

It is clear that, resulting in significant measure from the fact that in Russia, public protest against the Communist system could adopt neither Russian nationalist nor truly democratic forms, there exists a distinctive 'materialism' in the Russian consciousness of the Soviet and post-Soviet eras. Thus, in every poll conducted by the Levada Center (formerly VTSIOM) between 1989 and 2008, when respondents were asked to name 'the primary thing a person lacks in contemporary Russia', a large majority – between 53 per cent and 83 per cent – answered 'material prosperity'. 'Political rights' was chosen by between 2 per cent and 13 per cent, 'morality' by between 11 per cent and 24 per cent.[30] (In this we may see reflected the influence of more than seventy years of Marxist propaganda, which in popular

---

only 'nearly insignificantly', control the operations of official bodies, while only 23% believe the same to be true in the West. But at the same time, 51% believe the Western democratic model to be ill suited to Russia (p. 148), and 76% that there is already enough, or too much, freedom in this country (p. 88). In 1997, 60% agreed that order is more important than human rights, and in 2008, that number decreased to 51%; in 1997, 27% supported the opposite statement, and in 2008, 39% (p. 102).

   30   *2008 Yearbook*, 13.

consciousness took the form of a primitive materialism that dictated, 'What matters is money, profit, material interests.') In Russia, the slogan of Estonia's protests, 'We'll live on potato peelings if we can do it in freedom!', would simply have been unimaginable. Clearly, the valuation of 'material well-being' and 'order' above all else does not create the ideal moral-psychological climate for a transition to democracy.

Another factor that made Russia's transition to democracy in 1991 tremendously unlikely (even practically impossible) was the extreme atomization of Russian society. The totalitarian Communist system almost completely precluded the formation of the public structures independent of government that would have constituted a 'civil society', contributing instead to the atomization of every society it dominated. In Russia this atomization proved especially thorough. In the other republics of the former USSR, there existed either regional (especially strong in Ukraine) or clan- and tribe-based (in the Asian republics) affiliations and communities that could to some extent stand in for a civil society.[31] Even in the Soviet period, authorities in Russia succeeded in creating a colossal homogeneity of culture among the Russian people from Vladivostok to Kaliningrad. Lacking any sufficiently articulated ideologies that could create closeness between individual people and find organizational expression, and in the absence of the habits and skills of creating structures capable of defending common interests across huge geographical distances, Russians were never afforded the opportunity to rely on the support of 'their own' through clan and regional affiliations. For protection they could look only to supreme

---

31 In Ukraine, strong regional cultural pluralism, and, accordingly, strong regional loyalties, undoubtedly imposed powerful restrictions on authoritarian tendencies and contributed to the establishment of stable party structures (see Dmitrii Furman, ' "Centers" and "Peripheries" [The Political Systems of the Three Eastern Slavic Republics]', *Free Thought* [in Russian], no. 6 [1998]). The role of this kind of loyalty in central Asian and Caucasian countries remains unclear and demands further study. Still, there is little doubt that in confronting power, a person in these countries may rely much more confidently on the help 'of their own people' than a person in Russia.

power – and for protection *from* that power, they could look nowhere.

All this led to psychological conditions that hindered the formation of a democracy and instead favoured the creation of an authoritarian regime of imitation democracy. When a society offers no 'serious' alternatives to democratic ideology, but cannot itself easily establish an actual democracy, then imitation democracy – the creation of an authoritarian system attired in democratic camouflage – becomes the most natural way forward; this is the situation in which Russia found itself with the collapse of the Communist system.

As for what particular form of imitation democracy would arise out of the revolutionary crisis Russia faced as the eighties turned into the nineties, this was determined by the specific course of history – that is, by a number of arbitrary and subjective factors. 'Yeltsin's Russia', to be sure, was not the only one that might have emerged. (Let us briefly imagine, for example, what would have happened had Yeltsin fallen into a river under murky circumstances, caught cold, and died, or if one of the architects of the 1991 coup had given an order to occupy Russia's White House, and so forth.) Other possible outcomes range from the quite probable to the unlikely to the simply implausible. A return to the old Communist system would have been simply implausible (even if the Communists had won). Equally implausible, or nearly so, would have been a transition to actual democracy on the model of the Central European and Baltic countries. Various forces might have won the struggle, but they all carried similar 'political DNA', suggesting the advanced development of some version of an imitation democracy political system (with some particular people at the helm, or some particular ideological shading, or being of greater or lesser viability). But it is impossible to conceive any version of events that could have offered a direct transition to actual democracy. Theoretically, we cannot completely rule out such a possibility, but its realization would have required a very unlikely concentration of arbitrary factors that the author of this book, frankly, cannot imagine.

One of these possible transitions was realized. The accession in

1991 of Boris Yeltsin's anti-Communist democratic movement marked the birth of this particular system of imitation democracy, which has continued to develop according to its own internal logic.[32]

---

32 Since in any country there are a number of ways for a regime of imitation democracy to come to power; actual imitation democratic regimes arose in various ways in different post-Soviet countries. They were created by the last Soviet leaders, who renounced Communist ideology and the USSR, declaring democracy as their goal while holding tight to power (Nazarbayev in Kazakhstan, Karimov in Uzbekistan, Niyazov in Turkmenistan), or who returned to power after uprisings that overthrew the former dissidents and national-democratic movement leaders who had taken office (Shevardnadze in Georgia and Aliyev in Azerbaijan), or by those from the lower echelons of the nomenklatura like the collective farm leader Lukashenko, who rose to power in Belarus after the first and only rotation of power there, or Rahmon, who rose to power in Tajikistan after the civil war.

But leaders need not originate in the nomenklatura, nor power in non-revolutionary or counter-revolutionary sources, to form regimes of these kinds. In Kyrgyzstan, a comparable regime was created by Akayev, an academic nominated by the democratic anti-Communists as an alternative to the prior leadership, and himself a democrat and 'Westernist'. In Armenia, a regime of this same type was established by the intellectual and 'half-dissident' leader of the National Democratic Movement, Levon Ter-Petrosyan. And the overthrown leaders of Azerbaijan and Georgia, Elchibey and Gamsakhurdia, built regimes by the same plan, though theirs did not turn out to be strong. Moreover, the passionate 'Westernist' Mikheil Saakashvili, who rose to power in the Rose Revolution that overthrew Shevardnadze's imitation democratic regime, is following the same path (or trying to) as Bakiyev, who rose to power in Kyrgyzstan's Rose Revolution. The emergence of an imitation democratic regime from the victory of a democratic movement is thus not a situation unique to Russia.

In contrast, the rise to power in Moldova of a clearly 'counter-revolutionary' wave of Communists did not lead to the creation of an imitation democratic regime. Ideological differences (or perhaps we should speak of 'ideological nuances', since both former dissidents and former KGB agents now speak of their devotion to democracy in identical terms) played no fundamental role.

1.4 The Strengths and Weaknesses of the Democratic Movement

The Russian democracy movement Democratic Russia was one of many anti-Communist democratic movements that arose out of Gorbachev's perestroika in this period. A great number came to power in countries that had been part of the USSR or the socialist camp. Its slogans (democracy and the market), ideological structure (amorphous, lacking a single coherent ideology and programme), social composition (its main 'shock troops' being the mass intelligentsia concentrated in Moscow and other large urban centres), organizational features (not a party but a 'movement' whose formation would have been impossible in a totalitarian state), and methods of struggle (at first extra-parliamentary by nature, though peaceful) all found close analogues in other countries of the former Soviet and socialist sphere, dictated by the general conditions prevailing under decaying and collapsing Communist regimes. The evolution of these movements followed a pattern. All democratic movements in the Soviet republics began with slogans of support for Gorbachev and 'the party's policy of building perestroika', accompanied by language supporting 'Leninist principles', and so forth. And all of them, as their participants began to overcome their anxieties and express once-inhibited thoughts and feelings, swung toward radically anti-Communist positions, turning on the very Gorbachevian power that had liberated them from fear.

The movement in Russia, however, was also marked by significant, though at the time not easily discerned, differences from these other movements, deriving from the cultural and historical peculiarities of Russia.

A unified culture could be found equally on the right and the left, among both nationalists and 'Western-style' cosmopolitans ('Russophobia' is no less nationalistic than 'Russophilia'). All-Russian cultural features exerted no less decisive an influence on Russia's democratic movement than on its opponents; the struggle for democracy and markets took on no less nationalistic a tone than had the struggle to forestall them.

The weakness of Russia's democratic tradition, the difficulty of appealing to the Russian past in the name of democratic ideals, the misalignment between democratic anti-Communist and nationalistic vectors, and the inability of pro-democratic forces – Westernists and anti-Communists alike – to present themselves as a national liberation movement are all both pan-cultural characteristics of Russian society and characteristics of the democratic movement. If comparable movements in Central Europe, the Baltics, and even the Caucasus could depend on a spontaneous and natural national feeling and claim (or even actually achieve) a nationwide character, Russia's movement could not. A number of other psychological and ideological characteristics are involved here.

A propensity to exaggerate the Russian people's anarchic and antidemocratic totalitarian tendencies was to some degree characteristic of all the country's social strata and political currents. The fear that the same social groups who in 1917 had fallen in behind totalitarian strength would now do so again was nowhere stronger than among the pro-democracy intelligentsia. Ethnic concerns factored in as well. Thanks to the official (albeit disguised) anti-Semitism of the post-war USSR, Jews played a tremendous role in the democratic movement (to some degree recapitulating the situation of the Russian revolutions of the early twentieth century). Their fear of the 'dark, anti-Semitic masses' was, naturally, tremendous (and as unfounded as the actual anti-Semites' hope of rallying the masses against the Jews). The democrats systematically exaggerated the threat of 'Russian fascism', and, in their minds, the minuscule ultranationalist organization Pamyat assumed dire and outsize importance. The mass emigration to the West of Jews and, indeed, nearly everyone who could leave, at exactly the moment when democracy was triumphing, can be explained only by these profound fears and the deep-seated belief that Russia, whatever it did, could never become a free society.[33]

---

33 The large number of Jewish participants in the democratic movement does not mean much; while participating in public life in various societies, Jews naturally follow the internal logic of those societies. In Russia, Jews are

In their struggle against the Gorbachevian centre, Russian democrats used spontaneous Russian nationalism to great effect – their propaganda painted Russia as 'oppressed' and exploited by the other Soviet republics.[34] In a meeting with the public in Ufa in August 1990, Yeltsin commented, 'Russia feeds everyone, makes sacrifices constantly. Russia has always contributed what it could . . . It is no longer acceptable for us to continue sending aid off to other countries, and even other Soviet republics.'[35] The propagandization of ideas like these resonated widely in Russian mass consciousness and provided support for the establishment of Russian sovereignty. But the democrats here were making use of a dark power in which they were deeply unversed; no union between Western-leaning democrats and spontaneous Russian nationalism could ever be organic and stable. The democrats simply could not adopt a 'nationalist' character, and their appeals to nationalism were in the end quite demagogic.

Russians; in the USA, Americans; in Bukhara, Bukharans. The basic characteristics of the Russian movement would be the same even if no Jews had participated. Still, it is only natural that among Jews, a fear of Russian nationalism and the people's totalitarian potential manifested itself more sharply, more distinctly.

34 Indeed, there were a number of 'status markers' enjoyed by other Soviet republics that Russia lacked – their own central committees, academies of sciences, and trade unions. The usual explanation for this was that the Soviet Union was itself a kind of 'greater Russia', an expansion of Russia, and the USSR's Central Committee and academies of science were 'basically Russian'. Besides, any possible disunity of opinion – let alone outright disagreement – between Soviet and Russian authorities would pose a far greater threat than friction between central authorities and those of any other republic. But from the perspective of spontaneous Russian nationalism, of course, this looked like unequal and oppressive treatment of the Russian people. It is among the paradoxes of the late Soviet period that the adherents of Russian nationalism and Communist orthodoxy, the 'red-and-brown' Communo-fascists, unhappy with Gorbachev's liberal reforms, fought to strengthen Russian institutions, effectively allying themselves with the democrats surrounding Yeltsin and contributing to the destruction of the Soviet state. The creation of an orthodox Russian Communist Party was no less a blow to the Gorbachevian centre than the creation of the Russian presidency.

35 *The Union Could Have Been Preserved: The White Book* [in Russian] (Moscow, 2007), 165.

At the same time, spontaneous nationalists could not be inculcated with their Western-democratic ideas, and very quickly found that they had been 'ensnared'; while supporting Russian 'sovereignty' they had materially contributed to the downfall of the 'empire' in which Russians remained the predominant ethnicity.[36] In Russia, unlike in other countries, there was and could be no synthesis of nationalism with democratic anti-Communism.

The fear of the Russian people so characteristic of the Russian sensibility was manifest in the Russian democratic movement in other ways as well. Objectively, the 'democrats' were revolutionaries, but they were revolutionaries of a most idiosyncratic kind, more afraid of the popular elements and popular revolution than anything. As far back as 1969, the dissident Andrei Amalrik, reflecting perceptions and anxieties by no means unique to him, wrote, 'It is not difficult to imagine what forms and directions popular discontent will take if the regime loses its hold. The horrors of the Russian revolutions of 1905–7 and 1917–20 would then look like idylls in comparison.'[37] It is characteristic that while a revolution was in fact taking place in Russia in 1991, that frightful word was itself avoided.

---

36   The idea of Russia's seceding from the USSR was first voiced at a May 1989 meeting of the Congress of People's Deputies, in a speech by the Russian nationalist writer Valentin Rasputin, who used it to demagogic effect in disputations with the Baltic deputies: 'Here, at this congress, the actions of the Baltic deputies are laid bare: they seek to introduce constitutional amendments that would allow them to say their farewells to this country. What can I say in such a situation? You will choose your own fate in accordance with law and conscience. But if you must blame Russia for all your difficulties, and your underdevelopment and clumsiness encumber your progressive aspirations, then maybe Russia should secede from the Union? It would solve many problems for us, as well.' Tatyana and Valery Solovei write, 'By one of history's ironies, the Soviet Union was destroyed by exactly the weapons with which the nationalists were trying to fortify it ... Democrats skilfully absorbed the doctrine of Russian sovereignty, not blinking at its origin in Russian nationalism' (Solovei and Solovei, *Failed Revolution*, 271). *See also* Dmitrii Furman, 'The Great Russian State: A Conceptual Trap', *Free Thought* [in Russian], no. 1 (1992).

37   Andrei Amalrik, *Will the Soviet Union Survive Until 1984?* (New York: Harper & Row, 1970).

Later on, Yeltsin (or his ghost writers) wrote, 'What we denote by cumbersome language like "restructuring"[38] or "market reforms" is described more concisely and directly in the Western press as a "democratic revolution". Domestically, however, this designation has not caught on. The explanation is at once both simple and complex: Russia is tired of revolutions. It is tired even of that very word . . . We are against revolutions. We have left them in the twentieth century.'[39] And the word 'Bolshevism', which in the language of that time suggested radicalism and revolutionary zeal, was becoming the most popular of accusations (especially among the elite of the society Bolshevism itself created, as they struggled to maintain their position). The democrats portrayed their rise to power – and not just demagogically, but in a spirit of true belief – not as a revolution but as the alternative to some other, more frightening revolution, the notorious 'Russian revolt, senseless and merciless',[40] which never actually took place but seemed ever to be looming. Yelena Bonner wrote in April 1991, 'We . . . are scared to death of what we have been imbibing since childhood . . . God save us from witnessing a Russian revolt, senseless and merciless.'[41]

This was the product not of contemporary reality (Russia's anti-Communist revolution was nearly bloodless, there were no violent revolts to speak of, and had the democrats who came to power not opened fire on the defenders of the White House in 1993 and gone to war in Chechnya, bloodshed might have been avoided altogether), but of historical memory and culture. Russia's fear of its own people, with

38   The literal meaning of 'perestroika'. —Trans.
39   Boris Yeltsin, *Presidential Marathon* [in Russian] (Moscow, 2000), 238. As obviously as this comment reflects the self-interest of a person who has risen to power in a revolution only to ardently oppose revolutions, it is also an accurate reflection of one facet of Russian mass consciousness. Later, Putin would discuss how 'Russia had exceeded its capacity for revolution and civil strife in the last century'.
40   A phrase from Aleksandr Pushkin's 1836 novel, *The Captain's Daughter*. The book is set during the Pugachev Rebellion of 1773–5, the largest peasant revolt in Imperial Russian history. —Trans.
41   *Russian Thought*, 12 April 1991.

all their destructive potential, played an extremely complex role. On the one hand, it undoubtedly restrained revolutionary violence, and Yegor Gaidar is quite correct in labelling it a 'preventive dread' and observing that 'where the intelligentsia at the century's beginning were eager to hit the gas, their grandchildren are now scrambling for the brakes'.[42] On the other hand, it also created a desire to constrain the populace, reining in their destructive tendencies and forcing them onto the right path, while at the same time retreating from them under cover of authoritarianism. All the more so if this authoritarianism was seen as homegrown, as Yeltsin's was by Westernist democrats.

We have already discussed the particular materialism of Russian mass consciousness and the way economic value dominates it. In the ideology of Russia's democratic movement, this was reflected in the particularly large space occupied by market mythology, the idea that a transition to markets and private property would quickly bring material prosperity, and the notion that, in the related concept of free-market democracy, it was the market that would undoubtedly serve as the basis, the necessary source from which democracy, as it were, would grow autonomously.[43] This notion gave ideological sanction to the 'temporary' (necessarily so, for the sake of democracy's ultimate triumph) use of illicit and undemocratic methods in introducing the market. Insofar as the market and private property form the basis of democracy, the undemocratic transition to them was not itself perceived as inimical to democratic belief. Market romanticism led to both a tendency to romanticize 'pro-market' dictatorships and

---

42 Yegor Gaidar, *State and Evolution* [in Russian] (Moscow, 1995), 138.

43 In this sense, the tremendous roles played by antisocialist economic journalism and by actual economists (Gaidar, Yavlinsky) are characteristic of the Russian democratic movement. In other countries, where ideas about cultural revival played a bigger role, humanitarians and the creative intelligentsia were at the forefront of things. In Lithuania, there was the musicologist Vytautas Landsbergis; in Tajikistan, the filmmaker Davlat Khudonazarov; in Uzbekistan, the poet Muhammad Salih. The Caucasus during this period was a 'tsardom of philologists' (Elchibey in Azerbaijan, Ter-Petrosyan in Armenia, Gamsakhurdia in Georgia, Ardzinba in Abkhazia).

the popularity, among Russian democrats in particular, of figures like Pinochet and Stolypin, who were not 'democratic' but were 'pro-market'. It created the possibility of sanctioning and authoritarianism, and of authoritarian power's 'plunder privatization'.

In these features of Russian democratic ideology, to be sure, we see an authoritarian psychology formed by the whole of Russian history and inherent in Russian Western-leaning democracy, and the peculiar influence of a Marxist economic determinism not recognized by the democrats themselves. If we can locate Marxism's influence on the materialism of the popular masses only by way of assumption, its influence on the intelligentsia – democratic ideologues who, long after studying Marxist texts, became virulent anti-Communists – is beyond doubt. The more radically the ideology was denounced, the positive and negative trading places in the ideological narrative, the more easily its structure was preserved. Economic determinism made its presence felt in the ideology of the democrats through inverted signifiers – public property became the source of all evil, and almost any means of destroying it was seen as beneficial; private property, on the other hand, was the source of all good, and almost any means of creating it was, likewise, beneficial.[44] Russia's democrats came to regard their own victory as utterly inseparable from that of democracy. There was simply no awareness of the straightforward and obvious notion that democracy is affirmed not through the victory of any one party, not even the most democratic, but rather through the cycle in which one party is defeated and an opposition –

---

44   For a more detailed discussion, *see* Dmitrii Furman, 'Inverted Historical Materialism? From the Ideology of Perestroika to the Ideology of Building Capitalism in Russia', *Free Thought*, no. 3. This kind of 'market romanticism' prevailed not only among Russian democrats, but also among the democrats under their influence in other post-Soviet countries. Akezhan Kazhegeldin, the onetime prime minister of Kazakhstan later ousted by Nazarbayev and a fierce opponent of his authoritarianism (mirroring Mikhail Kasyanov in Russia, expelled by Putin and thereafter an opponent of his authoritarianism), writes, 'I and my fellow reformers believed that wherever there was a market, there would be democracy' (Akezhan Kazhegeldin, *Opposing the Middle Ages* [in Russian] [London-Moscow, 2002], 247).

one that upholds the importance of the rules of the game common to all participants in the political process – rises to replace it.

At the time, these principles were perceived as minor nuances that helped form the idiosyncratic Russian democratic movement and made it significantly ideologically and morally weaker than its Central European and Baltic counterparts, which tended to view themselves (accurately, as it happens) as movements of the entire country, unafraid of the domestic masses and calling most urgently for the immaterial values of national and personal freedom rather than the promise of a wealthier lifestyle 'as in the West'. This relative ideological and moral weakness naturally alloyed itself with authoritarian tendencies: the undifferentiated masses must be held in check and brought with an iron hand to the market, which will become the basis of democracy. With its signifiers inverted, and in a powerfully softened form, the ideological scheme of the 1917 revolution was restored (which is why, after the democrats' victory, this resemblance between ideological schemes would be mirrored in their political consequences).

The Russian democratic movement's conceptual and moral weaknesses are connected with its relative 'physical', numerical, and electoral weaknesses – two sides of the same coin. Russia's democratic anti-Communist movement, even at the peak of its influence, was not even a nationwide movement, let alone one of the majority.[45]

It was the movement of a vigorous, forceful minority. In varying ways and to different degrees, a majority of the intelligentsia elite took part. Its base in the masses constituted the 'grassroots' intelligentsia concentrated in large, 'strategically important' urban centres – Leningrad and Moscow most of all. Naturally, a capital's denizens play an

---

45   At the peak of the democratic movement's popularity, at the First and Second Congresses of People's Deputies in Russia in 1990, about 20% of the deputies were on the 'Democratic Russia' list, and 44% voted for DR propositions at least two-thirds of the time. After this, the number of democratic deputies only decreased – more and more deputies took up other positions (*see* Viktor Sheinis, *Rise and Fall of the Parliament* [in Russian] [Moscow, 2005], 1:281–3).

especially critical role during a revolution, far more so than the majority of the people, as we see illustrated clearly in French history. The Moscow intelligentsia could exert significantly more pressure on the organs of power located there than could the numerically predominant but far-off periphery.

This socially active minority with a more or less definite anti-Communist and Western-democratic ideology could depend on ideologically unformed, indefinite social discontent among wide swathes of the masses. The moods and inclinations of these masses, however, were far from the pro-Western stance and cult of markets that characterized Russian democrats. Polling throughout the late Soviet and post-Soviet periods demonstrates a majority of the population's attachment to the socialist system of social guarantees and egalitarianism, and their rejection of 'full-scale' capitalism.[46] But the democrats were able to make use of the masses' social protest against the nomenklatura elite, their growing discontent with the liberal, Gorbachevian centre, and even their spontaneous Russian nationalism, which they sought to channel into anti-Union activities.

The democratic movement could also find support among elements of the ruling Soviet nomenklatura elite, who had lost faith in Communist ideology, acquiring in the process an eagerness to shed the burden of party discipline and their envy of Western elites. The democratic anti-Communist ideology occupied a strong position within the echelons of formally Communist power, including the

---

46   Even today, with much of the populace acclimated to capitalism, an April 2008 survey found that 41% of respondents believed 'all large enterprise should be state-owned', 53% believed the state should own 'the enterprises most important to the country', and just 2% said all enterprise should be in private hands. Not once in the nineteen polls carried out by VTSIOM and the Levada Center between 1997 and 2008 did the supporters of capitalism outnumber the supporters of socialism (*2008 Yearbook*, 32–3). To the question 'What kind of economic system would you like to see in Russia?' the answer 'a market economy' was given by 16% in 2003, 17% in 2006; 'mixed' by 45% and 44%; 'planned' by 20% and 25% (*Public Opinion – 2006 Yearbook* [in Russian] [Moscow, 2006], 38). It all creates the impression that a majority of Russia's people hold as an unarticulated socio-economic ideal something akin to Lenin's New Economic Policy.

Central Committee and the Politburo. Fully prepared to abandon
Communist ideology and the USSR completely (so long, of course, as
their social position could be maintained), the nomenklatura
'proposed' a leader to the Russian democratic movement – 'rebellious' Politburo member Boris Yeltsin.[47]

Yeltsin (whom Bill Clinton once called 'the father of Russian
democracy', not realizing the phrase has, through the influence of
Ilya Ilf and Yevgeny Petrov's classic novel *The Twelve Chairs*, acquired
a satirical tone in Russian[48]) played what can only be called a colossal
role in the victory of the Russian democrats and the emergence of the
new Russian government. Gennady Burbulis, his closest adviser at
the time (later dismissed), commented, 'Yeltsin as a figure made a
good sort of "bridge" between the past and the systems being created.
His experience in wilful public policy, the desire and capacity to
exploit in every way the forms of power afforded him as a leader, have
turned out to be just what was urgently required'.[49] Yeltsin's ideological disposition was hazy, amorphous, labile (his transition from a
Lenin-citing Communist[50] to a fervent anti-Commmunist and

---

47   Russia's 1991 revolution occupies an intermediate position, as it were,
between the anti-Communist revolutions seen in Central Europe and the
Baltics and what took place in central Asian countries like Kazakhstan,
Uzbekistan, and Turkmenistan. That is to say, it was not a victorious movement embraced by the whole country, but neither was it a transformation
'from above'. It is no coincidence that Yeltsin, too, occupies an intermediate
position between Soviet leaders who maintained power in their countries, like
Nazarbayev, and dissident revolutionaries like Lech Wałęsa and Landsbergis.
He may have been a former Politburo member, but he was, at the same time, a
'rebellious' one.

48   *The Twelve Chairs* is a classic Soviet satire dating to the 1920s. In a
particularly well-remembered line repeated several times in the book, con
man Ostap Bender disingenuously refers to the hapless protagonist Kisa Voro-
byaninov as 'a giant of thought, the father of Russian democracy, and a person
close to the emperor!' —Trans.

49   Gennady Burbulis, *Occupation: Politician* [in Russian] (Moscow,
1999), 196.

50   Gorbachev recalled: 'Up until 1991, he was a Leninist Communist.
Having become the chair of Russia's Supreme Soviet, he sent me a card on
Lenin's birthday, urging me to fulfill his mandates' (*Unfinished History: Three*

pro-market democrat was astonishingly fast even for the time), but his thirst for power was deep, and in the struggle to slake it, he would say anything that worked, often convincing himself. He had acquired a loathing for Gorbachev and the rest of the party leadership,[51] who had 'failed to appreciate' and humiliated him, and his political activities to a significant extent took on the character of a personal vendetta.

Yeltsin and the democrats found each other. In joining the democrats, Yeltsin acquired a ready army of loyal supporters. The democrats got a leader who could be understood both by broad portions of the masses – who were impressed by his 'decisiveness', roughness, and authoritarian behaviour – and by the nomenklatura elite, who, under the peculiar conditions of Soviet social mobility,

Colors of Time. Conversations between M. S. Gorbachev and Political Scientist B. F. Slavin [in Russian] [Moscow, 2005], 53).

Yeltsin's speeches in the Politburo tended to be of a more orthodox cast than those of his colleagues. In January 1987, he objected to the term 'industrial democracy' in a Central Committee report, insisting this was 'not Lenin's position, but Bukharin's and Trotsky's'. From the notes of A. Chernyaev, V. Medvedev, and G. Shakhnazarov, *In the Politburo of the CPSU Central Committee* [in Russian] (Moscow, 2006), 130.

51   Yeltsin's conflict with Ligachev and Gorbachev, reflected in Yeltsin's speech before the plenum of the Central Committee on 21 October 1987, which branded him a member of the opposition and got him kicked out of the high leadership, is very hard to understand, even though both Yeltsin and Gorbachev wrote about it. It is harder still to locate some ideological distinction in it. One begins to suspect the sources of the conflict were personal and psychological. Yeltsin's speech before the Central Committee, which led to his downfall, is completely incomprehensible; his associates later wrote and distributed an apocryphal reconstruction, with more or less clear critical content. But Yeltsin's prompt dismissal at once cast him in the role of 'protector of the people' in the mass imagination, which under the circumstances opened up great political possibilities, while the democratic movement and its ideology provided a conceptual basis for his actions.

Yeltsin would later write of his meetings with Lech Wałęsa and Václav Havel, 'What united us was the fact that never before had former dissidents walked so bravely onto the political stage. We who had been persecuted' (Yeltsin, *Notes of a President*, 179).

were positioned significantly closer to the 'simple folk' than to the 'middle-tier' intelligentsia. By his own 'nationalness' and proximity to the party apparatus, Yeltsin mitigated fears of a revolution and a 'leap into the unknown'. The emergence of such a leader strengthened the democratic movement immensely, allowing it to transcend the limits of a relatively narrow stratum of the intelligentsia. It is quite difficult to imagine the democrats' victory without Yeltsin.

The strong democratic minority had even stronger allies outside Russia. The concentration of democrats in the struggle against the Union centre made all the other republics' separatist forces and movements their allies. Other allies outside the USSR included Western countries, which, though at the time they feared the collapse of the USSR and so put their support behind Gorbachev, nonetheless regarded the 'democrats' sympathetically, approaching them with understanding despite fearing both Communist and nationalist imperial reactions in Russia – all based on impressions gathered through reports of the 'Westernist' intelligentsia then flooding into the West, shared at innumerable conferences and gatherings.

So it was that the democrats counted themselves a powerful minority, blessed with a fortuitous leader, as well as powerful allies and 'fellow travellers' both within and beyond Russia. This vigorous, powerful minority was opposed by dispersed and demoralized forces, as well as the atomized, bewildered majority, unsure what it wanted after losing its faith in the old ideology and its sense of the USSR's Gorbachevian centre as a psychologically necessary form of 'strong power'. A vigorous, powerful minority with a fortuitous leader could well rise to power, as it had in 1917 and as indeed it would again in 1991. What it by definition could not do was rise to power – let alone entrench itself firmly in power – through democratic means.

Even though among those RSFSR deputies elected in Soviet Russia on 4 March 1990, only around 20 per cent represented Democratic Russia, the democrats managed, on 28 May of that year, their first major victory when, on the third try and by a margin of four votes out of more than a thousand cast by the deputies, Boris Yeltsin was elected chairman of the Supreme Soviet of the Russian Soviet

Federative Socialist Republic. Viktor Sheinis, a witness to and partic-
ipant in these events, writes, 'Yeltsin's election was the combined
result of a rally orchestrated by democrats and a series of closed-door
agreements pledging an "outpouring of generosity" after their victory.'[52] Yeltsin's memoir *The Struggle for Russia* contains a vivid
recollection of the newly elected leader walking into his new office:
'All this shimmering comfort gently pricked at me. "Well, now what?"
I thought. "We've snapped up not just this office, but all Russia." A
subversive thought – it frightened me.'[53]

Until this point, democrats had worked their way into the power
structure as an energetic, but still markedly numerically inferior, faction among the people's deputies of the USSR, an opposition
counterposed to the majority of that assembly exerting pressure on
Gorbachev, as well as a sizable minority of the RSFSR's deputies.
Now they had risen to a position of power from which they could
contest the power of the Union centre. Yeltsin and the democrats
gradually forged a path to victory and actual power: the path of erad-
icating the USSR and 'sovereignizing' Russia. Their most idealistic,
radical representatives called directly for the liquidation of the Soviet
state. Bonner writes, 'The totalitarian, Communist empire can be
disassembled only through the formation of independent governments to replace it.'[54] Elsewhere: 'The only way it is possible to break
apart the imperial, totalitarian government is by establishing many
governments in its place. Fifteen, twenty, or fifty.'[55] Meanwhile, the
'responsible' leadership among the democrats dared not speak, nor
even think, this way. Nine months before the Belovezh Accords,
Ruslan Khasbulatov wrote, 'Any talk of Russia's considering secession is brazenly untrue. Objectively, we are for preserving the Union,
a position dependent on neither Boris Yeltsin nor myself. No
matter which politician leads Russia, he will proclaim: "Yes, I am

52   Sheinis, *Rise and Fall of the Parliament*, 1:306.
53   Yeltsin, *Notes of a President* (in Russian), 33.
54   'The Landscape after Combat', *Russian Thought* [in Russian], 15
March 1991, 1.6.
55   *Kuranty*, 12 May 1991.

pro-Union!"'[56] All the same, the logic of their struggle for power against the Gorbachevian leadership inexorably led them to separatists in other republics and spontaneous Russian nationalism.

On 12 June 1990, the Congress of People's Deputies ratified the Declaration of State Sovereignty of the Russian SFSR (907 yeas, 13 nays, 9 abstentions), proclaiming the supremacy of Russian laws over Soviet ones. (Later, it was this date that would be declared an official holiday, first called 'Russian Independence Day', and later, when the assertion that Russia had achieved actual independence in 1991 made that too awkward, simply 'Russia Day'.) The primitive Russian patriotism of the bulk of deputies and their aspirations toward greater power and status made them unable to resist the allure of 'sovereignization' – besides which a number of republics had already adopted such declarations and Russia could not let itself be 'worse'. The Communists (who founded the Communist Party of the RSFSR on 20 June) and the 'patriots' followed behind the 'democrats', aiding Yeltsin and his circle in the destruction of the Soviet state. The Congress of People's Deputies and the Supreme Soviet of Russia began to adopt laws and regulations that, one after the other, redistributed power from Soviet to Russian leadership. Under the chairmanship of Ivan Silayev, Russia's government was busily bringing Soviet enterprises under Russian subordination. The irreversible disintegration of the USSR had begun – a process that could be arrested only through a use of force the Gorbachevian centre did not attempt.

On 17 March 1991, on Gorbachev's initiative, a USSR-wide referendum was held on the fate of the Soviet Union. In Russia, 71.3 per cent of participants voted to preserve the unified state. But 26.4 per cent voted not to. This is a rather large percentage – slightly lower than in Ukraine (28 per cent), but larger than in the other republics that participated (the Baltics, Armenia, Georgia, and Moldavia – which had already come the longest way toward separatism – did not participate). But this must not be taken literally; a 'no' vote was most of all an expression of protest against Gorbachev – in both style and

---

56   *Smena*, 14 March 1991.

policy – rather than a sincere expression of the desire to liquidate the USSR, which was not yet on the table in earnest. At the same time, another question included on the initiative of Russia's Congress concerned the establishment of the office of president of Russia; 71.38 per cent supported it. That is, a tremendous number of people voted for both the preservation of the USSR and the establishment of a Russian presidency that would make it practically impossible.

On 12 June 1991, Yeltsin was elected president in the first round of voting, receiving 57.3 per cent of votes. At the last moment, Yeltsin 'brought on' as his vice president Aleksandr Rutskoy, a hero of the Afghan War and leader of the 'Communists for Democracy' faction among the deputies. Despite being held under Soviet authority, these elections were immeasurably freer and fairer than any that would be held after the victory of the democrats. The election of Boris Yeltsin is the closest thing to an authentically democratic rotation of power in all of Russian history. Still, it did not amount to the democratic rise to power of the opposition by constitutional means.

Those who voted for Yeltsin by and large held little support for his platform (indeed, Yeltsin had no particularly distinctive platform,[57]

57   This fact notwithstanding, Yeltsin was not shy to offer promises: 'The transition will take . . . a year, maybe a year and change. During this time, the people's standards of living will remain consistent. And in the third year, they will soar! Support us for these two or three years' ('The Union Might Have Been Saved', 166). Among Yeltsin's many and varied mottos, a particularly significant one was the egalitarian dictum to 'fight the prerogatives of the nomenklatura', suiting as it did the general mood of social protest. 'I can't dine on sturgeon and black caviar while the country lives in such poverty and squalor. I can't jump into cars and rush past traffic and through red lights, can't gulp down imported superdrugs knowing full well that the woman next door can't afford aspirin for her child. I would be too ashamed' (Boris Yeltsin, 'Confessions on the Topic at Hand', *Rush Hour* [in Russian], 1990, 126). 'If something is lacking in our socialist society, the burden of its absence should be shared equally by all' (p. 169).

One of the many paradoxes of the 1991 Russian revolution is that, thanks to Yeltsin and the democrats' rise to power, the nomenklatura, most of whom had been transformed by privatization into a new bourgeoisie and bureaucracy, became unbelievably wealthy. The disparity between living standards at

besides promising everything to everyone, and it is likely he had
scarcely even contemplated the liquidation of the USSR). What
mattered was that a vote cast for him was by definition also one with-
held from the supreme power then invested (and, most importantly
of all, *seen* as invested) in Mikhail Gorbachev. Yeltsin was elected not
so much as head of state, but rather as head opponent of the head of
state, who was now beginning to seem too soft, too indecisive, both
to reformists and to supporters of 'order'. As the opponent of the
head of state, he was protected by a popular vote that had legitimized
his status, but it had not granted him supreme power.[58] Practically no
Yeltsin voter, nor Yeltsin himself, could really have imagined that the
USSR would dissolve within the year, empowering him fully as the
president of an independent Russia.

Yeltsin's election did not suffice to bring him and the democrats to
actual supreme power. So long as the Soviet government existed,
Yeltsin's administration in Russia could only be incomplete and fragile. The dismantling of the USSR was a necessary precondition for
their actual rule. But it was practically impossible for the Russian
government to eradicate the USSR through constitutional, democratic means. Russian society did not and could not provide a
'popular mandate' for Soviet dissolution.

Yeltsin and the democrats were helped enormously by the doomed
August coup of the State Committee on the State of Emergency – a
timorous, indecisive, and belated attempt to halt the collapse of the
Soviet state not even through the *use* of force, but merely through its

---

the bottom and the top of society became huge – far larger than would have
been possible under the Soviet system and quickly surpassing the West – and
the masses who had been drawn in by the promise of 'fighting elite prerogative' became extremely poor. That Yeltsin quickly shed any compunction
about eating caviar hardly needs pointing out.

58   The meaning of a vote for Yeltsin in this period was psychologically
similar to the meaning of a vote for Zhirinovsky's Liberal Democrats or for
the Communists in Duma elections under Yeltsin's presidency. In both cases,
it was not power but rather its opponents that were being elected. Neither the
Dumas of the post-Soviet period nor the Russian authorities of 1991 were seen
as holding 'real' power.

demonstration. The coup's failure led to the suspension and then the outright banning of the CPSU, which had been holding the Soviet state together (in 1993, the CPRF was founded in its ashes), as well as to the extreme weakening of the Gorbachevian leadership's power. It also gave a green light to other Soviet republics' separatist aspirations and to their capture 'without permission' of more and more of the Union centre's new functions. On 16 October, Russia declared the termination of funding for all Soviet agencies, leaving the Soviet leadership without money. Yeltsin savoured the humiliation and disempowerment of his opponents, toying with them like a cat with a mouse, casually issuing promises, then refusing to make good on them. Yeltsin's relocation of his residence to the Kremlin, which would have to house two presidents until Gorbachev's departure, became emblematic of his elevation (and at the same time, of the half-conscious reorientation of the Russian government toward traditional symbols and values). Yeltsin would later write about the decision, 'The idea of moving to the Kremlin came as quite a surprise to many in my circle . . . I made it after weighing the pros and cons . . . To put it plainly, dislodging a person from the Kremlin would require, at minimum, another coup. The Kremlin is a symbol of stability, endurance, of the strength of the political line being pursued.'[59]

Power was swiftly 'leaking' from Gorbachev and the Soviet centre. This ended on 8 December 1991, when the leaders of Russia, Ukraine, and Belarus signed the Belovezh Accords, liquidating the USSR and creating the Commonwealth of Independent States. The other republics were presented with a fait accompli, and on 21 December in Almaty, most of them joined in the agreement.

Not only did Russian society not provide a mandate for these agreements, it was woefully unprepared for them. Apparently, even Khasbulatov (who succeeded Yeltsin as chairman of the Supreme Soviet after his election to the presidency) and Rutskoy were unaware this had been in the offing. Moreover, it is clear that the very idea of such a dissolution of the USSR occurred to Yeltsin and his associates

---

59   Yeltsin, *Notes of a President,* 161–2.

very late. After the August coup, Yeltsin evidently intended to preserve the Union, somehow reformatting it with officials of the Russian government at its centre and himself in Gorbachev's place. Until the very last moment, he could be heard touting his readiness to come to a new Soviet agreement, pledging that Russia 'would never precipitate the collapse of the Union', and even threatening to redraw the borders of the Soviet republics interested in secession – which would have amounted, in practice, to a version of the 'Yugoslav scenario' playing out in a nation packed with nuclear armaments. But Yeltsin quickly understood that great dangers awaited down this road – he had the example of Yugoslavia to study, and nuclear weapons playing their role as a deterrent[60] – and chose instead an easier, safer path.

It is characteristic that although Yeltsin managed to secure the ratification of the Belovezh Accords by the shocked and bewildered deputies of Russia's Supreme Soviet, who had learned of them only through the mass media (an overwhelming majority of 188 yea votes, including both the Communist and the 'patriotic' opposition striving to rid themselves of Gorbachev, with 6 nays and 7 abstentions), he nonetheless declined to legitimate them post factum with any sort of referendum. The Belovezh Accords, which had decided the state's fate in secret, without any consultation by the masses nor any popular mandate, were unequivocally undemocratic and unconstitutional.[61]

---

60   When reports surfaced that Yeltsin's circle had been discussing the possibility of Russia and Ukraine trading nuclear strikes, Yeltsin remarked, 'Technically – and I have discussed this with the armed forces – it is absolutely impossible.' Cited by Yegor Gaidar, *Power and Property* [in Russian] (Moscow, 2009), 127.

61   Yeltsin's situation differed fundamentally from that of his Ukrainian counterpart in the Belovezh Accords, Leonid Kravchuk, who did possess a popular mandate, in the form of a declaration of independence that Ukrainians had endorsed in a referendum. Clearly, this difference between their situations in Belovezh is emblematic of the differences between Russia's and Ukraine's political evolutions. The referendum protected Kravchuk from charges of treason or revolt; he could afford to lose in the upcoming elections, leave power, and still retain tremendous political influence. This was not an option for Yeltsin.

And it was exactly this act that made Yeltsin the actual head of an independent Russian state and elevated his fellow democrats to the political elite of that state.

Thus, the key peculiarity of Russia's 1991 'velvet revolution' was that a movement that had appeared democratic in its postulated and subjective ideological goals nonetheless came to power through thoroughly undemocratic means.

It is precisely in this situation that we see the embryo of Russia's political system of imitation democracy; no other system could have developed from such a beginning. The victory of the democrats meant the elimination of the vague prospects for Russia's democratic development in this period of history.

For all the immense differences between the revolutions of 1917 and 1991, they share one critical similarity. In both 1917 and 1991, a minority rose to power through illicit means, fully convinced that it alone could carry the benighted masses to a brighter future. And after that, that minority could no longer leave power, doomed instead to create a system that rendered such a departure impossible. This similarity between the incipient regimes of Soviet and post-Soviet Russia in turn led them along comparable paths in their subsequent evolutions.

1.5 One Liquidation for All, with Different Consequences for Each

The USSR's liquidation had various, and sometimes even opposite, consequences for the republics that had once constituted it, depending on their cultural and psychological readiness for democracy. Their membership in the USSR had heretofore prevented the divergence in their political systems that now began in earnest. Neither the full-fledged democracies of the Baltic nor the Türkmenbaşy regime would have been possible within the Soviet state. With the centre no longer holding, the political systems of the republics began rapidly evolving in different directions.

Thus, for republics that had prepared for a transition to democracy, like the Baltic states, the dissolution of centralized Soviet power came undoubtedly as a blessing. But in most republics, including Russia, the dissolution struck a terrible blow to prospects for democracy. Those buds of democracy that had begun to sprout in these places could thrive only where power was divided between Soviet leadership and that of the republics. Less the control of Soviet power, most of the republics, no longer needing to turn toward Moscow and Gorbachev, pursued the most natural course – building authoritarian systems of imitation democracy.

In Russia, the actual democraticness of the June 1991 presidential elections was safeguarded precisely by the presence of the liberal Union centre; these would be the last elections to offer real alternatives. The victory of the democrats meant an end to democratic development. Following the Belovezh Accords, the path to relinquishing power became impassable for Russian democrats and their leader Boris Yeltsin. The very terms of their rise to power ruled out the possibility of establishing a standard system with a loyal opposition of the kind that had unified the elites of the old regimes with the radical democrats – the victors in the 'velvet revolutions' that had overtaken Central Europe, to whom it was naturally odious (but far from fatal) for democrat revolutionaries to hand over power. From now on, those opposing the authorities in Russia would have to formulate their grievances not as proclamations of misguided policy but as accusations of the usurpation and destruction of the state by a group ruling with no mandate (for example, 'Put Yeltsin and his gang on trial!'). The Belovezh Accords meant that political protest and the opposition would become 'extra-systemic', radical, 'counter-revolutionary'. Thus, to vacate power and allow the opposition to assume it, would for Yeltsin and his associates now likely mean immediate exile, or even prison. From that day, the struggle to remain in power would be motivated not only by the drive to realize their socio-political plans (that is, the carrying out of their 'reforms'), nor just by ambition and the 'will to power', but by their very survival instinct. It had become a struggle for their political lives. No alternatives remained open besides the establishment of no-alternative power.

The minority inevitably consolidated power by the same illegal or quasi-legal means that had brought them to power. That is, with every step on the path to consolidating their power, Yeltsin and his retinue made their eventually leaving power all the more fraught with the prospect of ruin, and, thus, less practicable. If it was still theoretically possible to imagine Yeltsin surrendering power to the opposition after the Belovezh Accords, then privatization and the constitutional crisis of 1993 would soon foreclose that possibility. Thus, Yeltsin and his circle had only one path available to them, not backward but forward, to the ever-stronger consolidation of power in the presidency, and then to his 'dynasty', those whom the president would name as his successors, continuing to hollow out ever more of the content of democracy while maintaining its form.

This path – the only one viable (with perhaps the exception of open dictatorship[62]) – was at the same time, for the victors of 1991, a relatively easy one to walk. Terrified by the prospect of anarchy (and to some degree actually collapsing into anarchy), a confused and atomized society was all too happy to accept measures aimed at restoring 'order', traditionally conceptualized in the Russian psyche as strong, centralized power held by a single person. How much more expedient if the emerging system of consolidated power could

---

62   Several times Yeltsin and his circle considered a transition to open dictatorship. A majority of Russian 'democrats' would surely have accepted a transition to dictatorship as a way of accelerating the transition to markets and guarding against 'Communist revanche'. But there simply weren't the resources to establish such a dictatorship, neither militarily (Yeltsin was hardly popular within the armed forces; it was only with tremendous difficulty that he persuaded military personnel to join the 1993 coup) nor 'morally'. Besides, an open dictatorship could only have been understood as a temporary emergency measure.

There was one further reason why open dictatorship was difficult to achieve in this period: Russian power's substantial dependence on the West. Fearing the rise to power of the Communist opposition, the West might well have sanctioned a dictatorship, as it had anti-Communist dictatorships in a number of countries (and had even helped foster their growth). But such sanction would be given only under extreme circumstances, with all kinds of qualifications, and accompanied by substantial pressure to liberalize and restore democratic norms. Besides, a dictatorship would have made it impossible for Western leaders to regard Yeltsin 'as an equal'.

disguise itself as democracy and Russian society could understand it at least partly as the legitimate outcome of their own electoral decision-making.

As society's influence on power waned in the course of subsequent political development, it grew increasingly pacified, returning to its accustomed, traditional ways, and even becoming content with power. The reaction to the revolutionary power vacuum of the late eighties and early nineties, the desire to leave 'revolutionary chaos' behind as quickly as possible, led paradoxically to the strengthening of the power that revolution had forged.[63]

To put it figuratively, it is as though in 1991 we stepped onto an escalator – one with essentially no exit, which carried us forward to the current fully developed (and already showing signs of 'ageing') system of imitation democracy.

---

63   The nostalgia for the Communist past that arose in response to the anti-Communist democratic revolutions was perfectly natural, considering all revolutions come with high expectations that inevitably lead to disappointment. But where circumstances were different, this reaction could lead to different and even opposite consequences. In countries with strong democratic traditions and cultures conducive to democracy, the radicals who had led these revolutions were swept from power in lawful elections, replaced by the 'moderate' representatives of the 'restructured' old nomenklatura; this is the pattern we see in Lithuania, with the replacement of Landsbergis by Algirdas Brazauskas, and in Poland, with the replacement of Wałęsa by Aleksander Kwaśniewski. It is these first rotations that prompt us to assert the primacy of democratic norms, of 'the rules of the game', in transforming a victory of democrats into a victory of democracy. On the other hand, in countries like Russia, Kazakhstan, and Uzbekistan, similar responses produced the opposite result – fortifying the personal power of the president. Responses of the former type are directed against those in power, strengthening democratic institutions. Those of the latter type are directed against weak democratic institutions, and so fortify the power of individuals.

2

The Development of Russia's Political System

The primary driving force behind the development of Russia's post-Soviet system and the direction it has taken has been its step-by-step eradication of threats to the preservation of supreme presidential power and the transfer of that power to successors of those presidents' choosing. Here again, the development of a political organism is not so different from that of a biological organism. It starts out weak, vulnerable to destruction by outside forces or growing pains, and must fend off very real dangers, overcoming crises that could easily prove fatal. In the development of Russia's political system, these crises fell during the Yeltsin era, when its foundations were being laid. But thwarting these crises, the organism continued to develop, growing stronger and stronger.

In the following period, under Putin, the organism was already strong enough, the regime sufficiently forceful, that no threats could pose a serious danger to it. (We will see these threats re-emerge later, in the next, final stage of development.) But ensuring the guaranteed no-alternative nature of supreme power required the continual elimination of ever more remote dangers. In the Putin era, power is contending not so much with actual threats as with potential ones that may someday become immediate.

The gradual elimination of first immediate, then potential threats means expanding the sphere of power's control over society. The development proceeds from no-alternative presidential power to a no-alternative parliament (that is, one defined by that presidential power), no-alternative gubernatorial appointees, and even no-alternative political commentary on TV. This development continues ever higher, until at the very peak of the system's power, new limits on growth are announced and new signs of weakness appear.

In modified and much weaker form, this cycle recapitulates Soviet development. Soviet power, too, progressed from such a 'childlike' weakness in the period from 1917 to 1921 that it might well not, under a different set of circumstances, have survived. But overcoming one crisis after another, it instead grew ever stronger, eliminating the most distant potential threats and expanding its control over society until the symptoms of a new weakness began to show – this time not childlike but, rather, senescent. Soviet and post-Soviet development are like two images, depicting the same subject with the same composition. The first is monumental, carved in stone. The second is drawn in pastels on paper.

At the same time, Russia's cycle resembles those by which other post-Soviet systems developed. These systems shared the same starting point – the collapse of the Communist system and the proclamation of democracy amid a cultural and psychological unreadiness to live under the conditions of democracy.

2.1 Conflict with the Parliament and Ratification of the Constitution

The Yeltsin era was marked by the emergence of three major political crises. The first was the crisis of 1993. It manifested primarily as a conflict between the branches of power – the president and the parliament – and its earliest signs had been observable at the end of 1991. It was also partly visible in the conflict between the president and the Constitutional Court. The court, witnessing the fierce struggle between the two basic political forces – the presidency and the parliamentary 'party' – took on relative independence and attempted to guide the opposing sides through legal channels. A series of further contradictions were superimposed on this basic conflict between branches of power. A whole bundle of maladies arose, complicating matters for each of them. The crisis of 1993 was especially dangerous to a young and weak system still being formed, and could have proved fatal to it.

*

Conflict between presidents and parliaments was a natural phenomenon in the earlier stages of the imitation democracy systems
emerging in the post-Soviet space, and practically all CIS countries[1]
experienced conflicts comparable to Russia's, though varying in form
and intensity. While the presidents of other post-Soviet states took
inspiration from the example of Russia,[2] it is clear they acted out of
more than straightforward imitation. The conflict among the different branches of power was prompted by causations shared among the
republics. The conflict in Russia differed only in the particularly
brutal, bloody forms it took, partly because it was the first chrono-
logically (having witnessed the defeat of the Russian parliament,
other parliaments surrendered almost without a fight), and, perhaps,
partly through the influence of more personal factors – in particular,
the personality of Russia's first president.

Relations between presidents and parliaments were, at the start
of the 1990s, objectively 'conflictogenic'. From the start, the
power of 1991's victors lacked adequate institutional formalization.
The constitutions under which this power was exercised consisted
of the basic laws of Soviet republics, ill suited to the new conditions under which they were being applied, necessitating the
introduction of amendments, many in number and various in
effect. The constitutions that resulted were contradictory in the
extreme. Regardless of other political circumstances, such constitutions, lacking in clear and concise delineations of power, could

---

1 Many post-Soviet presidents have dissolved parliaments that stood in
their way: Akayev in Kyrgyzstan in 1995; and Nazarbayev in Kazakhstan
twice – first in 1993, then, when the new parliament turned out to be equally
unruly, again in 1995; Lukashenko in Belarus in 1996. In one case – that of
Moldova – a conflict between President Petru Lucinschi and the parliament
ended with the parliament victorious, and the nation transitioning to a
parliamentary republic.

2 Russia's influence may not always have been limited to its ability to
serve as an example. It was rumoured in Kazakhstan that Yeltsin had directly
asked Nazarbayev to dissolve his parliament, lest Yeltsin himself stand out too
much for doing so (*See* Y. Yertysbayev, 'Kazakhstan and Nazarbayev', *The
Logic of Change* [in Russian] [Astana, 2001], 355). Nazarbayev, of course, could
hardly have declined such a request.

not but generate constant conflicts between the branches of power. New constitutions were needed, and this in turn further inflamed the struggle around how various branches would define their prerogatives.

The conflicts were also aggravated by particular ideological traditions. Besides the dominant authoritarian tradition of undiluted, personified power resting, unified, in a single set of hands, the Soviet period also left behind one specific, democratic-populist dictum: 'All power to the Soviets.' In Russia, it was of especially great importance. In the early days of the struggle for power, Russia's democrats, appealed, as had Gorbachev, to 'the ideals of 1917' and forcefully made the call for 'power to the Soviets'.[3] But after their victory, the phrase began to cut against them and their presidential standard-bearer. Article 104 was added to the text of the Russian Constitution, specifying that the Congress of People's Deputies 'may consider and resolve any question related to the management of the RSFSR'. It hung over Yeltsin's administration like the sword of Damocles.

---

3   These are the words with which the 1 December 1989 'Appeal to the People of the Group of People's Deputies' [in Russian], signed by A. Sakharov, G. Popov, Y. Afansiev, V. Tikhonov, and A. Murashov, concluded: 'Property to the people! Land to the peasants! All power to the Soviets!' (rfbr.ru). Sakharov's draft 'Constitution of the Union of Soviet Republics of Europe and Asia' included language specifying 'The Congress of People's Deputies . . . holds the highest legislative power in the country' (Andrei Sakharov, *Anxiety and Hope* [in Russian] [Moscow, 1991], 273). There is a photograph that shows Sakharov standing at the entrance to the Kremlin Palace of Congresses before the opening of the First Congress of People's Deputies, holding a poster that says, 'All power to the Soviets!' After the First Congress of People's Deputies of the Russian SFSR, Sakharov said in an interview, 'The Congress, in my view, failed to fulfill the historical mission embodied in the slogan "All power to the Soviets!" Without the power of the Soviets, there is no way to supersede the dictates of various government departments. There is no way to create truly self-regulating free enterprise. There is no way to achieve land reform' (Sakharov-archive.ru).

In the light of subsequent history, this all looks like shameless demagoguery, but at the time, clearly, people put some real stock in these slogans.

Both traditions contradicted the separation of powers. Incompatible claims to total power by the president and the parliament made any kind of compromise difficult to achieve.[4]

Conflict between presidents and parliaments should be analytically differentiated from conflicts of other types, which, however, in the early post-Soviet period, were always overlaid on the conflict between the branches of power and entwined with it. Clashes of new rulers with the 'old comrades' who had helped usher them to power have recurred hundreds of times throughout history. In the USSR, each new ruler tried to rid himself of those alongside whom he had struggled for power, and who had helped him attain it (for Stalin, it was the old Leninist guard; for Khrushchev it was the Anti-Party Group; for Brezhnev, it was Shelepin, Podgorny, and others). And each new ruler in the post-Soviet period would come to do the same.

All the presidents of the independent states that emerged from the collapse of the USSR, regardless of whether they rose from the Party elite or as the leaders of mass democratic movements, came to power with teams of their own, within which they were 'first among equals' rather than 'chiefs' or 'bosses'. When they became rulers, their old associates, adapting with great difficulty to their new roles as subordinates and missing no opportunity to remind their leaders of their former positions, began to interfere. Conflicts ensued. In the early nineties, a wave of these conflicts swept through all the newly independent republics.[5]

---

4 'Isomorphic', similar conflicts were at the same time unfolding between the Soviets and regional executive powers throughout Russia. During the decisive conflict between the president and the parliament, sixty-three Soviets, but only four regional administrative heads, supported the parliament. *See* Rutskoy, *Bloody Autumn*, 55.

5 In Kazakhstan, there was conflict between Nazarbayev and Supreme Council chairman Serikbolsyn Abdildin, and Nazarbayev's firing of Vice President Yerik Asanbayev; in Kyrgyzstan there was a clash between Askar Akayev and Vice President Felix Kulov; in Uzbekistan, a confrontation between Islam Karimov and Vice President Shukrullo Mirsaidov; in Azerbaijan, between Heydar Aliyev and Rasul Quliyev; in Belarus, the struggle of Lukashenko against many of his onetime supporters and associates. Almost everywhere, we find presidents in contention with vice presidents and

Russia experienced this mode of conflict in the confrontation between Yeltsin, who had gone from the leader of a democratic movement to the head of the Russian state, and his former allies and comrades-in-arms: Gorbachev, the State Emergency Committee, Vice President Rutskoy, and Speaker Khasbulatov, who had organized the 'defence' of the White House with Yeltsin in August 1991. Rutskoy and Khasbulatov stood at the head of the parliamentary party. With disarming candour, Yeltsin writes of his conflict with Rutskoy, 'His main ... mistake ... was a stubborn unwillingness to comprehend and accept his own status.'[6]

The conflicts between presidents and parliaments were everywhere intensified and aggravated by the generally nervous atmosphere incipient market reforms were creating. Privatization worsened general social tensions and impacted the material interests of every party to the conflict; the question of who carried out privatization and the associated reforms and how they went about it also determined who would grow rich and who would miss their chance and be forever branded a 'loser'.

Everywhere, presidents demanded additional reform powers, citing the necessity during a 'transition period' that power be concentrated and action taken decisively and energetically. Democratic movements (especially Russia's), with their market romanticism, supported this, and the deputies, in whose minds lurked both a nationwide hunger for strong power and poorly organized masses thronging in protest (in Russia, where the Supreme Soviet coexisted with the Congress of People's Deputies, crowd psychology was of greater concern to parliamentarians than in the other republics), were at first happy to join them. At the Fifth Congress of People's Deputies of the Russian SFSR in late October and early November

---

speakers of parliaments – that is, with their closest comrades, who occupy the most critical offices besides the presidency. Of course, the presidents always win. Their opponents variously join the opposition (Abdildin), leave the country (Mirsaidov, Quliyev), or wind up in prison (Kulov).

6   Yeltsin, *Notes of a President*, 49.

1991, Yeltsin received special powers to issue decrees with the force of law. But the deputies soon came to regret this, realizing they had in effect surrendered their influence over the privatization process and that the real power was now flowing from the president and his circle.

As market reforms proceeded, ideas that had once been popular among the democrats, like worker autonomy and rights for labour collectives, were hastily discarded and forgotten, and the ideology of the reforms was transformed into one of acceleratedly 'constructing capitalism'. The reforms were everywhere accompanied by a decline in living standards for most of the population – the cost of enriching the ruling elite and those nouveau riche who had won the favour of the government. Market democrats, in accordance with their ideology, welcomed the orgiastic plunder of state property (and took part themselves, to some degree). One member of Anatoly Chubais's privatization team, Aleksandr Kazakov, wrote, 'We proceeded from the understanding that after some time, the logic of market self-development would drive property into the hands of efficacious owners.'[7]

Predictably, social tension and protests by broad segments of the population sprang up. The deputies, more tightly tethered to the masses than were the bureaucrats and the democratic political intelligentsia, to some degree 'accumulated' this social protest and appealed to it. The conflict between branches of power took on the sense of being one between 'high' and 'low', the centre (where the 'high' were concentrated) and the periphery. The administration of the radical 'marketist' Yegor Gaidar, whose youthful appointees Rutskoy once called 'the boys in pink trousers', became the symbol of antipopulist policy and the main target of attacks by people's deputies and social protests by the majority.[8]

---

7   Anatoly Chubais, ed., *Privatization, Russian-Style* [in Russian] (Moscow, 1999), 66, 208.

8   Yegor Gaidar was the grandson of a famous children's author, a Communist and Chekist, and was himself part of the Soviet nomenklatura, an economist and member of the editorial board of *Communist* magazine. He had become a radical 'marketist' and exponent of the 'Chicago School'. His

While its social aspects are obvious, it is difficult to discuss the conflict between the president and the parliament as a clash of ideologies. Both sides appealed to democracy, and each accused the other of plotting to revive totalitarianism. The leaders of the parliamentary party could hardly be called opponents of market reforms. Both 'parties' adopted vague, eclectic positions, and each included people with the most varied and unstable ideological orientations. Still, some ideological differences did exist between these 'parties'.

The democrats' market romanticism, their awareness of their own minority standing, and their fear of the masses' 'reactionary' tendencies – all concerns that found voice among the deputies – pushed them to support presidential authoritarianism. Fear of the reactionary potential of the masses became fear of the Soviets. With astonishing swiftness and ease, the motto 'All power to the Soviets!' was abandoned, as were all that appealed to the discarded ideals of the Soviet era. They were replaced by new slogans, diametrically opposed to the old: 'The Soviets and democracy are incompatible!' and 'The Soviets are the final stronghold of partocracy!' Bonner writes of her feelings watching the Congress of People's Deputies in 1992: 'The whole time, I kept wishing Boris Nikolayevich would pound his fists and declare, "Enough! End this nonsense!" '[9] Radical

---

evolution perfectly embodied that of the Soviet elite. Burbulis introduced him to Yeltsin, and he proceeded into a meteoric career, serving first as finance minister than first deputy prime minister. When in September 1991 Silayev vacated his post as prime minister, Yeltsin himself took over the prime minister's responsibilities, with Gaidar playing the main role in shaping economic policy. From June to December 1992, Gaidar served as acting prime minister (the deputies refusing to confirm his permanent appointment).

To this day, the mass imagination equates Gaidar and all his reforms with pure evil. In both 1997 and 2008, only 3% of the population agreed that Gaidar's reforms 'had undoubtedly benefited the economy'; in those same years, 19% and 20%, respectively, agreed they had been 'painful, but necessary'; 15% and 21% that 'there had been no need for them in the first place'; and 41% and 33% that 'they had had a destructive impact on Russia's economy' (*2008 Yearbook*, 31).

9   Yelena Bonner, 'Neither Earth nor Will' [in Russian], *Kurranty*, 25 April 1992.

Westernist democrats were directly pressuring Yeltsin to put an end to the Soviets by force, accusing him of indulgent 'liberalism'. 'Yeltsin's biggest mistake', Bonner writes, 'and the true democrats' along with him, poorly represented as they were in executive and especially legislative power, turned out to be the absoluteness of their conception of democracy, their adherence to democratic institutions and democratic modes of power, excessive to the point of fanaticism, in a nondemocratic country. They remained committed to working only by legal, constitutional means, despite doing so in an unconstitutional, lawless state whose parliament had been elected before democratization, in what in fact was a different country – thus rendering it, strictly speaking, illegitimate.'[10] But if the Westernist minority, subjectively radically democratic and radically pro-market, actively supported the creation of a system of presidential authoritarianism, the parliamentary defenders' camp naturally became attractive to anti-Western elements, and began to project a certain anti-Western, anticapitalist mood growing among the people, connected with nostalgia for the Soviet 'empire'. The democrats' actions, and their support for presidential authoritarianism, were to a significant degree motivated by fear of the reactionary and totalitarian potential of the masses. But these actions themselves created a situation in which mass protest was unable to avoid taking reactionary forms. The more reactionary the forms it took were, the more tightly the democrats would embrace the necessities of authoritarianism and the forceful suppression of protest.

The parliament, of course, was neither Communist nor Bolshevik, and did not endeavour to restore the Soviet order, as Yeltsin and the democrats had portrayed it.[11] But the parliamentary party had

---

10   Yelena Bonner, 'Boris Yeltsin's Victories and Defeats', *Russian Thought* [in Russian], 19–25 March 1993. This rebuke to Yeltsin for being too democratic sounds to me very much like a rebuke to Stalin for being too humanistic. Bonner forgets not only that her own late husband, a democratic 'icon', had himself repeated the call for all power to go to the Soviets, but also that the president, just like the parliament, was elected 'in a different country', and one that was not an independent state.

11   'These past months', Yeltsin writes of the parliamentary party's leaders, 'they had been living in the fantasy that with little more than a nudge,

the appearance of a motley, amorphous bloc, and the logic of struggle against the radical democrats began to draw Communists and Russian nationalists – even the nearly fascist ones – toward it. They shared an outrage at the destruction of the USSR, 'Russia's humiliation', and the market reforms. During the blockade of the White House, televisions broadcast an astonishing image of people dressed in black uniforms, marching and lifting their hands in the Fascist greeting of Aleksandr Barkashov's Russian National Unity movement, acting out their role as defenders of the Constitution and parliamentarianism. As for the leaders of the parliamentary 'party', the logic of struggle pushed them into positions that corresponded to the moods of their social base. Rutskoy and Khasbulatov now accused Yeltsin of destroying the USSR, their appeals to the experience of Western democracies paradoxically accompanied by accusations that the president was selling Russia to these very democracies[12] and tinged, especially in Khasbulatov's case, with a certain amount of thinly disguised anti-Semitism. (Later, he would go so far as to claim 'detachments of Jewish youth' had taken part in the assault on the White House.)

On the other side of the pro-authoritarian democratic Westernist paradox was the paradox of the anti-Westernist as defender of constitutionalism, separation of powers, and democracy.

In Russia, with its Soviet-federal structure[13] and its many national

---

the whole country . . . might rush headlong to follow a Bolshevik Communist parliament into its own past' (Yeltsin, *Notes of a President*, 373).

12   'We need not borrow another country's laws, another country's morality, another country's values . . . We should under no circumstances allow that same violence we saw visited on the Soviet Union to be visited on Russia' (Report of Ruslan Khasbulatov to the Tenth Extraordinary Congress of People's Deputies of the Russian Federation, Rutskoy, *Bloody Autumn*, 67).

13   We cannot, of course, speak seriously of the RSFSR as an actual federation, just as we cannot speak of the USSR as a federative state, a Union of republics. A totalitarian state cannot in reality be federal; it can only possess federalism as a formal feature. But both the equality of Soviet republics and the presence within the RSFSR of autonomous national entities were more than just formal features – they were unshakable ideological dogmas. Toward

minorities, the conflict between the branches of power was further complicated by the growth of separatist movements and totally undefined relationships between regional authorities.

The collapse of the Soviet Empire did not tidily observe the borders of the Soviet republics, which had been drawn quite arbitrarily. Separatist and irredentist movements of varying intensity now emerged in all the post-Soviet republics, with the exceptions of ethnically homogenous Turkmenistan and Armenia. In Russia, it was hard for ethnic minorities like the Chechens, whose entire history was one of bloody struggle against empire, to accept the idea that peoples who had never particularly striven or fought for their independence, like the Belarusians, were now being 'forced into' independence, for no better reason than their former, ficticious status as Soviet republics, while minorities within Russia did not have the right to form their own states, because their republics had only 'autonomous' status. In the various autonomous republics of the Russian Federation, as in former Soviet republics, relations between the nomenklatura elite and spontaneous national movements developed in different ways. A truly revolutionary change of power took place only in Chechnya. But both national movements and the more cautious among the 'partocrats' strove for greater or complete independence. The autonomous republics began to proclaim their 'sovereignty' and 'independence'.

Conflicts in the centre (first between Russian and Soviet authorities, then among Russia's branches of power) created a tremendously favourable situation for authorities in all the ethnic republics,[14] which all the conflicting parties sought to win over. (A famous line from

---

the end of the Soviet period, the formal features began to take on some actual content, as the republics – both the Soviet republics and the autonomous republics of the RSFSR – were ruled by the local nomenklatura, while the central government, desperate for stability, increasingly backed away from real governance. Formal federalism gradually gave way to the contours of 'vassal principalities'.

14   Vladimir Shlapentokh compares this struggle between the growth of regionalism and separatism to the struggle between emperors and popes in medieval Germany (*see* Vladimir Shlapentokh, *Modern Russia as a Feudal Society* [in Russian] [Moscow, 2008], 171).

Yeltsin when he was rising to power and tossing off promises: 'Get as much sovereignty as you can swallow.'[15]) The once-autonomous republics could appeal to the right of nations to self-determination that had been so prominent in the democrats' early ideology (before they came to power and began their struggles against the Union centre). In Andrei Sakharov's utopian-idealist plans, the autonomous republics were, like the Soviet republics, to become independent, and as such to participate in the development and implementation of a new Union agreement.

The Federation Treaty, signed in 1992, which to some degree inhibits the uncontrolled accumulation of power by the republics,[16] calls the formerly autonomous zones 'sovereign states' within the Russian Federation. Seeking allies and institutional support in his struggle against the parliament, Yeltsin even created a council of heads of the republics – which, of course, disappeared without a trace immediately after he won.

National autonomism and separatism also had some influence in areas of Russia where the local authorities looked on national republics with jealousy, even envy. They, too, strove for greater self-reliance, seizing property within their own territories (as the autonomous republics had done, and the Soviet republics before them had done to Soviet property) and refusing to send their tax money to Moscow (once again mirroring the Russian government in its dealings with Soviet power). In certain parts of Russia, separatist movements emerged, albeit significantly weaker and more artificial than the national movements in the former autonomous republics. The phantoms of Ural, Siberian, Far Eastern, and other republics loomed.

---

15 The phrase is from 1990. By 1993, Yeltsin was speaking differently: 'First of all, absolute sovereignty does not exist. The rights of any republic are limited by those of other federal subjects. Second, the sovereignty of the republics within Russia is subordinate to the preservation of Russia as a unified and indivisible state' (kommersant.ru/doc.aspx?DocsID=56630).

16 The treaty was not signed by the two republics with the most active separatist movements: Chechnya, where a national movement had overthrown the partocracy leadership, and Tatarstan, where the Soviet party leader Shaimiev used it in his trade war with Moscow.

Everything about the 1993 crisis developed in accordance with predictable patterns, but the way various aspects of it came together, the forms the conflict took, and the way it was finally resolved all resulted from a number of coincidental and subjective factors. This was a crisis that presented real dangers to the system and, just like in 1991, offered a spectrum of possibilities for its resolution. One cannot ignore the possibility that the parliamentary party might have won in Russia. This theoretically possible victory would have meant the liquidation of the very weak Yeltsin regime, still taking its first steps, and the re-emergence of some kind of chance at democratic development. The construction of a new regime of imitation democracy would have been significantly more complex (though by no means impossible), since the ideological significance of constitutionalism and the separation of powers would suddenly spike, Yeltsin's unsuccessful attempt at authoritarianism would stand as precedent, and, besides all that, there simply was no one else like Yeltsin to take on the leadership of the parliamentary party. But power, and so opportunity, were distributed unevenly between the parties, and the odds had always favoured Yeltsin and the 'democrats' to win.

It was no surprise that Yeltsin continued to enjoy the support of most of the democratic intelligentsia that had carried him to power (and been to some degree brought to power by him), though their ability to bring the masses along with them declined precipitously after the fall of the USSR and the onset of market reforms. The reforms did to some degree contribute to the consolidation of power around Yeltsin and the old nomenklatura elite, insofar as they opened up the prospect of property ownership and enormous enrichment. These new owners (both representatives of the old nomenklatura and the nouveau riche whose wealth had come from arbitrary official decision-making, the 'millionaires by appointment') wanted to strengthen Yeltsin's grip on power, which meant consolidating their properties. Spontaneous protests by the lower classes, relayed by the deputies, scared them.[17] But in Moscow, where

---

17 Maxim Boiko, a member of the Gaidar-Chubais privatization squad, would later write, 'If not for privatization, then in the spring of 1992 and the

intelligentsia, bureaucrats, and business elites supporting Yeltsin were concentrated, the deputies found themselves in hostile terrain, under the pressure of constant demonstrations, protests, and attacks by democrat-controlled mass media. Their support in the provinces did not count for much.

Nor was the international climate particularly favourable to the parliamentary party. The leaders of all the CIS countries, who, like Yeltsin, aspired to funnel as much power to themselves as they could and become no-alternative leaders, supported the Russian president, understanding full well that the dissolution of Russia's parliament would offer them an opportunity for retribution against their own parliamentary oppositions. Yeltsin further enjoyed the support of Western leaders, who held only the foggiest idea of what was happening here, gathered from a 'Westernist' intelligentsia in Russia that feared Communist revanche and had grown alarmed at the nationalist rhetoric of parliamentarians and the growing nostalgia for the USSR.

Despite the shock of the USSR's unanticipated collapse, and the general immiseration and protest brought on by market reforms, the desire for a return to order and strong power made a resurgence in the popular mind.[18] Although the parliamentary 'party' was actively directing its appeals to the mass social protests, the masses themselves tended to associate order and strong power not with the deputies – who rather personified the very revolutionary chaos they were seeking to swiftly overcome – but with the sole power of the president, in which traces of the venerable, customary prerogatives of

---

autumn crisis of 1993 . . . the balance of political forces might not have tipped in favour of reforms' (Chubais, *Privatization, Russian-Style*, 66). In the author's ideological idiom, 'in favour of reforms' really means 'in favour of presidential power'.

18   In a poll that asked them to list the state's various goals (one could choose the most important and second most important from among four options), 79% of respondents named 'maintaining order' as their first or second goal in 1991, and 86% in 1993; 'giving the people greater opportunity to influence government decision-making' got 57% and 31%; 'combatting rising prices', 50% and 70%; 'protecting freedom of speech', 13% and 7% (*see* Dmitrii Furman and Kimmo Kaariainen, eds., *New Churches, Old Believers – Old Churches, New Believers* [in Russian] [Moscow, 2007], 34).

general secretaries and tsars could be discerned. The desire for strong power was more forceful than the desire for social protest, and the nostalgia for bygone Soviet stability worked for the president, himself one of the primary antagonists of that stability. The desire to leave the revolution in the past abetted the power that emerged from that revolution.

A war of position between the president and the deputies spanned all of 1992 and the start of 1993. Neither the parliamentary opposition's attempts at impeaching the president in December 1992 nor the president's attempts at dissolving the parliament in March 1993 proved successful. Flare-ups alternated with passing periods of calm and even retreats by Yeltsin (the most significant was the replacement of Gaidar, loathed by the deputies and most of the electorate, with Viktor Chernomyrdin, a representative of the old Soviet elite of bureaucrat bosses).

But in April 1993, Yeltsin won overwhelmingly in a referendum on confidence in the president and the parliament. Not only did a majority (58.7 per cent) express confidence in Yeltsin personally, but a slightly smaller majority (53 per cent) approved of his socio-economic policy despite the extreme economic difficulties the country was undergoing; 44.8 per cent in the referendum had participated in early presidential voting, and 67.2 per cent in early voting for the people's deputies. The referendum did nothing to resolve the conflict,[19] but it did demonstrate the balance of power between the presidential and parliamentary parties and uplifted the president and his supporters. Sheinis, then an active member of the democrats' camp, described it as polling 'the presidents' analysts wouldn't have dared imagine in their wildest dreams'.[20] It turned out that the

---

19   The Constitutional Court had ruled that in order to resolve the elections in early voting, a majority not of actual voters but of the total electorate itself was required. No such majority appeared to support the election of either the president or the deputies.

20   Viktor Sheinis, *Collected Essays* [in Russian] (Moscow, 2005) 2:301. Yeltsin's press secretary, Vyacheslav Kostikov, also writes, 'The scale of victory surpassed even the most optimistic analysts' predictions' (Vyacheslav Kostikov, *Romance with the President* [in Russian] [Moscow, 1997], 180).

people's fear of anarchy had outstripped their dissatisfaction with the authorities, their fear of want, their resentment at the pilfering of 'public' property. They were far likelier to support the president than the parliament. With so much support for Yeltsin – and even for his economic policy – it was clear that he had little to fear from the electorate. The referendum had in effect cleared the way for Yeltsin to resolve his conflict with the deputies by force.

Yeltsin finally overcame his 'tortured contemplations', which he described with characteristic naïveté. 'Oh, how I wished I didn't need to break the law to extricate us.'[21] He proceeded to openly announce that he would conduct artillery preparations in August, and would resolve the situation in September. In the memoirs of Yeltsin's press secretary, Vyacheslav Kostikov, we find a good description of the atmosphere prevailing in the democratic camp that had supported the president and pushed him to be more decisive. In the transcripts of the 10 August 1993 session of the Presidential Council (composed in its entirety of well-known democrat-intellectuals), one of those assembled (Kostikov is discreet with names) says, 'Better to work legitimately, of course. But you need to have other options on reserve. The situation in the army is tolerable. But the situation in the Ministry of Security is concerning . . . Where television is concerned, I'm an extremist. We must maintain control. The indefatigable opposition must never be allowed a toehold.' Others more or less agreed.[22] On 21 September, Yeltsin issued his decree suspending the Constitution and dissolving the parliament, whereupon the White House fell under siege. Electricity, water, and all communications were cut off. On 4 October 1993, TV channels the world over broadcast images of the shooting of the White House by tanks. Somewhere between 123 (the official figure) and 2,000 people died in street skirmishes.

---

21 Yeltsin, *Notes of a President*, 372.
22 Kostikov, *Romance with the President*, 204–5. These comments by the author do not restrain him from writing on the same page, with stunning naïveté, 'The records of our discussions around the armed forces show that we considered only peaceful means of resolving the conflict.'

Whereas in 1991 the democrats – Yeltsin's supporters – had organized the defence of the White House against tanks sent by the State Committee on the State of Emergency, in 1993 they found they were the ones ordering tanks to besiege it. But in contrast with the 'reactionaries' of the SCSE, the democrats were not overly concerned by the prospect of spilling (other people's) blood. The most prominent members of the intelligentsia welcomed the revolt. A group of writers, including the best known literary figures of the time, names like Bella Akhmadulina, Daniil Granin, Viktor Astafyev, and Bulat Okudzhava, appealed to the citizenry and the president, 'These stupid scoundrels respect only strength. Isn't it time to make a demonstration of such strength before our democracy, which, young as it is, we are gladly persuaded has been sufficiently fortified?'[23] The actor Liya Akhedzhakova even went on TV to shout, 'Where's our army? Why isn't it protecting us from this damned constitution!?' The leaders of the parliamentary 'party' were hoping to see mass demonstrations backing them; none materialized.

Most people did not support the revolt, but even those who found Yeltsin's conduct outrageous breathed a sigh of relief. The threat of civil war receded, order was restored, and the crisis was over. The bloody events of October 1993 had given Russian society a good scare. A culmination of the anarchy Russia had so feared, they stoked the desire for strong power. Fears that had been preserved in historical memory since 1917 and even the Time of Troubles were supplemented by the fresh fear October 1993 generated.

The presidents of the other CIS countries sent Yeltsin a message that read, 'We have every faith that Russia's president and government will take whatever measures are required to halt the provocateurs and protect democracy.' Western democracies, too, breathed sighs of relief. George Mitchell, the majority leader in the US Senate, said, 'President Yeltsin has no choice but to do whatever is required to restore order in Moscow, by any means.' British prime

---

23   Rutskoy, *Bloody Autumn*, 441. Even many years later, Gaidar writes, 'The majority in the Supreme Soviet was subordinated to people who had no concept of ethics or democratic norms' (Gaidar, *Power and Property*, 179).

minister John Major: 'I wish to express my full and unconditional support for President Yeltsin and for the actions he has taken to restore law and order in his country. There can be no doubt this is a critical moment for the reform process, and, indeed, the future of Russia.' The OSCE Ministerial Council adopted a statement that read, 'All democratic states must loudly and emphatically express their support for the democratic forces in Russia, including President Yeltsin.'[24]

After the victory in Moscow, regional councils disbanded or were dissolved without resistance. Proceedings in the Constitutional Court, which had condemned the revolt, were 'suspended'.

The shelling of the White House obviated any further compromises by Yeltsin on the text of the new constitution, and on 12 December 1993, a referendum held by presidential decree ratified a constitution completely satisfactory to Yeltsin. According to official data, it was supported by 57.1 per cent of the 54.8 per cent of voters who took part. There can be no serious doubt that the results were falsified, but we cannot know to what degree (it is no coincidence the Central Election Commission swiftly destroyed all the ballots).[25] All the same, it is clear that more people voted for the Constitution than against it – a reflection of the widespread desire for order and stability.

Yeltsin's decision to combine the referendum with the Duma elections was, so far as his own interests were concerned, inspired. The Communist and Liberal Democrat leadership quickly understood that with Rutskoy and Khasbulatov now in prison, their seats were up for grabs. Opposition parties' focus surged to the ballot, and they largely ignored the issue of the new constitution, in effect sanctioning a coup d'état. Consequently, popular protest was expressed in votes *for* these parties, rather than *against* the Constitution.

The results of the Duma elections came as a terrible disappointment to the pro-Yeltsin democratic bloc 'Russia's Choice'. They even

---

24   Rutskoy, *Bloody Autumn*, 435–7.
25   *See* A. Sobyanin and V. Sukhovolsky, *Democracy Limited by Falsifications* [in Russian] (Moscow, 1995).

had to interrupt the broadcast of their 'winner's banquet', at which democratic leaders had intended to celebrate their victories while returns poured in on a monitor. When the outcome had become clear, Yuri Karyakin, one of the democrats' intellectual leaders, cried out, 'Russia, you've gone mad!' People who did not dare vote against the authorities in dichotomous elections had voiced their protest in party-list voting. Russia's Choice, despite a vigorous media campaign, received only 15.5 per cent of the vote. The shock-populist Liberal Democratic Party of Russia (LDPR) got 22.95 per cent; the Communist Party, 12.4 per cent. In elections to the Second Duma in December 1995, the successor party to Russia's Choice, the 'Democratic Choice of Russia – United Democrats' bloc, received only 3.86 per cent of the vote, while the Communist Party got 39.4 per cent and the Liberal Democrat Party, 11.3 per cent.

The opposition vote was undeniably an expression of protest against Yeltsin and the democrats' policies, but it did not signify a sincere desire to see a change in top-level power. The protest was in effect just so much 'punching after the fight', totally unimportant. Under the new constitution, an opposition parliament could no longer pose a direct threat to the president's power. The figures who had led the parliamentary 'party', once an actual danger to Yeltsin, exited the stage, to be replaced by the new opposition of the Communist Party and the eccentric, but utterly harmless, quasi opposition of Vladimir Zhirinovsky. In contrast to its predecessors, this 'systemic' opposition fully accepted the new 'rules of the game'.

Naturally, the new constitution offered a comprehensive enumeration of rights and freedoms. It also significantly expanded the president's authority.[26] The president was now the head of state, the 'guarantor of the Constitution, and of the rights and liberties of all persons and citizens'. He was the supreme commander in chief and

---

26 An article by Soili Nysten-Haarala, 'A Comparison of the Political Functions and Constitutions of Russia and the Baltic States' [in Russian], offers a good analysis of the Russian Constitution (Dmitrii Furman, ed., *The Baltic States and Russia: Societies, States* [in Russian] [Moscow, 2002]).

director of all foreign policy. The president appointed the government, presiding over its sessions and demanding resignations within
it as he saw fit. These appointments did require Duma approval, but
the president had the right to dissolve the Duma if it rejected his
nominee for prime minister three times (and there was no rule by
which a rejected candidate could not be renominated) or voted no
confidence twice within a three-month period. Moreover, the head of
the government could call for a confidence vote, and if the Duma
voted no confidence, the president could dissolve it within seven
days. Thus, the Constitution placed a sword of Damocles over the
deputies' heads and made legislative power completely dependent on
the executive, which remained free to dismiss an unruly parliament.
The president would issue decrees; propose bills; sign laws (or veto
them, which could be overturned only by a two-thirds vote in
both houses); declare extraordinary states and, in the case of military threats, martial law; and nominate candidates for high courts,
prosecutor general, and chair of the Central Bank. There was an
impeachment process spelled out, but – in contrast to the very straightforward process for dissolving the parliament – it was so complex
that it made impeachment practically impossible. (This provision,
Article 93, had clearly been given especially meticulous consideration.) The position of vice president was eliminated – there would be
only one official elevated through 'nationwide election', and in the
event of the president's unanticipated death or incapacitation, the job
would be performed by the prime minister he had appointed.

In the lower house, the State Duma, half the deputies were elected
through a party-list system and the other half in single-member
districts. To counterbalance it, an upper house was created: the
Federation Council, with two representatives from each of Russia's
federal subjects. The Constitution does not spell out the procedure
for staffing the Federation Council. Its members were initially chosen
by direct vote, but starting in December 1995, administration chiefs
and the heads of the legislative assemblies of 'Federation subjects'
could sit in ex officio. (The opposition-led Duma supported the law,
too, by prior agreement, in exchange for the adoption of a different
law providing the direct elections of regional chiefs – which Yeltsin

categorically did not want to become a kind of victory of the 'reactionary opposition' over 'democratic power', the sole strengthening of democratic institutions during the entire post-Soviet period.)

The Constitution halts the process of the country's 'drifting apart', equalizing the rights of Russia's 'federal subjects' and autonomous republics, declaring the supremacy of federal law and the presidential prerogative to abolish local laws that conflict with federal ones. The Constitution contains no references to the Federation Treaty, which it decreases in force. With the conflict between the branches of power ended, the regional and national powers within the republics had lost their chance to play on their divisions, and a way was cleared for the president to constrain federalism, by degrees, ever more tightly.

Under a regime of imitation democracy, it is not the constitution that establishes the inflexible rules of the game by which winners and losers exchange positions. Those rules are set by whoever comes to power, who will quickly establish new rules that suit them, subject to periodic change, guaranteeing their perpetual victory. Of course, for no-alternative presidential power, any constitution is, to one degree or another, an obstacle. But it is for precisely this reason that what would in a democratic society have been disadvantages in the constitution approved in the December 1993 referendum – the unclear language, all that was missing – are, under an imitation democracy system, strengths. Radical changes in our political system, all of them tending to strengthen official control over society (the transition from the election of the Federation Council by the regional populations to a council on which governors and heads of regional assemblies sit ex officio, and from that to one whose members are in fact appointed; the transition from governors' being elected to their being appointed; the extension of the presidential term), could now be implemented without violating the Constitution or necessitating amendments that would trigger referenda. Those in power could continue fortifying their no-alternative system without entering into sharp or evident dissonance with the 1993 Constitution.

Peter Reddaway and Dmitri Glinski note that 'Putin's presidential powers have exceed those of the American and French presidencies combined, and approximate the powers of Tsar Nicholas II under the 1905 quasi-constitutional system'.[27] It is no accident that the lower house of parliament was named a 'Duma', just like the organ that advised the tsars before Peter I and the parliament that functioned in the final, 'semiconstitutional' days of the Russian Empire. Yeltsin himself was half-jokingly known as Tsar Boris, and became famous for utterances like, 'Not the tsar's problem!' There was even some talk of reviving the monarchy, though it never became too serious. But this was both eccentric and superfluous – Yeltsin's power had already grown complete.

The period of revolutionary chaos was now in the past. The post-Soviet system had a while yet before it would reach its heyday, its 'acme', so to speak – that would come only under Yeltsin's successor – but it had now overcome the most acute crisis of its childhood, emerging in a stronger, more consolidated adult form.

2.2 The First Post-Soviet Presidential Elections

The 1993 and 1995 Duma elections brought defeat to the democratic, pro-presidential parties and marked a tremendous victory for the Liberal Democratic Party of Russia and the reborn Communist Party. One could plainly see that the democrats' electoral base had quickly shrunk as a majority of voters rejected the democrats' radical-Westernist ideology and the president's policies. For huge numbers of people, the words 'democracy' and 'democrats' had become obscenities (indeed, some started using the neologism *der'mokraty*, from the Russian *der'mo* [crap] – meaning something like 'demo-crap-ts'). With nostalgia for the Soviet past on the rise, it became clear that Yeltsin's main rival in the 16 June 1996 presidential elections would be Communist leader Gennady Zyuganov. As the elections approached, Yeltsin and his circle felt increasingly insecure. It could do little to soothe Yeltsin's nerves that in 1994, two of the

---

27   Peter Reddaway and Dmitri Glinski, *The Tragedy of Russia's Reforms* (Washington, DC: United States Institute of Peace, 2001), 633.

three signatories to the Belovezh Accords – Ukraine's Leonid Kravchuk and Belarus's Stanislav Shushkevich – had been driven from power by electoral defeats.

That power would not be handed over to the Communists, regardless of the electoral results, was obvious to everyone and discussed openly. The possibility of the ruling group's handing power over to the opposition was simply out of the question. We get a revealing glimpse of the mood prevailing among the ruling elite in a note that Aleksandr Korzhakov, head of the Presidential Security Service – at this time operating as a powerful secret police force – made in his memoirs of a conversation with Chernomyrdin. Korzhakov recalls saying, 'I told [the Communists], "Look, guys, let's not joke around. You ran things for seventy years. Time to give us seventy. If we can't get anywhere after that, we'll give power back to you." ' Chernomyrdin replies, 'There's no going back'. To which Korzhakov says, 'I know. I was speaking hypothetically.'[28]

At first, Yeltsin, uncertain of the vote and fearing tensions around the elections (by this time he had suffered two heart attacks, with a third coming between the first and second rounds of voting and a fourth immediately after his reelection), concocted plans to postpone them by two years, dissolve the Duma, and ban the Communist Party. The relevant orders had already been prepared. Later, Yeltsin would write, 'I conceived of the situation in this way: At the cost of . . . transcending constitutional limits, I would complete one of my main tasks. The Communist Party in Russia would be done with forever.'[29] The *siloviks* had pushed Yeltsin down this path under the leadership of a man whose fealty had been repeatedly proved: the president's then-all-powerful favourite, Korzhakov. But another point of view, and another court group of intelligentsia and progressives hostile to Korzhakov and his 'plebeian' *siloviks*, prevailed

---

28 Aleksandr Korzhakov, *Boris Yeltsin: From Dawn to Dusk* [in Russian] (Moscow, 1997), 367, 369.

29 Yeltsin, *Presidential Marathon*, 32. Note that this did not prevent his saying, in the 2000 address in which he announced his resignation, 'I've always maintained that I would not take so much as a step outside the bounds of the Constitution' (p. 422).

instead, under the leadership of First Deputy Prime Minister Anatoly Chubais – a leading force in Russia's privatization who had called for the president to proceed with the election and win. Chubais's group enjoyed the support of the Yeltsin family – particularly the president's wife, Naina, and daughter Tatyana, who pushed Boris, himself barely alive, through the paces of the exhausting campaign. Korzhakov and his retinue were driven out. He would go on to write a memoir that painted an absolutely ghastly image of the state of affairs in Yeltsin's 'court' (in my view, the most vivid and interesting memoir of the period).

In terms of the stability of the system, Chubais's group was unquestionably right. Another revolt was eminently possible, and it would create a temporary situation of emergency from which the country would need to be extricated. This in turn would mean immediately again violating the Constitution that had just been adopted, dealing a blow to the 'normalization' that adoption had achieved. Russia would become a country of coups, organized one after another by the same president, constantly betraying his oaths of allegiance to a long series of constitutions. It would undermine the legitimacy of power and destroy the illusion of Russia as a society that endeavoured, whatever the challenges, to walk a democratic path – and could well have proved, for the pro-Yeltsin West, a bridge too far. In the meantime, Chubais's proposal for organizing an electoral victory seemed bold and risky only from the outside. Not only was Yeltsin's victory possible, it was, in fact, certain.

There was, in 1996, little nationwide support for the policies of those who had won contests for power in 1991 and 1993. Yeltsin was, at the start of the year, tremendously unpopular. That the president was quite unwell, suffering from excessive drink (officially, his periodic absences were explained by 'paperwork') and mentally not necessarily 'up to the task'[30] before him, was plain. The president's

---

30   Yeltsin had a strange proclivity for flights of fancy, telling what couldn't quite be called lies because he came, at least to a degree, to believe them himself. He spoke of his own unparalleled achievements in sports. He concocted a story

inevitable defeat was forecast by observers and politicians who had failed to understand the peculiarities of the Russian national consciousness – in which a fear of change in the upper reaches of power and the acceptance of that power as inescapable and independent of the people readily coexist with displeasure at the actions and personal qualities of whoever is wielding it. They were as mistaken as those who had doubted Yeltsin's victory in the 1993 confidence vote.

However unpopular Yeltsin may have been, traditionalist loyalty was already being forcefully redirected toward the new powers of the presidency. There is a story that so clearly and beautifully illustrates this that I will recount it here, though I cannot, unfortunately, remember where I read it. A journalist was speaking with an old woman who lived in poverty. The woman was going on, tearing Yeltsin apart, while speaking wistfully of the Soviet regime. When the journalist asked her whom she would support in the upcoming presidential election, she answered, 'Yeltsin'. 'But what about Zyuganov?' 'When Zyuganov's president, we'll vote for Zyuganov.' There were a great many such old women; in fact everyone, including both Yeltsin's active opponents and the democrat-intellectuals, was to one degree or another an old lady of this kind.

The fear of a change in power, of a return to revolutionary chaos, proved stronger than dissatisfaction with the government. Yeltsin's supporters' avowals that power would not be handed to the Communists even if they won the election, which in some countries would have stirred mass indignation, worked in the president's favour in Russia. Journalist Boris Vishnevskii wrote, 'Many people I knew, with no sympathy for the president, followed a cynical but precise

---

that his falling off a bridge in 1991 resulted from being pushed by political enemies. In 1996, he claimed to have planted potatoes for his family in every year of his presidency. He told wildly improbable stories about a raid by Chechen militants on the village of Pervomaiskoe. All manner of despotic antics, in the spirit of a merchant in one of Aleksandr Ostrovsky's plays – pushing an annoying press secretary off a motorboat into the river, conducting an orchestra in Berlin – doubled as clear manifestations of the pained mental state that followed being catapulted, helplessly, to the pinnacle of power.

logic: If Zyuganov gets more votes, Yeltsin will not leave the Kremlin, but call in the tanks. There will be bloodshed. Better not to allow such a situation to develop.'[31] (My own acquaintances said similar things.) Voters vented their discontent only in the Duma elections – that body was (accurately) not seen as a seat of real power. In actually significant dichotomous voting, where a defeat of those in power could lead to a change in that power and serious destabilization, majorities in both April and December 1993 cast their votes for those in power, seeing no alternative and fearing major jolts to the system. Chubais's group, both democratic and reformist, propelled Yeltsin through the elections, betting on precisely this authoritarian and traditionalist mindset among the masses.

Yeltsin agreed with Chubais because he himself had long known (or at least felt) how key this powerful traditionalist support was – more important for him than the support of the democratic minority. Yeltsin distanced himself from and drove from power the democrats who were obstructing him with their ideologization and ambition, and who had splintered into a number of parties. He sought to position himself not so much as the 'leader of a democratic movement' but as a traditional Russian ruler, a 'president of all Russians', even a Tsar Boris, establishing order and 'gathering' the Russian lands anew. He actively entered a game of integration with Lukashenko in Belarus, intending to demonstrate that the process of rebuilding the USSR had begun. This, to a significant degree, was the purpose of their undertaking a war with separatist Chechnya (as in October 1993, the new democratic government was demonstrating that it was not constrained by the fear of bloodshed that had characterized the late, 'totalitarian' regime). It did not end well, but that failure – already apparent by the 1993 elections – had little impact on the no-alternative nature of the presidency, which continued to suit the majority's traditionalist sensibilities.

In addition to the fear of anarchy and of a repetition of 1991, 1993, or even 1917, the particular character of the opposition contributed

---

31   Boris Vishnevskii, *To Democracy and Back* [in Russian] (Moscow, 2004); available at yabloko.ru.

meaningfully to Yeltsin's victory. When a minority has come to power by illegal means, and fortified that power through equally illegal means, the opposition will naturally become 'extra-systemic' – either 'revolutionary' or 'counter-revolutionary'. Outwardly, this exactly describes the main opposition force in Russia at the time we are discussing: the CPRF. The CPRF can be considered a successor to the CPSU only conditionally, since the overwhelming majority of the old Party and nomenklatura elite steered clear of it. Instead, they allowed themselves to be integrated into the new 'democratic' regime, swapping out ideologies without apparent difficulty. The CPRF thus was a party headed by the representatives of the second and third tier of the Soviet nomenklatura, with an electoral base composed of the lower social classes – those who had lost their baseline social welfare support and customary way of life in the anti-Communist revolution. At the heart of the new party's ideology was a nostalgia for the social guarantees of the Soviet past and the USSR as a great power. The CPRF attacked the Yeltsin regime as an antipopular occupation. At their rallies, one could hear exhortations to 'put Yeltsin's whole gang on trial!' Zhirinovsky, who had threatened to send the democrats to Siberia and called for a 'break southward', presented himself rhetorically as a leader of 'extra-systemic' opposition. This extra-systemicness was, however, superficial, a mere façade.

For one thing, precisely by virtue of its own outward revolutionariness, such an opposition worked objectively for power, enabling Yeltsin to claim that the only alternative to him was a horrific one, and stoking fears that an opposition victory in the elections would spell the return of chaos and the threat of civil war. The superficial extra-systemicness of the opposition thus served the system, operating as a constitutive element of it.

For another thing, peculiarly reflected in the opposition's ideology and policy was not just mass protest – which, unable to assume an 'ordinary' democratic form instead became necessarily 'revolutionary' and 'extremist' – but also mass readiness to accept power, and mass fear of a change in power. The opposition's radicalism and extremism were to an enormous extent rhetorical, compensatory, and aimed at achieving shock. After 1993, the superficial radicalism

of the Communist (and, even more so, the Zhirinovskian) opposition
came mixed with a readiness to make compromises and deals with
power, its hollering about the 'occupation government' accompanied
by votes for that government and its budget. The main target of the
opposition's attacks was the 'antipopular course' and the presidential
appointees who embodied it – the likes of Gaidar and Chubais –
rather than the president, who could always 'course correct' and
drive out his most despised officials. Opposition leaders had attained
a comfortable and relatively stable political niche for themselves and
had no desire to risk it in a power struggle. Many observers noted
that Zyuganov conducted his 1996 presidential campaign with
neither any hope for victory nor any real enthusiasm – rather, it was
all 'for appearances'.

Another characteristic of the opposition that reduced its ability to
threaten power was extreme disunity. A union of the basic opposition
force, the Communists, with the Zhirinovskians was impossible.
Instead, the two camps were competitors, working in a narrow electoral field of 'protest', their leaders fearful of losing their positions,
with Zhirinovsky prone to periodic bursts of passionate anti-
Communist philippics. In point of fact, Zhirinovsky was acting as a
spoiler for the more serious and ideological Communist opposition.

Communist quasi extremism at the same time made it impossible
to unite the leftist Communist opposition with the liberal one that
had also been taking shape. This opposition, represented most
prominently by the Yabloko party, had a limited social base, drawn
mainly from the intelligentsia, and drew a segment of democrats
displeased with the authoritarian transformation of the regime.[32]
But however much opposition democrats protested Yeltsin's authoritarianism and the Chechen War (though these protests did not
extend so far as the demand for Chechen independence – 'the right

---

32   Even light attempts at 'feeling things out' between the Communists
and the foremost opposition party, Yabloko, provoked great concern among
those in power. But in fact Yabloko leader Grigory Yavlinsky had said,
'Communism is like lice – it's spread by poverty.' Both Zyuganov and Yavlinsky preferred comfortable niches to risky alliances.

of peoples to self-determination' stayed safely in the romantic past), Yeltsin remained for them a lesser evil compared with the terrifying prospect of Communist revanche.[33] In critical situations, Yeltsin could absolutely rely on their support. In early 1996, when asked whether democratic forces would support him in the elections, Yeltsin responded, 'Where else are they going to go!'[34]

In short, it was exactly the kind of opposition – just radical enough in its pronouncements to voice some feelings of protest, just externally 'frightening' enough to keep voters afraid of its coming to power, content enough with its relatively stable political niche to have no interest in expanding beyond it, compromising, sluggish, seeing more evil in other opposition forces than in Yeltsin – needed to make the president's 1996 victory possible. The Communists' quasi extremism and the democrats' dogmatic anti-Communism complemented each other, together guaranteeing the no-alternative nature of Yeltsin's power.

The nearer the elections drew, the higher Yeltsin's ratings soared. According to polling data, in January 1996, when asked whether, if the elections were held the following Sunday, respondents were prepared to vote for Yeltsin, 8 per cent answered yes; in February, 11 per cent; in March, 15 per cent; in April, 18 per cent; in May, 28 per cent, and in June, 36 per cent.[35]

The regime organized a fantastical electoral campaign. As it ran its course, objective information disappeared from mass media

---

33   In 1995, Yavlinsky wrote, '[Power] . . . creates a breeding ground for fascists and orthodox Communists. Therefore, we are power's democratic opposition. In relation to the Zhirinovskians, the patriot-nationalists, and the orthodox Communists, we are an implacable opposition.' Grigory Yavlinsky, 'On Russian Politics', *Speeches and essays, 1994–1999* [in Russian] [Moscow, 1999], 68. A month before the 1996 elections, he declared, 'Democrats and liberals are the logical opponents of the "party of power", and, of course, of the "party of Communists"' (p. 169). Writing of the Soviet past, he speaks of 'the power of impudent scum who detested and reviled their own people' (pp. 408–9).

34   Yavlinsky, 'On Russian Politics', 154.

35   'The Presidential Elections and Public Opinion' [in Russian] (Moscow: VTSIOM), 64.

altogether. As Yeltsin's main rival, Zyuganov never appeared on television without the accompaniment of negative commentary.
Money – taken from both the budget and frightened 'oligarchs' – was
passed around in notorious boxes of Xerox copy paper. Innumerable
propaganda concerts featuring pop stars were organized to attract
youth. Yeltsin travelled across the country, dancing with the young
and promising anyone absolutely anything they wanted. Germany
and France provided emergency loans to ensure Yeltsin could pay on
debts owed to government workers (these loans were arranged by
Mikhail Kasyanov, who would go on to serve as Putin's first prime
minister). American campaign specialists were invited, despite
understanding little about the realities of Russian life, 'just in case'
help was suddenly needed. Before the elections, a special, free newspaper called *God Forbid!* was published, with a circulation of 10
million, dedicated to portraying the horrors that awaited Russia in
the event of a Communist victory. To make it more persuasive, they
even included a faked version of the CPRF's economic plan. And, of
course, all the available 'administrative resources' (a euphemism that
gained currency at this time, denoting various kinds of illegal and
semilegal influence on voters, even the falsification of electoral
results) of local authorities were used. (One of the jokes that circu-
lated at the time: 'Yeltsin will win with 52 per cent – Zyuganov will
only get 51 per cent.') But the entire campaign was to a significant
degree superfluous.

The tremendous rise in Yeltsin's ratings in 1996 owed less to the
efforts of propagandists than to deeper causes. People who feared
both a change of power and the very prospect of voting for the
opposition were ready to convince themselves Yeltsin wasn't so bad –
at any rate, better than his rivals. The 'triumph of professional image
makers' could take place only because their propaganda fell on
well-prepared ground.

In the first round of elections on 16 June, the president managed
to overtake the rest of the field, receiving 35.3 per cent of votes
(Zyuganov got 32.03 per cent, and the rest were divided among
non-Communist opposition candidates: 14.32 per cent to the charismatic general Aleksandr Lebed, 7.34 per cent to Grigory Yavlinsky,

and 5.7 per cent to Zhirinovsky). After the first round, Yeltsin named Lebed as secretary of the Security Council, after which he began supporting reelection. Yabloko let its members and supporters loose to vote as they wanted; in most of their 'hearts' (one of Yeltsin's campaign slogans was 'Vote with your heart!'), voting for the Communists was out of the question. And so it was that in the second round on 3 July, most of the votes for non-Communist candidates who had not made it to the second round naturally fell to Yeltsin, the 'lesser of all evils'. In the end, Yeltsin received 53.8 per cent of the vote, and Zyuganov 40.3 per cent.[36]

Had Zyuganov prevailed, this would have been the first case in Russian history of an opposition victory in elections for the nation's highest office. This in turn could theoretically have been the first step on a path to true democracy, considering that the goal of restoring the Soviet past was entirely unrealistic, and Zyuganov was immeasurably less well situated to build a regime of no-alternative power than was Yeltsin. But no such victory was possible. Unlike during the 1993 crisis, there was no mortal threat to power in 1996. (The only real threat was that Yeltsin, unable to take the pressure of campaigning, might die.)

The Yeltsin era's second crisis posed fewer dangers to Russia's presidential power and system of imitation democracy than its first. The atmosphere of fatefulness that had been created around the 1996 elections ('Vote or you'll lose!') was partly the product of natural fears held by Yeltsin and his retinue, and partly a deliberate creation,

---

36 There are those who believe Zyuganov was the actual winner, and Yeltsin had to falsify the results to claim victory. Mikhail Delyagin writes, 'Today there is practically no room to doubt that in 1996 a majority voted for Zyuganov . . . Zyuganov, however, fearful of the responsibility and of angering Yeltsin's circle, decided not to protest the obvious fraud, choosing instead to surrender power. At the same time, he guaranteed himself a lifelong title as 'head of His Imperial Greatness's opposition' (Mikhail Delyagin, 'Default?' [in Russian], *Novaya Gazeta*, 14 August 2009, 6). I do not doubt there was some fraudulence in Yeltsin's favour; nonetheless, since most of Yavlinsky's and Lebed's votes, as well as many of Zhirinovsky's, passed to Yeltsin, his victory seems easily explainable without recourse to accusations of fraud.

intended to scare the populace with the horrific prospects of the chaos and civil war that might arise in the case of an opposition victory.

Nonetheless, the 1996 elections were an important landmark in the development of our post-Soviet system. They served to demonstrate, to both power itself and the society that had taken shape, in general terms, the full potential of a system in which supreme power operated independently of the popular approval of policy or the general assessment of its bearer's human qualities. Neither the people's will nor their approbation determined who would be president – on the contrary, it was precisely his being president that ensured their approbation. The elections of 1996 go a very long way in elucidating the later popularity and electoral support enjoyed by Vladimir Putin. If Yeltsin could win in 1996, having done everything in his power to squander the popularity he enjoyed in 1991, it seemed clear that any successor he appointed would be 'doomed' to further electoral triumphs.

The 1996 elections fully dispelled the illusion that a constitutional change of power remained possible within the framework of Russia's developing political system. It had become obvious that, henceforth, the goal of the opposition would not be to achieve power, but rather to achieve ever-less-attainable seats in the impotent Duma and to exert ever-weaker pressure on the authorities. The electorate was losing its incentive to vote for the opposition, which it now understood would never come to power (nor was it even trying). And so the opposition began to wither away.

2.3 The Succession Crisis

In 1999, a new crisis emerged, capable of bringing down the entire system. It centred on the question of how power would be transferred. Like every crisis, it was characterized by both unforeseeable elements and regular, systemic ones. Sooner or later, it was inevitable.

Russia's post-Soviet system was created around Yeltsin's personal power. But any such power, even if it remains unlimited by politics, will be limited by biology. In an authoritarian system, the transfer of power from one person to another always presents a crisis to some degree, as the new ruler makes changes to the circle and policies he has inherited. For some, this will mean disaster; for others, happiness. When a ruler dies suddenly, in the absence of legally prescribed order of succession, a very acute crisis can ensue, a struggle for power. Naturally, the crisis will prove less acute where a ruler has announced his successor in advance, though this possibility is in turn complicated by the fact that the very designation of a successor cannot but diminish the ruler's power. Some dissatisfied contingent will always dream of the ruler changing his mind. A kind of 'successor's party' – those impatiently waiting for the old ruler to die or step down – inevitably forms.

Under Russia's autocratic system, a crisis ensued nearly every time a ruler died. Even after the adoption of a law on succession aimed at minimizing uncertainty in the transfer of power, a 'successor's party', with agreement of the successor himself – Alexander I – planned the murder of his father, Paul I. The transfer of power from Alexander to his brother Nikolai I twenty-four years later was marred by the Decembrist uprising.

Under the Soviet system, too, the succession of power had inevitably been accompanied by struggle among the ruling elite. Intrinsic to the Soviet system was a contradiction between, on the one hand, true autocracy and the irreplaceability of the leader, and on the other, the formal process of electing leaders through organs of the Communist Party, which inevitably contributed some uncertainty. Leaders did not formally hold office for life; Khrushchev had even been removed without dying. Such a system made it impossible for authorities to announce their successors in advance and gave the ruler little power to choose who would take power after his death; in practice, the Politburo would choose a successor, who would then be confirmed (though this was mere civic ritual) by the Central Committee and Party Congress. Nobody could rise to power from outside the tight, familiar circle of the Politburo, and the transfer of power was far more institutionalized and orderly than in post-Soviet systems.

In imitation-democratic systems, the chasm between the formal and actual mechanisms of governance is broader than in the Soviet system, let alone tsarism, and there is accordingly broader uncertainty in the process of transferring power and authority. In Russia, the Politburo had become 'the family', an informal circle of those close to the ruler, regardless of their duties. Its boundaries were sketchy, its membership highly labile. Under Yeltsin, it included Korzhakov, as well as billionaires Boris Berezovsky and Roman Abramovich. According to the Constitution, the president was elected by the people – but this was a mere formality, and there was in fact no institutionalized, orderly way of transferring power. The president could name any successor he wanted, but there was nothing in place to ensure his entourage would implement his wishes when he died.[37] Here a kind of gap arose that could lead to splits among the ruling elite, the activation of society, even the dismantling of the system. Outside Russia, the post-Soviet space has seen only two cases where a ruler died in office and had to be succeeded, in Azerbaijan and Turkmenistan. Both were accompanied by succession struggles that precipitated severe crises.[38]

---

37 Naturally, rulers have often named their children as successors, and the 'pseudo-dynasties' this has created in systems of imitation democracy strongly resemble normal, monarchic dynasties, with the added twist that the successor-child is popularly elected. (This has been the path of the Somozas in Nicaragua, the Assads in Syria, the Gaddafis in Libya, and the Mubaraks in Egypt. There is also the Kim dynasty in Communist North Korea.) In the post-Soviet space, such a dynasty has so far emerged only in Azerbaijan – but it is very unlikely to be the last. In Russia, the idea of transferring power to Yeltsin's daughter Tatyana Dyachenko was discussed, but no serious plans were drawn up. One wonders how our history might have turned out differently if Yeltsin, like Aliyev, had had a grown son with serious designs on power.

38 Although a successor had been named in Azerbaijan long since (Heydar Aliyev's son Ilham), his rise to power was made more difficult not only by a power struggle within the Aliyev clan but also by the opposition's attempt to instigate a 'colour revolution' at the time of Ilham's election. Niyazov's death, too, led to fighting among the ruling elite of Turkmenistan. Assembly chair Öwezgeldi Ataýew, whom the Constitution named as the president's successor, was quickly arrested and relieved of office, and

Russia underwent its crisis of transferring power first, when Yeltsin – very much alive – announced that he would leave office, requiring the investment of authority in a successor.

There is no point seeking some deep reason for this in the details of Russia's culture or political system. A simple, obvious explanation is likelier correct. Yeltsin's health had deteriorated horrendously after the 1996 elections, and he now faced the choice of either leaving office to prolong his life or amending the Constitution to make it possible to seek a third term, which he would be unlikely to draw breath for much of. His family and circle conceptualized the choice differently: either take charge of a process by which the president could step down and transfer power to someone they trusted, or run the risk of being persecuted after the rise of some outsider beyond their control.

At first, Yeltsin made use of the problem of succession to test his circle's loyalty (from time to time he told various people, like Chernomyrdin and Yuri Luzhkov, that he was considering them to succeed him – whereupon they, no fools, would categorically proclaim their own unworthiness and Yeltsin's indispensability), and to play possible contenders off one another. At the same time, Yeltsin hastily distanced himself from anyone who really believed himself a likely successor – Rutskoy, Lebed, Chernomyrdin. He was in no hurry to weaken his power by being seen with some official successor, a constant reminder of his own eventual disappearance. A successor would also strip from ruler and society alike the no-alternative aura of the presidency as a 'successor's party' that inevitably began forming. Now that the position of vice president had been eliminated as incompatible with the consolidation of presidential autocracy in the 1993 Constitution, the second-ranked position in the government hierarchy was the prime minister, appointed by the president. In the event of the president's death or resignation, presidential power

---

Gurbanguly Berdymukhammedov took power. The anticipation of Nazarbayev's death in Kazakhstan has likewise stirred up fierce dynastic disputes there.

would be transferred to the prime minister until new elections could be held. Thus, the office of prime minister took on an added dimension: it indicated the president's likely successor. So long as the president was in good health and planned on remaining in office, this remained a relatively minor aspect of the job; but as Yeltsin quickly deteriorated and lost his ability to work, it took on ever-greater significance.

From 1992 to March 1993, while Chernomyrdin served as prime minister, the post continued to accumulate power. Though Chernomyrdin himself remained totally loyal to the president, the public increasingly viewed him as a successor. In 1996, he even served as president for 24 hours while Yeltsin underwent heart surgery. (The very first thing Yeltsin did on waking up was rescind the decree transferring power.) Chernomyrdin began conducting himself with greater assurance and self-possession. He grew even more popular after his public role resolving the Budyonnovsk hospital hostage crisis of 1995 while the president was overseas. Yeltsin simply could not abide the rise in his prime minister's popularity and power. The last straw was a visit Chernomyrdin paid to the US, where he was received as Russia's future head of state. The president demanded his resignation – a move he would later describe as a mistake. Transferring power to Chernomyrdin would have been easy, and left Yeltsin's 'family' free of the fear of persecution. Yeltsin's thirst for power and egotism had landed him in a difficult spot: he now had to find not just a prime minister, but a successor to whom he was essentially promising power. A frantic search for successors – and a game of prime-ministerial leapfrog – ensued.

Having jettisoned Chernomyrdin, Yeltsin named Sergei Kiriyenko as his prime minister. Young and little known, Kiriyenko was a former minister of fuel and energy who had recently arrived in Moscow from Nizhniy Novgorod (and had been nicknamed Kinder Surprise). Having no party of his own, he was wholly dependent on the president. He made Yeltsin feel younger, while at the same time enabling him to play the role of the wise old man taking an apprentice under his wing. He also served as a demonstration of Yeltsin's power: 'I'll appoint who I want.' In the Duma, a majority of deputies moved swiftly to confirm Kiriyenko, lest Yeltsin dissolve the body. Yeltsin himself crudely and undisguisedly used his influence over deputies' material interests as leverage, and could be seen across the airwaves saying he would have his administration resolve parliamentarians' worldly dilemmas (which mostly concerned getting apartments in Moscow).

But in August 1998, a severe financial crisis broke out under Kiriyenko's 'reformist' government. The Russian Central Bank sharply devalued the ruble and defaulted on its debt. Bewildered, Yeltsin dismissed Kiriyenko and reinstated Chernomyrdin, resigning himself to the latter as an official successor. In a televised address on 24 August 1998, Yeltsin explained, 'Another important consideration motivates this decision: to ensure the continuity of power in the year 2000.'[39] But here, events took a turn the president had not managed to foresee.

There was a combination of factors: the default; the debasement of the Duma at Kiriyenko's appointment; and a general feeling that the president was lost, impotent, his days numbered. Together, they awakened the Communist opposition and rallied the political elite to organize among themselves and name a presidential successor of their own. The same parliament that had obediently confirmed Kiriyenko twice refused to vote for the far more acceptable Chernomyrdin. This frightened Yeltsin so badly that not only did he not dare dissolve the parliament, he went so far as to forget his anti-Communist scruples completely and nominate Yuri Maslyukov, a Communist, as prime minister.[40] Moscow mayor Yuri Luzhkov began openly eyeing Yeltsin's legacy, which tremendously irritated the president and his circle. In the end, they settled on a candidate more acceptable to Yeltsin: former intelligence chief turned foreign minister and academic Yevgeny Primakov. Proposed by Yavlinsky, he had the support of a Duma majority.

The Primakov government was the first and last in post-Soviet Russia to have a leader put forth by the majority of a parliament

---

39   Yeltsin, *Presidential Marathon*, 218.

40   *See* Yevgeny Primakov, *Eight Months Plus* [in Russian] (Moscow, 2001), 8.

chosen through relatively free elections. Gathering courage from the situation, this parliament even went so far as to initiate a vote to impeach the president (there was practically no chance this would succeed, but it did manage to play on Yeltsin's nerves and strengthen his resolve to leave office).

If Chernomyrdin had become an alternative to the president only gradually by virtue of his limiting Yeltsin's power and serving as his obvious successor, then the popular Primakov, supported by a parliamentary majority and widely credited with resolving the 1998 crisis, had been such an alternative from the very start. The elite began reorienting themselves in his direction, seeing him as an embodiment of the stability, poise, and solidity that had characterized the ever-more-longed-for late Soviet period. To Yeltsin, Primakov came to symbolize the end of his era. To the Yeltsin 'family', this potential successor – independent of the president, owing him nothing, already launching anti-corruption campaigns[41] – took on the appearance of a mortal threat.

It wasn't only to particular people – Yeltsin, his friends and family, those closest to him – that Primakov posed a threat. He objectively became a threat as well to the system itself. Under the Primakov government, something resembling an authentic separation of powers emerged – not well-defined branches of authority, exactly, but still two centres of power, limiting each other and creating the conditions for the legislature and judiciary to take strong, 'normalized' roles. Besides that, there were elections looming, threatening to offer actual alternatives. Had Primakov declared his candidacy over Yeltsin's objections and defeated any last-minute Yeltsin-protégé nominees, Yeltsin would have been followed by an unappointed successor, and Russia would have been very close to seeing no-alternative power replaced by a system of democratic rotation. By the eve of the

---

41   Primakov had proclaimed the need for an amnesty that would 'free up space in jail for everyone we'll imprison on economic charges'. Yeltsin's response was to aver that 'it has finally become clear this popular prime minister . . . lives in thrall to Soviet stereotypes' (Yeltsin, *Presidential Marathon*, 298).

presidential elections, Primakov had formed something like an alliance with Luzhkov to create a political bloc. Yeltsin and the system in turn coped with the danger.

On 12 May 1999, Yeltsin fired Primakov. In the memoirs he wrote shortly thereafter, Yeltsin muses, 'Did I have the right to let Primakov . . . walk the country back to socialism . . . ? I am deeply persuaded that the answer is no.'[42] Yeltsin had already informed the Speaker of the Duma that he planned to appoint Rail Minister Nikolai Aksyonenko as the next prime minister, but at quite literally the last moment, he changed his mind (or was otherwise persuaded). Instead, he named Sergei Stepashin, minister of Internal Affairs and onetime head of counterintelligence and the FSB. But Stepashin was 'weak' and did not suit the president, who may have conceived of him from the start as a temporary placeholder. In the end, Yeltsin and his circle chose a successor about whom little was known, by the masses and the elite alike. Quite without warning, in August 1999 Yeltsin fired Stepashin as prime minister and replaced him with Vladimir Putin, who had risen swiftly from a modest posting in the St Petersburg city government to head of the FSB, having been a midlevel KGB functionary during the Soviet period. Putin's case had been taken up especially vigorously by the oligarch Boris Berezovsky, then enjoying tremendous influence in Yeltsin's 'family'. Berezovsky had good reason to fear Primakov, who had opened a criminal money laundering investigation against him.[43]

The choice of Putin, made under great time pressure, was no doubt somewhat haphazard. Yeltsin might easily have landed on someone else. In his book *Presidential Marathon*, he claims to have decided on Putin well in advance and then kept the secret, but it seems clear that in fact he had vacillated for some time between Putin and

---

42 Yeltsin, *Presidential Marathon*, 295.

43 Even years later, after he had become Putin's sworn enemy and fled the country, Berezovsky told an interviewer, 'Had Primakov become president, it would have meant catastrophe for Russia' (F. Medvedev, *"I'm Tired of the Twentieth Century": Interviews on the Verge of a Foul* [in Russian] [Moscow, 2009], 472).

Aksyonenko, who had become first deputy prime minister in Stepashin's government. Nonetheless, the choice of Putin reflects certain
predictable tendencies.

Most important, to be sure, was that Putin had shown himself to be
a man 'of understanding', able to serve his patrons honestly, free of
excessive constraint from 'abstract legality', capable of pulling off
'special operations'. After his former boss, Anatoly Sobchak, a mayor of
St Petersburg who had been a democratic leader during the Gorbachev
era, suffered electoral defeat and was accused of corruption, Putin,
now director of the FSB, refused to turn on him, instead helping him
escape to Paris. Later, in February 2000, he would be seen weeping at
Sobchak's funeral. Putin proved his loyalty to the Yeltsin 'family' by
helping to gather compromising information on the 'insurgent' prosecutor general Yuri Skuratov, freeing the Yeltsin circle from the threat
that its corruption would be exposed. This combination of extraordinary personal loyalty and a talent for carrying out special operations
represented everything the Yeltsin 'family' wanted in a successor. It was,
of course, hardly a coincidence that Yeltsin found himself looking to the
ranks of the special services for his successor – first Primakov, then
Stepashin, finally Putin. The transfer of power from Yeltsin – a leader
among 'democrats', an associate of Sakharov's and in certain ways his
successor, a man who had once had ample reason to fear the KGB – to
a 'KGB man' presents an irony of history. But it is only one of post-
Soviet history's many ironies, a manifestation of the systemic
transformation that followed the democrats' victory in 1991.

In other ways, Putin was a natural choice. Yeltsin selected a
successor quite different from himself psychologically. Yeltsin
hungered for power, behaved impulsively, exhibited little self-control,
and was unpredictable, unbalanced. He chose someone who had
harboured no aspirations to the presidency, someone disciplined,
effective, almost grotesquely secretive and 'buttoned up'.[44] The

---

44 In later years, Putin more than once 'lost his cool' and started talking like a criminal. But these were either deliberate attempts to win the people
over or the outbursts natural in a person constantly holding himself back.
This is quite different from Yeltsin's mode of intemperance.

differences between these two men, I think, highlight the progressive stages of the system's development. Yeltsin, power hungry and impulsive, represents the revolutionary stage. The 'charismatic', the destroyer of the old system – a role Putin could never have played. But the same qualities that brought Yeltsin to a lead role in the destruction of the USSR and to an ascent into revolutionary power also made it impossible for him to function through the consolidation and ordering of the new system. That called for someone with very different qualities. It is clear Yeltsin on some level understood this. About choosing Putin, he wrote, 'The new Russia is past the stage of democratic revolution. We now return to the concept of statehood.'[45] It may also be that Putin's relative obscurity, having played no political role in the events of 1991, appealed to Yeltsin's desire to limit the association of power with the post-Soviet revolution and the destruction of the USSR.

Thus, in the naming of Putin by Yeltsin and his 'family', the haphazard entwined with the predictable, the fortuitous appearing as a form taken by natural tendencies.

As in 1996, of course, the authorities were nervous, seeking to insure themselves against unforeseen developments. One form this need for insurance took was the Second Chechen War (the lead-up to the first presidential election brought the First Chechen War, and with the second election, the process repeated), whose onset was accompanied by dark, mysterious events – explosions in Moscow apartments, a thwarted bombing in Ryazan that was declared an FSB exercise, and the Chechen invasion of Dagestan, which came in the wake of talks between Berezovsky and Chechen commanders. We are unlikely to ever find out whether these resulted from 'special operations', as was widely believed at the time by both Putin's supporters and his opponents (the journalist Vitaly Tretyakov wrote of 'a brilliant operation by the special services, which lured Basayev and Khattab to Dagestan'), but there is no question that the attacks, and then the war, helped rally society around the authorities – and more than anything, around the prime minister who was leading the fight.

---

45   Yeltsin, *Presidential Marathon*, 238.

Putin took savvy advantage of the situation to craft an image as a tough, decisive leader – the very 'strong hand' so many had longed for. At one point, he was quoted as saying, 'We will pursue the terrorists everywhere . . . If you'll pardon the expression, when we catch them in the toilet, we'll wipe them out in the john.' The war overshadowed everything else and spared Putin from having to advance any other policies – he was 'saving Russia', after all.

Before elections to the Third Duma, scheduled for 19 December 1999, seemingly 'out of nowhere', the 'Unity' movement was founded to support Putin, with the help of Berezovsky's uncontainable energy and vast wealth. There was, in fact, only one plank in its platform: support for the prime minister as successor. Putin also enjoyed the support of the right-wing Union of Right Forces (SPS) – the last surviving outgrowth of a once-vigorous democratic movement – which saw Primakov as tainted by his connections to the Communists and insufficiently 'pro-market'. For all the democrats' traditional antipathy toward the KGB, their anti-Communism was even stronger, and it pushed them to once again opt for imitation, rather than actual, democracy. Power was doing all that it could to ensure Unity and the SPS overtook the Primakov-Luzhkov bloc, 'Fatherland – All Russia'. They threatened governors with blackmail and lured them with fiscal subsidies. 'Fatherland – All Russia', a timorous attempt at self-organization by the elite, was melting under the rays of a new rising sun. As soon as a 'true' successor had been identified, the elite began reorienting themselves toward him. In the election, Unity came in second to the Communists. The CPRF got 24.2 per cent of votes; Unity, 23.3 per cent; Fatherland – All Russia, 13.3 per cent; the SPS, 8.5 per cent; the Zhirinovsky bloc, 6 per cent; Yabloko, 3.9 per cent.

On 31 December 1999, Yeltsin announced his resignation, making Putin acting president in accordance with the Constitution. As power was being transferred, his valedictory 'statement for posterity' was 'Take care of Russia!' (Years later, in a televised address shortly after Yeltsin's death on 23 April 2007, Putin would say, 'We will do everything to ensure that the memory of Boris Nikolayevich Yeltsin, his noble thoughts and his words, "take care of Russia", will always act as our moral and political watchwords.'[46]) Naturally, Putin used his first official decree to guarantee Yeltsin and his circle immunity from prosecution in connection with their conduct during Yeltsin's presidency. The scene on TV was like something out of a political thriller: Yeltsin taking the exculpatory decree from Putin in one hand, before extending his appointment to serve as acting president in the other.

Putin entered the snap election fully vested with power, with mass support organized by Unity and the SPS. Only two opponents posed a real danger to him. First was Primakov, an eminence after the late Soviet mould, psychologically incapable of open struggle. The Berezovsky-controlled media dogged him constantly. Second was Luzhkov, the Moscow mayor. The airwaves were soon awash in accusations of not only his family's corruption (Luzhkov's wife headed a construction company that had made her, over his time in office, the richest woman in Europe) but his having actually arranged the death of a businessman who'd gotten in his way. Primakov and Luzhkov withdrew from the field. There remained only Yeltsin's old rivals, defeated in 1996 – Zyuganov, Zhirinovsky, Yavlinsky – and entirely unserious candidates who had filed just to see their names in the news. Putin, understanding (or sensing) the traditionalist source from which his support flowed, did not behave like a candidate running against other candidates. He put forward no programme and offered no polemics. Putin was power. A vote for him was not one choice from among possible alternatives, but an expression of loyalty to the authorities. All the more so when the country was in peril, its very integrity under threat. On 22 March 2000, Putin won in the first round – an achievement that had eluded Yeltsin in 1996. Putin got 52.94 per cent of the vote; Zyuganov, 29.2 per cent; Yavlinsky, 5.2 per cent; Zhirinovsky, 2.7 per cent. The Fatherland – All Russia bloc quickly broke apart, its remnants merging with the pro-Putin Unity to form United Russia.

A majority of people enthusiastically cast their ballots for the new president, who replaced the disliked Yeltsin and embodied the return of power in its more traditional form, truly independent of the people

---

46   'Vladimir Putin's Address on the Occasion of Boris Yeltsin's Passing', 23 April 2007, kremlin.ru.

(including the elite). There were elements of the lower social strata, those who had lost the most in the reforms and had the most traditionalist consciousness, who had once voted against Yeltsin and his power, which they had not perceived as actual or legitimate, but who now voted for that power, in effect recognizing it.

The most perilous crisis, the succession of power, which had threatened to bring the system down and lead to an actual democratic transition, had been successfully navigated. In overcoming it, the system had been dramatically fortified. Power had demonstrated its colossal force and independence from society. An unpopular president made a last-minute appointment, of someone no one had even heard of, and this person went on to an electoral triumph. The elite's attempt at self-organization had been nipped in the bud. The system could be 'depersonalized', breaking the bonds that connected it to the personality of its creator, freeing it from dependence on his life. It had reached maturity, fully bloomed.

With Putin's election, the construction of a no-alternative system for presidential power was basically complete. The system had undergone its most acute political crises, its 'growing pains'. There seemed to be no crises capable of posing a serious threat to power for the rest of the Putin era. Putin did not fight, as Yeltsin had, to protect his power (nor, indeed, his life) from his numerous enemies. Rather, he 'calmly completed' the edifice his predecessor (or all of Russian society under his predecessor) had started constructing. Thus, I will henceforth describe the evolution of the system not in chronological order, moving from crisis to crisis, but in functional directions.

2.4 Suppressing Separatism and Subordinating Regional Power

One of the most pressing tasks before Putin was the centralization of control over the Russian space and the suppression of separatist, autonomist, and federalist tendencies. Putin seems to have seen this ('preserving Russia's integrity') as his main task. In his book *First*

Person, he offers an eschatological image of how the state might have collapsed if the Chechens weren't stopped and relations between the centre and the periphery were not steadied. 'The whole Caucasus would have seceded. That much is clear. Then, up the Volga – Bashkortostan, Tatarstan. You know, when I imagined the real consequences, I was struck dumb. I thought . . . how many refugees can Europe, America take? . . . Or would we have to consent to breaking apart the country?'[47] Psychologically, the hyperbole is understandable; the task of strengthening his power takes on the fervour of a mission to save not only Russia but almost the whole planet, Europe and America – ends that justify a generous range of means. In reality, though, as in other spheres, the basic work had already been done by Yeltsin. The adoption of the Constitution had already arrested the 'drifting apart' of the Russian space, and Chechnya, battered, collapsing into anarchy, left without hope or certainty after the Khasavyurt Accord, could no longer serve as an inspiring example for other republics. Putin just consolidated what had been achieved before him and walked further down the path of centralization.

He also embarked on the Second Chechen War (a clear understanding of how this war started has not been possible; it will likely arrive only after many years). This time, the Russian army was able to demolish organized Chechen resistance, and Chechnya was formally readmitted into the administrative space of the Russian Federation. (It is probably better understood as an authoritarian vassal state, in whose internal affairs Moscow rarely interferes.) The victory helped create an upsurge in Russian society, as well as in Putin's popularity ('Russia has ceased retreating, our armaments are victorious again'), opening a path for the new president to further centralize management of the country.

Under Yeltsin, central control of regional power, especially once governors began being directly elected, had been highly relative and rather indirect. The levers that operated it were financial, pulled by regional representatives of the president (themselves not so effective,

---

47   Vladimir Putin, *In the First Person: Conversations with Vladimir Putin* [in Russian] (Moscow, 2000), 135–6.

often rejected or co-opted by local elites) with support from the
mayors of regional capitals who competed with governors. Now
Putin sought to collect regional authorities into a single, vertical line
of bureaucratic power. In May 2000, the country was divided by
presidential decree into seven federal okrugs, each encompassing a
number of federal subjects. They were headed by appointed representatives of the president, mainly *siloviks*. Control over the elected
governors and local elites was tightened; the status of the national
autonomous regions ('constitutive republics of the Russian Federation') plummeted. National republics that had until recently
pretended to 'sovereignty' and 'treaty relations' with Russia found
themselves part of Russia's territory, ruled through its administrative
subdivisions.[48] Work was underway to bring regional legislation in
line with the Russian Constitution. Putin also severely limited the
regions' financial autonomy, concentrating most of the country's tax
revenues in the centre.

Changes were made as well to the way the Federation Council
would be staffed. At first (from January 1994 to January 1996), it was
composed of regional representatives elected by constituents. In
1995, the new Federation Council law provided that all elected governors and legislative assembly chairs would sit on the council ex officio.
Under a 2000 law, the council's 'senators' came to be appointed by
governors and legislative assemblies. This meant the governors' loss
of their deputy immunity and the diminishment of the significance
of the council, theretofore something akin to a gathering of regional
'barons' that had managed to demonstrate its obduracy a couple of
times.

The next stage came in 2004, when the direct election of heads of
oblasts and republics was phased out in favour of presidential

---

48   Later, a number of these federal subjects would merge, and some of
these small ethnic regions – the Komi-Permyak Autonomous Okrug, the
Ust-Orda Buryat Autonomous Okrug, the Agin-Buryat Autonomous Okrug –
would dissolve and be assimilated by the Great Russians. But the attempt to
enfold the Republic of Adygea into the Krasnodar Krai provoked strong resistance, and the mergers were ceased. Those in power were afraid to touch the
volatile republics of the northern Caucasus.

appointments. Regional legislative assemblies would now have candidates proposed to them by the president, who could remove a governor by decree or temporarily dismiss him from office. (Putin, for some reason, used the Beslan hostage crisis, which he thought demonstrated the need to strengthen the 'power vertical', as an opportunity to introduce this measure. A ruler looking to fortify his power will see anything as an argument in favour of it.) Just as the governors were now appointees, their representatives on the Federation Council, too, had become appointees of appointees. The Federation Council had been transformed from an influential body that represented regional elites into an assortment of random people, totally dependent on the regime and often bearing little connection to 'their' regions. (In 2009, during the Medvedev era, Putin's law on the form of the Federation Council was somewhat amended. Now, only deputies of regional assemblies or local self-government bodies are eligible to be voted or appointed 'senators'.)

While this was happening, Putin eliminated gubernatorial term limits. Thus, whereas a disloyal governor could be promptly removed from office, a loyal one might serve indefinitely. As of October 2009, the heads of two of Russia's federal subjects had been in office since 1990, six more since 1991, another since 1992, and three more since 1993.

The continual elimination of the threats to central power that could originate among regional populations and authorities ultimately robbed the state of its federal character, which was incompatible with the no-alternative nature of the presidency. As in the USSR, Putin's Russia combined formal, constitutional federalism with an almost complete centralization. And, as in the USSR, especially the later USSR, that centralization was also sharply limited and formal.

Local authorities in post-Soviet Russia, like those in the late Soviet Union, were expected to show utmost loyalty, and were in exchange given wide latitude in the maintenance of daily affairs. The system of relations between the centre (which strove most of all for stability) and the periphery in some ways resembled feudalism, where the vassal serves the suzerain, who in turn pledges not to interfere in the vassal's relations with his subjects. The comparison is particularly apt in the case of Russia's national republics, relatively closed societies where relations remained opaque to a Kremlin in constant apprehension of the possibility of separatism. The most independent in its internal affairs was 'pacified' Chechnya, whose ruler, Ramzan Kadyrov, demonstrated unconditional personal loyalty to Putin and turned out dream results for the regime in every election, but ruled at home with utter disregard for Russian law. Kadyrov and others in local power since 'time immemorial' – Shaimiev in Tatarstan, Rakhimov in Bashkortostan, Ilyumzhinov in Kalmykia – are perfect analogues for the likes of Kunayev, Rashidov, Aliyev, those who had been unquestioningly devoted to the 'leadership of the CPSU and, personally, to the general secretary', and who built relatively stable systems for the maintenance of their own republics, which in turn enabled those republics, eventually, to declare independence from the Soviet Union and transition without any major unrest.

2.5 The Submission of the 'Oligarchs' and the Media

The meaning of privatization was not merely economic; it was also political. There was an emerging class of property owners with a driving interest in the nascent socio-political system and a deep fear of Communist revanche – these being the same people who had become interested not just in the system, but in keeping power in Yeltsin's hands.

The issue was that privatization, which the no-alternative political system and unfettered power had made inevitable, had been achieved through the arbitrary use of that power and the brazen violation of any number of laws. Radical democratic ideology had enabled Russia's democrats to observe this calmly. They considered it their most urgent job to build capitalism, assuming that the market itself would then sort everything out. Chubais said of this attitude among privatizer-reformists, 'Onward, to private property, to capitalism. The other option is backward, to Communism (or to some new redness, which, I am profoundly persuaded, can only be blood). We have one job: to do everything we can to push the country away from Communism.[49]

The phenomenal enrichment and lack of interference enjoyed by the oligarchs were inextricably linked with the 'roof' – Russian criminal slang for 'protection' – to which presidential power amounted for them. The smaller property owners had their own, more modest 'roofs' within the apparatus of state. At the same time, oligarchic fortunes served as a kind of 'pocket' for the president. It is little wonder Abramovich was called Yeltsin's 'cashier'.

The doubtful origins of the largest fortunes, and the widespread presumption they had been dishonestly gained,[50] put the oligarchs ill at ease. Further, Jews were heavily represented among those with the largest fortunes (in 1998 they headed seven of the nine largest banks), which may be explained not only by cultural and socio-political factors, but also by the fact that it was easier for power to deal with 'ethnically vulnerable' populations and those who looked to it for protection from anti-Semitism, a force Jewish oligarchs tended to exaggerate.[51] Property owners understood that the rise to power of the opposition – not just the Communists, but any opposition – would carry the threat of having their fortunes investigated and their holdings redistributed. The thought of it became 'a bad dream that haunted their nights'. Cosy with crime and protected by private security forces staffed with prominent ex-KGB men, the oligarchs in control of the media were constantly fighting, intriguing against one another in the capital, blackmailing each other, even ordering assassinations. Yet when power came under threat, they were capable of acting in harmony. In 1996, the oligarchs closed ranks and dropped gargantuan sums into Yeltsin's election coffers, for which those in power compensated them by transferring over ownership of large,

---

49   Chubais, *Privatization, Russian-Style*, 313.

50   In two surveys, conducted in 2006 and 2008, 70% of respondents agreed that in modern Russia, there is no honest way to become a millionaire (*2008 Yearbook*, 94).

51   Interestingly, despite the proliferation of Jewish oligarchs and the widespread sense of their wealth as 'ill gotten', polls do not record an uptick in anti-Semitism during the post-Soviet period.

not-yet-privatized enterprises (through the administration's notorious loans-for-shares scheme).

After 1996, a tendency emerged in the oligarchs' relations with power: they were 'becoming impudent'. Having concentrated fantastic wealth in their own hands, having answered power's cries for rescue, they had sharply increased their own estimation of themselves. This newfound oligarchic self-esteem engendered a desire for wealth to spill over into political power and social status. Certain of them became deputies or joined the executive branch and quickly got to work advancing purely personal interests, taking down competitors, strengthening and enriching themselves ever more. In 1999, Berezovsky, the most ambitious of them all, helped ensure Yeltsin's nomination of Putin (there is no way to determine exactly how big a role he played; Berezovsky himself is naturally inclined to exaggerate it) and quite possibly the Second Chechen War. Berezovsky certainly participated in Unity and its electoral campaign.

The need to 'curb' the oligarchs first became apparent under Yeltsin (who once went so far as threatening to deport Berezovsky to Israel), but the task was not accomplished until his successor took office. While the oligarchs projected an image of great, nearly consummate political power to many, including to themselves[52] (the very use of the term 'oligarch' reflects this, as did the neologism *semibankirshchina*, a play on *semiboyarshchina*, the Russian name for the rule of the Seven Boyars who deposed and succeeded Tsar Vasily IV during the Time of Troubles), in fact, power's dependence on them was largely an illusion, whereas the dependence of the oligarchs on power was all too real. The semilegal nature of the privatization process that had built such immense fortunes for the oligarchs made

---

52   Berezovsky went so far as to propagandize for the notion that the power of big capital was natural. He could say to FSB director Mikhail Barsukov, 'If you can't understand that we have come to power, we will simply remove you. You will have to serve our money, our capital' (Korzhakov, *Boris Yeltsin: From Dawn to Dusk*, 289). It is likely that Berezovsky believed the West was actually ruled by big capital, as Soviet propaganda had always insisted, but considered this acceptable. Here again we see the monstrous influence of vulgar Marxism on post-Soviet anti-Communist sensibilities.

them hugely vulnerable to presidential control at the same time. Authorities could, at a moment's notice, pull charges 'off the shelf' and prosecute unmanageable or politically dangerous oligarchs for crimes arising out of privatization, taxes owed, and so forth – many of them perfectly legitimate. (This, of course, was made much more expedient by the subordination of the courts to the presidential 'power vertical'.) Yeltsin himself had written, 'Given the imperfections of our tax and financial accounting systems, practically anybody . . . can be "drawn in and tossed in jail." '[53]

Putin did exactly that to Russia's three strongest and most ambitious oligarchs. Two of them were forced to flee the country, having lost much of their wealth. (These were Vladimir Gusinsky, a media tycoon with ties to Luzhkov and his 'Moscow group' and Putin's active opponent during the succession struggle, and Berezovsky, to whom, in contrast, Putin practically owed his presidency, and who reported Putin had, while rising to power, told him, 'You mean more to me than a brother.'[54]) The third, Mikhail Khodorkovsky, was the richest and most dangerous of all (because, unlike the others, he was motivated partly by democratic and legal ideas; he strove for more transparent relations between power and business; and he supported the opposition – even the Communists – financially). He was in prison. Khodorkovsky's company, Yukos, had been bankrupted, its assets distributed among those close to the president. His 2003 arrest,[55] and the liquidation of his 'empire' that followed,

---

53   Yeltsin, *Presidential Marathon*, 274. With the assertion that 'any businessman, at the whim of the authorities, can be deprived of his business and his property, even his very freedom', 40% agreed in 2007, 35% in 2008 (*2008 Yearbook*, 95).

54   Dmitry Gordon, *Berezovsky and Korzhakov: Secrets of the Kremlin* [in Russian] (Kiev, 2008), 46. Naturally, once he had come to power, Putin could no longer tolerate the presence of someone like Berezovsky and would take the first opportunity to be rid of him. At a press conference on 18 January 2001, when asked about Berezovsky, Putin responded, 'Boris Berezovsky, who's that?' – paraphrasing, of course, the question put to the Russian delegation at Davos, 'Just who is Mr Putin?'

55   The authorities now appear terrified to release Khodorkovsky from prison. He has carried himself courageously and won sympathy among the

marked a turning point in relations between power and big business.

The people who hated the oligarchs welcomed reprisals against them, which in turn only added to the prestige of power. From this point on, there would emerge no further opposition activities among the oligarchic milieu. But anti-oligarchic messaging and persecution by the media were also ended. As it was with the regional 'barons', what power needed from the oligarchs before all else was loyalty. Once that loyalty was confirmed, they were free to dazzle the world with the extravagant use of their wealth, unhindered.[56]

The establishment under Putin of greater control over property holders aimed primarily to ensure their political subordination. But a strengthening of the president and ruling elite's control over business also took place in the purely economic sphere. The president sought to control the most vital sectors of the economy directly through subordinates and confidants, rather than through property holders whose loyalty would inevitably prove relative. The state was making its 'return' to economics in the form of powerful public-private companies that controlled the most 'strategically' important and profitable natural-resource companies. A system of 'state-monopoly' capital intimately connected with political power was beginning to take shape. Such a system was of course adequate for maintaining the imitation democracy that had already been created around no-alternative presidential power, which sought to insulate itself from political threats arising out of the economic sphere. In a system of

---

people. [Putin eventually pardoned Khodorkovsky in late 2013. He immediately went into exile; as of this writing, he lives in London. —Trans.]

56 Similar processes took hold in other post-Soviet states, with a number of figures that can be seen as analogous to the Russian oligarchs who entered politics and got into conflict with authorities. In Kazakhstan, Akezhan Kazhegeldin, who had once even served as prime minister, went into exile; Galymzhan Zhakiyanov and Mukhtar Ablyazov were imprisoned. In Azerbaijan, Speaker of the Parliament Rasul Quliyev, once called the 'cashier' of the Aliyev family, also went into exile. They were all accused of economic crimes. In Kyrgyzstan, Akayev accused and imprisoned Felix Kulov; in Belarus, Lukashenko treated Klimov and Leonov the same.

imitation democracy, 'actual' market relations are out of the question – only a quasi market is suited to quasi democracy.

In the early days of the system's evolution, gaining official control over the mass media, which perestroika had dramatically liberalized, was impossible. It was also unnecessary – most journalists (like most of the broader intelligentsia) counted themselves democrats and supported Yeltsin, 'not out of fear, but out of conscience'. The utterly biased coverage of opposition activities, particularly during the parliamentary conflicts and in 1996, might have looked like official control, but journalists and editors were simply 'following their hearts'. After 1993 and 1996, however, authorities' fear of the Communist opposition subsided. The media, gradually falling into the hands of the oligarchs, was increasingly a tool of lobbyists and a weapon in internecine political feuding. A media channel controlled by one oligarch would release compromising material about the officials and politicians who supported another. Nonplussed viewers might see a minister of justice cavorting with young women in a bathhouse, or 'someone resembling the prosecutor general' in bed with two prostitutes. Newspapers released the transcripts of a secret 1999 phone conversation between Berezovsky and Chechen separatist Movladi Udugov and published endless stories on corruption among the 'highest strata'. It had become necessary for the authorities to bring the mass media under control.

Clearly, television was especially important. During the 2000 electoral campaign, a true information war erupted between Gusinsky's anti-Putin NTV and Berezovsky's pro-Putin ORT. Of course, Gusinsky would lose NTV very quickly after Putin came to power. With that accomplished, Putin turned to the impudent Berezovsky. The liquidation of the unruly oligarchs, and the subordination of the other oligarchs, essentially meant government control over the media, either directly or through loyal proprietors.

Television had now become an amplifier for government propaganda. News was delivered more and more in the style of Soviet newscasts. While it never got quite as strict, control over print media was significantly tightened, too.

2.6 The Creation of United Russia, the Movement toward a Quasi-One-Party System, and the Establishment of Control over Parliament

The political inclination of power toward movements and parties in Russia was undergoing an evolution in which we can distinguish three distinct stages.

During the earliest stage, Yeltsin was the informal leader and 'standard-bearer' for the Democratic Russia movement, the primary striking force of the revolutionary process that would eventually bring him to power. In the course of Yeltsin's struggle for power, he realized that the minority supporting him, influential and vigorous as their support may have been, were not numerous enough, and, at the same time, that he could take that support for granted whenever he really needed it ('Where else are they going to go?'). But of course, he had little interest in letting an ambitious minority meddle in his affairs or tell him what to do. Yeltsin began distancing himself from the democratic intellectuals, first slowly, then, once he had risen to power, much faster. Meanwhile, the democrats began splintering into parties and factions, until elections to the First Duma made it plain that they had dramatically narrowed their electoral base. At the same time, the sheer strength of traditionalist support for supreme power that had manifested in the 1993 referendum became apparent. While this was going on, Yeltsin used the ideologically motivated demo-cratic intelligentsia to conduct his riskiest and least popular market reforms. In this role it was easy to make them scapegoats. Period-ically someone would be pushed out under pressure from the opposition, and another brought in from the cohort (which is how the 'unsinkable' Chubais fell and rose up again). In this way, the left opposition went from a struggle for power to one for influence on power and against one of the court circles – a struggle for the 'tsar' and against the 'boyars' deceiving him (Gaidar, Chubais, and so on), so to speak. The effective-sounding call for a 'change of course' did not particularly intimidate Yeltsin, a man who had radically changed course, and ideology, a number of times in his life. On the other hand, the democrats had no chance of becoming a true opposition, pinning their hopes instead on a desire to see the president 'staying the course of reforms', freeing himself from 'bad influences' (Korzhakov, Skokov, and so on), and, eventually, calling on them again.

Yeltsin positioned himself as 'a president for all Russians', non-partisan and in fact above the party system, which he and his circle were attempting to put in order. They envisioned a system of moderate, expedient left- and right-wing parties that would expel the Communists and evade complete control by democrats. But they did little to bring this about. The attempt at a 'pro-presidential' party, Our Home Is Russia (NDR), failed to win the president's support (what he mostly saw in it was a strengthening of Chernomyrdin's position, which irked him) and then failed in the elections (in voting for the Second Duma, NDR received about 10 per cent). Meanwhile, the Ivan Rybkin bloc, envisioned as a more moderate bulwark against the Communists on the left flank, failed to reach the electoral threshold altogether.

The situation changed during the transfer of power from Yeltsin to Putin and under Putin. Those in power started by creating the Unity movement, beginning in September 1999. By the time of the elections to the Third Duma, three months later, it received 23 per cent of the vote, achieving the goal for which it had been created: surpassing the Fatherland – All Russia bloc, formed from the spontaneous movements that emerged from elite attempts at self-organization during the political uncertainty of 1998. Then, in 2002, arrangements were made for Unity to merge with Fatherland – All Russia, which had been completely drained of purpose, to form the pro-presidential United Russia. Outwardly, it was beginning to look like the early Yeltsin era, with Putin playing in United Russia the role Yeltsin had established as the 'leader' of Democratic Russia. (The names of the pro-presidential movements reflect shifts in ideological emphasis: first Democratic Russia, then the more neutral Our Home Is Russia, finally United Russia.)

But the similarity was only superficial. If Democratic Russia was a spontaneous movement independent of Yeltsin and the authorities, with an ideology of its own and some chance of limiting Yeltsin's power, then United Russia was an organization created by the will of the authorities, with no distinctive ideology. Electoral support for United Russia essentially took loyalty to the 'sovereign' and handed it over to the party of 'servants of the sovereign'. The authorities needed United Russia to discipline the elite, to establish a mechanism for control over the Duma and the regional legislative assemblies, to act as a litmus test separating 'their own' – the unconditionally loyal – from those whose loyalty may have been questionable, and to facilitate the selection of operatives. What it could not do was exert any pressure on Putin or limit his power in the slightest way.

The general development of public sentiment, the gradual shift of loyalty to the president toward his party, the increasing concentration of media resources in the hands of power or those beholden to it, the enormous uses to be made of 'administrative' resources, measures to constrict the creation of 'spontaneous' new parties, the proscription of electoral blocs, the raising of the electoral threshold from 5 per cent to 7 per cent, the repudiation of elections by single-member districts in favour of party-list voting – all of this fed the party's tremendous successes. It even created its own analogue to Komsomol – the organization Nashi.[57]

The United Russia (ER) faction, strengthened by deserters from other factions and deputies from single-member districts, won a majority in the Third Duma. In elections to the Fourth Duma in 2003, ER got 37.6 per cent; the Communists, 12.6 per cent; the Liberal Democrats, 11.45 per cent; and Rodina – a spoiler party created by the Kremlin to split the Communist vote – 9 per cent. Liberal parties didn't make it to the Duma at all. In elections to the Fifth Duma in 2007, ER got 64.3 per cent of the vote; the Communists, 11.57 per cent; the Liberal Democrats, 8.14 per cent. A Just Russia – another pro-presidential party but seemingly a farther left one, created to offer the appearance of pluralism and act as a spoiler for the left opposition on the model of the earlier, unsuccessful Ivan Rybkin bloc – got 7.74 per cent. The parliament, at long last, would no longer

---

57 The word *Nashi*, which in Russian literally means 'ours' or 'our people', is also commonly used to mean 'Russians'. —Trans.

be a constant headache for the president. It had fallen under the control of United Russia, which in 2008 had 1.8 million members. The possibility loomed of a one-party system, or more exactly, a quasi-one-party system,[58] a return of the power of the Soviet party system 'at a new, higher (or lower) stage'.

The authorities, however, did not allow this to happen, stopping literally two steps short. Below, we will discuss the reasons why.

2.7 Politics as a Series of 'Special Operations' and the Increasingly Strong Role of the Special Services

The increasingly strong role under Putin of special services run largely by former KGB and FSB operatives[59] resulted partly from the coincidence of Putin's having started his career in the KGB. He brought many of the skills he acquired there into his government work, relying on only those who had proved their personal fealty and corporative loyalty. In a well-known remark made at the 2000 Chekist's Day banquet, Putin joked that his assignment, to seize power, had at long last been completed. A year later, at the same banquet, he told the same joke. It got riotous applause both times.[60]

---

58   I will explain precisely what I mean by 'quasi-one-party system'. First off, the establishment of a formal one-party system would contradict the very soul of imitation democracy. Thus, those in power must keep some alternates, or some pseudo-opposition parties, in play. Secondly, United Russia, unlike the CPSU (and unlike Democratic Russia), was without ideological foundations of its own outside of its support for presidential authority. It could be called a 'quasi party'.

59   On the tremendous rise of special services personnel – especially those from Leningrad/St Petersburg – into the national leadership under Putin, see Olga Kryshtanovskaya, *An Anatomy of the Russian Elite* [in Russian] (Moscow, 2005).

60   Putin's acquaintances from Leningrad, especially former KGB workers, played a role in his administration comparable to that played by leaders from the regions and clans of origin of those running the former Soviet republics of Asia, like Nakhchivans in Azerbaijan, or by Yeltsin's 'family'. If we look deeper into history, we may recall the elevation of Dnipropetrovskans under Brezhnev.

In both Yeltsin's hiring a KGB man to succeed him and the sub-sequent strengthening of KGBists' power, we can discern a predictable pattern. An imitation democracy cannot be managed effectively through formal legal norms. No-alternative power can be guaranteed only by circumventing or violating the rules, acting in grey areas of the law – or even well outside it. The elimination of candidates who pose a threat; the advance promise of the correct number of votes;[61] control over the higher echelons of the bureaucracy, oligarchs, and regional 'barons', inquiries into their loyalty, and the gathering of compromising materials on them; the arrangement of proceedings against unruly oligarchs; the recruitment of loyal personnel to staff senior positions; the transfer of strategically important materials to the ownership of trusted insiders; and so forth – all these activities, essential to the maintenance of the system, were in essence 'secret special operations'. Rather than rare exceptions, they were fast becoming crucial and lasting dimensions of all political activity. Carrying them off required operatives with suitable specializations.

We see the role of the special services being ramped up already under Yeltsin. Yeltsin had never really trusted the old special services, a holdover from the Soviet era, and even feared them. Instead he created a highly potent new special services, under his own personal command, based in the Presidential Security Service, which all Kremlin personnel feared,[62] whose director, Korzhakov, Berezovsky

---

61 Korzhakov's memoirs include a remarkable document: a statement of 'General Principles for Working with Opponents', approved by Yeltsin. It includes the following instructions: '4.2 "Severing" the opponent's lines of funding and information; 4.3 The implementation of hidden influences . . . through referent groups significant to him. 4.4 The implementation of special measures to deprive a challenger of allies', and so forth (Korzhakov, *Boris Yeltsin: From Dawn to Dusk*, 435).

62 'Everyone who worked for the president assumed we were being bugged. If we needed to have a conversation that was not for the "thirsty ears" of the Kremlin, we would simply exchange notes while we talked, and later destroy them' (Kostikov, *Romance with the President*, 11). Later, during his retirement, Yeltsin himself would complain to Kasyanov that 'they have all the phones bugged', urging him to buy a large number of phones, throwing each

bragged would have killed his rival Gusinsky had he asked. While, as we see, Yeltsin's selection of a KGB and FSB man as his successor was hardly an accident, the special services would likely have been empowered under any president. In other republics with comparable systems, but where leaders were not drawn from the ranks of the KGB – Belarus, Kazakhstan, Uzbekistan – the role of the special services came to be similarly enlarged.

The expanded role of the special services offered them a greater measure of independence, even the opportunity to partially escape control. (Here, again, we see the same processes undergone in the Soviet 'coil of the spiral' repeated in extremely softened form.) Some elements within these forces naturally took it upon themselves to begin identifying the enemies of power and of Russia and determining how to combat them. Besides that, a tremendously complex web was being woven from strands of personal, corporate-clan, and state interests (as these people understood them). During the Yeltsin era, and even more so under Putin, the news reported a seemingly endless series of unsolved murders; the victims were people who posed some threat to those in power or to power itself. (Someday, these will surely be portrayed in as many political thrillers.) The picture in Belarus and Kazakhstan was nearly identical. Of course, no one could accuse the executive powers in these countries of having orchestrated those murders. But the connection of these murders with the growing strength and independence of the special services is obvious.

All the same, the expansion of the special services' role, like so much else within our systems, reached such an extent that it became dysfunctional and began disquieting those in power. Putin's response to the murder of journalist Anna Politkovskaya, on his own birthday, is a case in point. Putin remarked that 'for those actively in power . . . Politkovskaya's death is far more damaging than her journalism ever was'.[63] By the same token, the establishment of a high

---

away after a single use (Mikhail Kasyanov, *Without Putin: Political Conversation with Evgeny Kiselev* [in Russian] [Moscow, 2009], 296–7).

63   'Putin: Politkovskaia caused great damage', [in Russian], 11 October 2006, polit.ru.

level of control over the political process ameliorates, to some degree, the need for 'extra-legal' controls. Practically no major political figures were left who could pose a threat to power.

There is thus every likelihood that at the new, more liberal stage of our evolution marked by the Medvedev presidency, the government will strengthen its control over the special services ('bringing the KGB under the control of the Party', as it were), limiting its influence.

2.8 Ideological Quests

When post-Soviet Russia emerges, it is as a society whose proclaimed goal is 'a return to world civilization' and the construction of a system modelled on those of Western democracies. The ways in which Russia differed from these countries were denied, glossed over, or explained 'transitionologically' as hardships unique to the establishment of democracy in a country with a 'heavy inheritance', one that had endured 'the horrors of Communist totalitarianism' and the embittered resistance of Communist revanchists. Every revolution produces a similar pattern. The early Bolsheviks had decried the 'damned autocracy' in every way they could, exaggerating its faults. Their time was depicted as one of hardship and struggle, to be endured through gritted teeth on the way to the promised land of socialism and Communism. The early democrats replaced the 'pluses' of the Bolshevik rubric with 'minuses'. With the 'damned autocracy' swapped out for the 'damned Communists', it was just as perilous a time, offering a road that had to be walked, no matter the costs, to reach the market and democracy.

But the Westernist democratic market ideology was always that of a minority, and over the course of Russia's social and political evolution it contracted rather than expanded. Politicians avoided the very words 'democrats' and 'democracy', which took on the ring of an obscenity. Those in power had to shift their ideological emphasis, accentuating the values of order, patriotism, and tradition as they oriented themselves ever more directly toward the traditionalist strata. Official ideological rhetoric began to take on an anti-Western

flavour. These changes were accompanied by a political transformation that brought Russia no closer to resembling a Western
country. On the contrary, it was pushing Russia further from both
the socio-political model of the 'Western world' that had been
successfully adopted and reproduced by the post-Communist countries of Central Europe and the principles that had been declared
during its own creation. As this went on, the traditional features of
Russian society and the Russian state came into ever-sharper focus.
These two processes – the traditionalist reorientation of ideas and
the construction of a system of imitation democracy – found themselves functionally bound together, each both presupposing and
reinforcing the other.

The ideology of stability, and of denying the need and even possibility of a new revolution, had become the ideology of the victors of
1991. Already under Yeltsin, and then more actively under Putin, we
saw a notion gaining ground that Russia had 'reached its limit on
revolutions and civil wars in the twentieth century', and had now
finally attained a reasonable structure. What had been sought in the
late eighties was, in the early nineties, achieved. Further development
could only be 'quantitative' in character; it could not impact the
foundations of the system. But this, in turn, meant that the transitionological explanation for Russia's peculiarities no longer sufficed,
and it became necessary to find another explanation for why the new
system so obviously failed to conform to both Western norms and
the glorious futures that had been predicted in the earliest days of
post-Soviet development. The need to find within the specifics of
Russian culture an explanation for the differences between Russia's
system and those of the West was obviously stronger than in Muslim
post-Soviet imitation democracies, where presidents insistently
pointed to the backwardness of their own people ('for them, there
can be no other way') and the dangers of Islamic fundamentalism.[64]

The system as it had actually developed could be explained only
by reference to Russia's national past – a gesture toward the organic

---

64 Nazarbayev: 'If there weren't five authoritarian regimes here [in
central Asia], there'd be ten Bin Ladens' (*Kommersant*, 12 May 2003, 11).

naturalness of such a system for Russia, its rootedness in Russian history. Under Yeltsin, a tendency emerged to find symbolic parallels in the tsarist period (and even some toying with the notion of restoring the monarchy, though this was never very serious). Orthodox Christianity took on the character of a kind of ersatz official ideology, with the patriarch acquiring huge importance as a symbolic-ideological figure whose physical proximity to the president sacralized his power, and being seen in church on holidays became a sign of loyalty among officials and businesspeople – many of them until recently Communists. (Vladimir Sorokin's dystopian novel *The Day of the Oprichnik* portrays a future grotesquely extrapolated from this traditionalist tendency.)

This trend continued developing under Putin, with the addition of symbolic ties to the Soviet past that would have been unthinkable under Yeltsin. These ties were not, of course, to revolutionary upheaval, nor socialist ideology, but rather to the USSR's stability and imperial greatness. The two-headed eagle was accompanied by the strains of the Soviet anthem (Yeltsin, now retired, raised his objections, but no one listened). In the pantheon of great names being created, tsars, their dignitaries, and White Guardists stood alongside Communist leaders like Andropov (all of them 'statesmen', founders of Russia). But revolutionaries were not welcome. On TV, heroic Soviet Chekists competed for airtime with no less heroic tsarist men-at-arms. This could produce absolutely monstrous juxtapositions, like the Kremlin solemnly marking the anniversary of Komsomol (the All-Union Leninist Young Communist League) at the same time academic experts on another channel were declaring Lenin a blood-soaked, syphilitic madman.

The meaning of the 1991 revolution, and of Yeltsin as the founder of a new Russian state, was being obscured (here we see one difference between the Soviet 'coil of the spiral', in which the figure of the founder, Lenin, was sacralized, and the post-Soviet coil), and the nineties were being presented as an era of 'difficulties' – one that was already, thank God, behind us. If in the early nineties the Soviet Union had been portrayed as a 'kingdom of darkness', now it was the wild nineties themselves being portrayed as a kingdom of darkness – one from which Putin had rescued Russia.

Ideas about the indispensability to Russia of a strong central government, and about the country's 'special path', were being promulgated. The words of the emigrant philosopher Ivan Ilyin, who had worked on Nazi propaganda and written on the inevitability of a Russian 'Christian dictatorship' that would succeed Communism, were quoted by Putin and took on an almost official significance.

The system under development sought an ever-greater measure of 'self-determination', hoping to create an autonym and develop its own language. The later days of the Putin era[65] even saw the emergence of a term whose inventors claimed it would define that system and express its distinctiveness and differences from Western systems; they called it 'sovereign democracy'. (I would argue that this term, by its meaninglessness and air of functionalism, is quite comparable to the late Soviet 'real socialism', or something like 'people's democracy'.) Another term coined to designate the specifics of the system and the special place of Putin's presidency was 'national leader' (itself perilously close to 'chieftain').

Like so much in post-Soviet development, this evolution somewhat recapitulates the evolution during the Soviet period, when, faced with a decline in official ideology and the system's taking on more traditionally Russian features, those in power tried to establish symbolic ties to the Russian Empire and attract traditionalist and imperialist ideological support.[66] As in the Soviet past, the process could not be completed.

Power could not fully break free of its democratic ideological roots, just as Soviet power had been unable to fully break free of its Marxist-Leninist roots. Firstly, the transition to a new ideology would mean the threat of the political destabilization that power feared most of all. Secondly, there was no ideological alternative to

---

65 Furman is writing, of course, before Putin's formal return to the presidency for a third term. —Trans.

66 'Here, an obvious similarity to the use of imperial (and, to a degree, nationalistic) motifs by Joseph Stalin in the forties and early fifties shows through' (Solovei and Solovei, *Failed Revolution*, 385). The use of these motifs is not confined to the Stalin era, however. While it decreased under Khrushchev, it was an active presence during the Brezhnev years.

democracy, and none could be invented. Thus, traditionalist tendencies within the ideological sphere remained on the level of 'symbolic
games'. Democratic rhetoric never disappeared from the lexicon of
power. The term 'sovereign democracy' was rejected. But with
Medvedev's rise to power, the importance of democratic rhetoric
once again increased sharply.[67]

2.9 Russia 'Rises from Its Knees' and Faces Increasing Confrontations with the West

Another facet of Russia's evolutionary processes, and of the project-
ion of its internal development into the sphere of foreign policy, is the
emergence and intensification of confrontations with Western democracies, which we can see beginning even in the Yeltsin era.

At first, it was thought that the creation of a new Russian state
would spell an end to conflict with the West, marking instead
Russia's entry into the union of democratic nations. Yeltsin writes
that, with the signing of the Belovezh Accords, 'Russia had abdicated
its traditional role as "ruler of half the world", of armed opposition to
Western civilization, its role as a global police force, to focus on
resolving internal issues.'[68] As early as October 1991, some were
speaking of the need for the USSR (then drawing its final breaths) to
join NATO. It was not Yeltsin who voiced this perspective, but the
more 'patriotically'-oriented Rutskoy. The thought of Russia's theoretically possible entry into NATO has been periodically raised by
various Russian politicians, Putin included, and admittance to the EU
remains a hazy but desirable prospect to most Russians.[69] As the Central

---

67 Medvedev's essay 'Forward, Russia!' even marks the return of some
transitionological thinking. The contemporary situation is viewed as one of
transition, with the future promising the establishment of full democracy, as
defined by the rotations in power of various political forces.

68 Yeltsin, *Notes of a President*, 151.

69 In 2000, 54% were for joining the EU, 25% against it. In 2005, 53% for,
24% against (*Public Opinion – 2005 Yearbook* [in Russian] [Moscow, 2005],
164).

European states' admission into NATO and the EU represented the logical and symbolic culmination of their post-Communist evolution toward democracy, it seemed only natural that these eventualities would carry the same meaning for Russia's evolution, at least if it followed a similar path.

In fact, however, Russia's real evolution was following a completely different path than the one that had brought the Central European countries into the Western embrace. Russia's integration in the Western world, which in the early nineties had seemed so natural and near at hand, had become impossible, thanks to the increasingly obvious incompatibility of the socio-political systems involved. In the meantime, Western countries continued to be seen as developed, advanced, and successful, and relations with them could confer tremendous status on a nation or ruler. But Russia's incapacity to be integrated into a system of states seen as advanced and bound by close alliances inevitably gave rise to a painful ambivalence. The reasons why were difficult to recognize or comprehend ideologically, especially since the system itself was growing to incorporate countries that had once been Soviet satellite states or even republics of the USSR.

Russia found itself nursing feelings of humiliation and neglect.[70] Over time, more and more developments in the country incited condemnation from the West, and Western states made timorous efforts to somehow guide our politics in the direction of liberalism, which Russians naturally experienced as insulting lectures, and meddling in our internal affairs.[71]

The Western democratic model – and still more so its propagation, expressed externally in the growth of Western alliances to

---

70   In 2001 and 2007, respectively, 6% and 20% of Russian citizens polled reported that they felt the West treated Russia with respect, 21% and 11% with contempt. Meanwhile, in the same years, 34% and 32%, respectively, said they felt Russia treated the West with respect, 3% and 5% with contempt (*2008 Yearbook*, 149–50).

71   In 2008, 51% of respondents described feeling that 'criticism from Western societies and politicians of the state of affairs in Russia with regard to democracy amounts to interference in our internal affairs', while only 27% did not (*2008 Yearbook*, 147).

include former Soviet republics – was experienced more and more as a threat to surround our 'sovereign democracy', to leave Russia as an island in a politically alien and hostile world, a besieged fortress. This threat was felt especially keenly during the 'colour revolutions' that swept the regimes of Leonid Kuchma in Ukraine, Askar Akayev in Kyrgyzstan, and Eduard Shevardnadze in Georgia. These men had headed systems highly comparable to Russia's, if substantially weaker, and their ousters aroused an irrational panic of the kind seen in tsarist circles after the French revolutions, or in Soviet circles in the run-up to the Prague Spring. To acknowledge the naturalness, the predictability of these regimes' collapsing would mean acknowledging the inevitability of the collapse of Russia's regime, too – an impossibility. Those in power in Russia thus concluded instead that these revolutions were all the work of Western security services (very much as Soviet leaders had blamed similar forces for unrest in Hungary, Czechoslovakia, and Poland). Vladislav Surkov, the foremost ideologue of the Putin era, appearing before a Nashi group in July 2008, said, 'Inspired by their successes in nearby countries, they have attempted to infiltrate the internal affairs of countries neighbouring Russia, and even of Russia itself. But we have overcome the threat of these shocks from abroad.'[72]

Ratcheting fears about the spread of democracy and Western support for the opposition, as well as, more generally, about 'interference in our internal affairs' during the formation of imitation democracy regimes, were far from a uniquely Russian experience. Nazarbayev, Karimov, Akayev, Lukashenko, and Kuchma had all had similar concerns. But Russia's increasingly confrontational relationship with the West was made more intense by particularities of history and culture – the 'complexes' arising from the loss of the USSR's imperial greatness, its role as a major power and counterbalance to the US – as well as by our ideological transformation; our tendency to draw connections to our imperial (and, to some degree, even our Soviet) past, which suggests some kind of struggle for a return to, if not

---

72 'Surkov praised the "Nashists" at Seliger' [in Russian], 21 July 2008, newsru.com.

'empire', then our 'sphere of influence' and identity as a 'major power'; and some competition with other 'power centres'. Russia's historical trajectory impelled an energeticness, globalism, and striving for leadership not found in other post-Soviet imitation democracies.

To some degree, Russia did become a centre of gravity for countries with comparable systems the world over. Instinctive solidarity with similar regimes, and ill-defined fears that outsiders would begin with Serbia or Iraq and make their way to Russia, meant that Russia would invariably accept its role as a more or less active defender of these regimes whenever they were threatened with sanctions or invasion. Russia felt especially strong solidarity with Serbia's Milošević regime. The presidents of countries that could not have been more different, save their having (or endeavouring to have) political systems of the same type, looked to Russia with hope and rejoiced at the first sign of its burgeoning involvement. We can vividly see how they played on Russia's resentments and fears. Daniel Ortega once said to a Russian delegation, 'Russia continues to illuminate the world, persecuted as ever by empire, which labours under the belief that the collapse of the USSR will make it possible to chop her into pieces.'[73] Hugo Chávez's active desire to build an imitation democracy in Venezuela and his rapprochement with Russia are as interconnected as the emergence of dictators in colonized 'third world' countries and their rapprochement with the USSR and adoption of 'scientific socialism' as an ideology. Just as many characteristics of the Soviet system had reappeared, in dramatically weaker form, in the next coil of the spiral, the Cold War itself was being revived, in likewise softer form. This was happening in any number of regions, but its core area was the post-Soviet space.

The ease with which the USSR fell had a downside – the fall was not experienced as natural, predictable, and permanent. The Russian mind had a tremendously difficult time reconciling itself with the actual independence of post-Soviet states. After the fall of the USSR, the post-Soviet space had come to be seen as a natural 'zone of Russian interest', or as a battlefield from which enemies were trying to chase Russia out.

---

73   NG-dipkuryer, 15 May 2009, 10.

In the early 1990s, Russia enjoyed a number of successes in the space of the CIS. We can account for them by several objective factors. First of all, many of these countries were even less equipped to thrive under the conditions of proclaimed democracies than Russia. Following a time of surging national democracy, there began a period of reaction and the construction of no-alternative systems of power like the one taking shape in Russia.[74] The construction of regimes of imitation democracy was everywhere accompanied by an increasing orientation toward Russia. 'Class instinct' told post-Soviet rulers that, whatever their democratic rhetoric, Yeltsin's Russia would serve as their main ally.

There were other factors that also contributed to these centripetal tendencies. The new states were terribly weak, and they had retained the habit of looking 'up from below' at Russia, perceiving Moscow as the natural centre of things, the place from which their fates would descend, a model for the successful resolution of the problems of post-Soviet development. Russia's progress toward the construction of an authoritarian system of power served as an inspiration to the presidents of other CIS countries. It conferred a certain kind of legitimacy – if the dissolution of Russia's parliament was meeting with approval from the West, it was as though the order to dissolve the Kazakh parliament had come 'from God Himself'. Russia saw tremendous opportunities to intervene in the internal conflicts of post-Soviet countries. With Russia's help, any number of separatist groups and 'frozen conflicts' arose in Georgia, Azerbaijan, and

---

74 In Georgia, the Gamsakhurdia regime was overthrown and Shevard-nadze came to power with help from Russia. Events in Azerbaijan went precisely the same way (Elchibey was overthrown, Aliyev came to power). Immediately after attaining power, both men brought their countries into the CIS. In Armenia, a bloodless military uprising removed Ter-Petrosyan, who had often spoken of Armenia's need to end its ancient orientation toward Russia. In Tajikistan, the threat of victory by the bloc of Islamist and national-democratic forces was liquidated, and, after a bloody civil war, Rahmon claimed the presidency, with Russian backing. In Moldova, the pro-Romanian Druc was toppled. In Belarus, Lukashenko rose to power, announcing the inevitability of reunification with Russia. In Ukraine, Kravchuk, a signatory of the Belovezh Accords, was replaced by the more pro-Russian Kuchma.

Moldova, and between Azerbaijan and Armenia. Russian power exploited these conflicts to bind these countries to Russia.

Alongside the return of authoritarianism in a new, softened form, there also emerged a kind of 'mini socialist camp'. A protective belt of authoritarian imitation democracy regimes sprang up, thanks to Russian efforts and their own, as the result of a natural process through which these regimes emerged in countries unprepared for democracy. Like systems 'reached out' to like, the weak seeking the protection of the strong. But this experience turned out to be very short lived. Centrifugal tendencies overtook centripetal ones.

A number of CIS countries whose cultures had laid fairly substantial groundwork for democracy were stepping onto the path of democratic development, albeit with torturous difficulty. Attempts to create regimes of imitation democracy in Ukraine, Moldova, and Georgia met with failure. In Georgia and Ukraine, they were swept away in colour revolutions. The regime in Armenia was 'softened' and transformed in a democratic direction. This naturally tended to be accompanied by a reorientation in foreign policy. The key goal of the foreign policy of those who had now risen to power in Ukraine and Georgia was joining NATO and, eventually, the EU. Moldova's constitution guaranteed non-alignment, but admission to the EU was nonetheless the dream of all its political forces and its whole society, and there was growing interest in seeking a rapprochement with Romania.

Meanwhile, Belarus and the Muslim republics managed to hold on to their authoritarian regimes of imitation democracy. In Kyrgyzstan, the fall of the Akayev regime was swiftly followed by the rise of a highly comparable regime led by Kurmanbek Bakiyev. The durability of these regimes, however, was relative. Almost no one doubted they were headed for deep political crises, the most severe of which would assume the form of spontaneous violent uprisings, along the lines of the 2005 unrest in Andijan, Uzbekistan.

But centrifugal forces in relation to Russia and the CIS also impacted countries with authoritarian regimes. For these countries to be integrated with Russia along the lines of Western Europe's integration was out of the question, thanks both to imbalances in size between them and to the fact that personalist authoritarian power cannot be divided and distributed to supranational bodies. Russia could relate to the countries with comparable systems in the post-Soviet space only as a hegemon to its 'satellites' or 'vassal' states. Such relationships are fragile. The republics began to develop a 'habituation to sovereignty'; their psychological reliance on Russia dissipated, and Russian cultural influence began to weaken. They were being pulled ever more strongly into the global market; their economic bonds were being reconfigured, with far less of a Russian orientation. The stabilization of authoritarian regimes itself led to greater self-assurance and less focus on support from Russia, especially since such support could only be of limited dimension.

In the event of threats to their power, Russia could come to the aid of authoritarian presidents – but as the experience of the colour revolutions shows, it could not guarantee the preservation of their power. Considering this, these authoritarian presidents found themselves less attracted to the proposition of becoming Russian vassals. Besides, partnership with the West could confer legitimacy on those holding power in CIS countries, as indeed it had done in Russia. The most advantageous and natural position for them was thus some balance between Russia and the West. Even Lukashenko, the so-called last dictator of Europe, the most despised by the West and formerly the most pro-Russian of these leaders, attempted something to this effect.

Here, too, we see analogues to the disintegration of the socialist camp. It assumes two discrete forms: firstly, as a result of the spontaneous democratic movements that emerged in Czechoslovakia, Hungary, Poland, and so on, and secondly, as a result of the increasing self-reliance of the most severe Communist regimes – China, North Korea, Albania, Romania. If the colour revolutions saw themselves as modelled on the Czechoslovakian and Polish movements, then the isolationist and independent position of the Türkmenbaşy regime seems to have been modelled on the likes of Kim Il-sung or Enver Hoxha.

Everything was 'coming full circle'. But as in other areas, in Russia's foreign policy, Soviet elements were returning in weakened form. The new Cold War was little more than a degraded copy of the older one – not only because Russia's resources were tremendously smaller than those of the Soviet Union, but also because the clear motivation of Soviet ideology no longer existed. Russia, lacking even a term for its own system, could not meaningfully oppose it to the systems of democratic countries. We could hardly struggle 'for the victory of imitation democracy around the world'. This absence of any clear ideological motivation, any basically adequate ideological 'language', or the kind of global perspective present in Soviet politics (albeit increasingly merely formal as the end of the Soviet period approached) imbued post-Soviet Russian politics with a particular impulsiveness and irrationality. Politics had become a series of scandals over a variety of things (from gas prices to the relocation of the Bronze Soldier memorial in Talinn), which flared up and then subsided, half-forgotten. At the same time, this lowered the temperature of confrontation, preventing it from reaching the intensity and consistency it had during the 'real' Cold War.

In all the interconnected processes outlined above, we see the predictable intertwined with the fortuitous. Predictable, most of all, is the unified logic of establishing power's control over society, eliminating present and possible threats to no-alternative power. The pattern to which this conforms can be seen clearly in comparisons between the development of Russia's system and the development of comparable post-Soviet systems.

All this – disputes with parliaments; the elimination of 'old comrades'; the exertion of control over regional elites, oligarchs, and the media; the change from a policy of distancing power from parties to one of creating presidential quasi parties – bears strong resemblances to other imitation democracy systems. United Russia is entirely comparable to the New Azerbaijan Party, Nazarbayev's Nur Otan (Radiant Fatherland) party, or the People's Democratic Party of Tajikistan. Khodorkovsky's trial can be likened to the trials in Kazakhstan of Galymzhan Zhakiyanov and Mukhtar Ablyazov. The mysterious murders of Altynbek Sarsenbayev and Zamanbek

Nurkadilov in Kazakhstan, and of members of the opposition in Belarus, strongly resemble the murders of Russia's Alexander Litvinenko and Anna Politkovskaya.

We can also see a pattern emerge if we compare the formation of Russia's post-Soviet system with the formation of the Soviet system itself. At first blush, the Soviet system, with its dogmatic totalitarian ideology, looks completely different from post-Soviet imitation democracy. But the two systems have something in common – under both, not only can power create conditions of no-alternative politics, it has no choice *but* to do so. There is no chance of escaping it. Consequently, the development of both systems follows a general logic of maximizing control over society.

Over the course of this development, threats to power are gradually eliminated, and the systems in turn become stronger. At the start of the 1990s, the post-Soviet system had not yet been codified; its contours were ill defined. It was still weak, and a crisis like that of 1993 might have taken it down, as the civil war from 1917 to 1921 might have destroyed Soviet power. But by 2000, it had become a powerful organism, with a clearly articulated structure, dealing with the threats it faced.

The developed system was strikingly different from its initial forms. If you read any portion of the minutes of the Tenth or Eleventh Communist Party Congress, and then follow it up with something from the sixteenth or seventeenth, you will have travelled to a completely new world. An identical effect can be achieved by perusing the records of the Congress of People's Deputies or the Supreme Soviet from the start of the Yeltsin era, and then the transcript of a discussion in today's Duma – whose speaker, Boris Gryzlov, recently uttered a phrase that will resonate through Russian history for centuries: 'The parliament is no place for discussion.' People dedicated to the ideals of a prior period (many old Bolsheviks under Stalin, many 'old democrats' under Putin) will inevitably find this horrifying, and will attempt to explain these contrasts in terms of leaders' differing personalities (as between Lenin, on the one hand, and Stalin, who 'deviated from the norms of Leninism', on the other, or between 'Yeltsin the democrat' and 'Putin the KGB man', who has become for many of them the incarnation of evil[75]). On a psychological level, this is perfectly understandable – for democrats of the 1991 model, discerning the pattern that leads from 1991 to Putin would mean acknowledging their own misdeeds and errors, just as discerning the development from 1917 to Stalin would for the Bolsheviks. It would mean admitting that they were reaping what they themselves had sown.

As I have tried to explain, however, what matters most is not demonstrating personal differences among these politicians, but rather identifying differences among the predictable stages of the system's development. Moreover, those differences among politicians are to some degree the result of these developmental stages. Putin could not have fulfilled Yeltsin's role any more than Yeltsin could have named as his successor a man like himself, or indeed anyone fundamentally different from Putin. And if Yeltsin had chosen someone other than Putin in 1999, it is only individual and stylistic elements of the situation that would have turned out differently. It might not have been possible to see the shape of the eventual, mature organism in the embryo of 1991, as indeed in the embryo of 1917; but in each case, there was only one organism that could finally emerge. The post-Soviet system's natural development was being realized through the medium of Yeltsin and Putin.

That said, the primary work of building an imitation democracy fell to Russia's first president. Putin inherited a system already largely in place; his work was rather to 'complete the construction' and 'add finishing touches'. Yet it was Putin who most benefited from the labour that had built that system.

---

75 Bonner writes, 'Putin has created an antidemocratic state. The destruction of the free press, the destruction of the upper house of parliament, the establishment of seven super-administrative structures with leaders personally answerable to Putin, and, of course, the war in Chechnya – all of this collectively testifies to a strong antidemocratic tendency. To all of this must be added the destruction of the electoral process – the hallmark of a democratic state' (insomi.ru). (All this from a person who in 1993 reproached Yeltsin for his excessive liberalism and directly called on him to dissolve the parliament!)

3

'The Golden Age': A Developed System

Putin's second term, clearly, will go down in history as the heyday of our system, its 'golden age'. Power had reached a stage at which no visible enemies or dangers could threaten it.

Chechnya had been subjugated, the parliament brought completely under control, regional elites locked in a competition to see who could demonstrate the greatest loyalty, oligarchs made completely dependent on power and discouraged from any independent political activities of their own, the mainstream media transformed into a tool for government propaganda. No actual opposition party had any real influence (except the Communist Party of the Russian Federation, which had found a niche for itself in the system but was rapidly losing influence) nor any chance of creating any. Putin's political enemies, like the oligarch Vladimir Gusinsky, and his rivals, like Nikolai Aksyonenko, had been thoroughly crushed. Yeltsin, with whom Putin 'had not recommended' his ministers communicate, would live out his days in a 'golden cage' and steer clear of government business. Within his own circle, Putin had purged not only everyone who believed they had earned the president's gratitude and his ear by their role in his rise to power, but anyone with any independence at all, any ability to raise objections, like Prime Minister Mikhail Kasyanov. Every post of even remote importance was filled with someone totally dependent on the president – many of them old friends and acquaintances from St Petersburg and the KGB.

Power took on tremendous strength domestically and strengthened itself substantially in the international arena. The favourable economic situation meant Russia no longer had to depend economically on other countries – on the contrary, both neighbouring countries and Western

Europe now depended on Russia to supply their energy, which sharply increased the country's sense of self-worth and fuelled dreams of an 'energy empire'. It was under Putin that Russia finally gained admittance to the G8, even hosting the 2006 summit in St Petersburg. Western leaders were seeking Putin's friendship.

The 2004 presidential elections clearly demonstrated the accomplishments of Russian power. As in 2000, Putin staked his electoral campaign on traditionalist, 'monarchic' loyalty – not 'stooping' to debate the opposition, not offering any proposals, not campaigning for himself, much like Yeltsin in 1996. It was the right approach.

In election after election, those in power triumphed ever more confidently. Yeltsin had prevailed in 1996 only in the second round, and only after mobilizing all the forces at his disposal; in 2000, Putin managed to win in the first round, albeit by a small margin, and in 2004, without breaking a sweat, he received a remarkable 70.08 per cent of the vote. The leaders of opposition and semi-opposition parties did not themselves run in these elections (lest they be embarrassed), instead nominating more disposable candidates. But even this triumph pales in comparison with Putin's abandonment of the presidency in 2008 and the election of his chosen successor, Dmitry Medvedev – which demonstrated his absolute control over the political process.

Until the very last moment, Russian society – including, to be sure, even the highest echelons of the elite – were wondering what plans Putin was carefully concealing. Did he truly intend to vacate the presidency, or were his comments to this effect designed to gauge public response and the loyalty of his circle, presumably before a last-minute emendation of the Constitution? And if he really did vacate the presidency, where would he go, and who would succeed him? Of course, it was universally understood that these decisions were Putin's alone to make, and his will would be implemented. There were no visible attempts to influence him (with the exception of a few rather ritualistic calls to stay in power from especially obsequious members of the intelligentsia). Not only did wide swathes of society play no role whatever in the decision-making process, but the highest strata of the power elite (a term that does not seem very apt in this situation) were completely in the dark, and ready to enact whatever decisions he made. The very top elite had been reduced to the role of silent actors.[1]

In the elections, Medvedev got 70.28 per cent of the vote – about equal to Putin's showing in 2004, though this time with the participation of the leaders of the CPRF and the LDPR. Zyuganov got 17.73 per cent; Zhirinovsky, 9.35 per cent. (Kasyanov, however – the only candidate who posed an actual threat – was barred from taking part.) Federal elections had at last been converted into a ritual for consecrating by mass assent whatever decision the president had made – somewhat akin to the 'elections' staged by the USSR, or a pledge of fealty to a monarch. The independence of power from society, and the dependence of society on power, had reached truly immense proportions. Neither the tsars, who could select successors only within their own dynasties, nor the general secretaries of the CPSU had enjoyed such liberty in bestowing their power.

3.1 Putin's Second Term

Putin's second term was the apex of Russia's post-Soviet system, not only because it found power at its most independent from society and society at its most dependent on power, but also because it saw the peak of the president's popularity and the height of society's satisfaction with the system.

---

1 We see the elite's submissiveness not only in their attitude toward the primary question – that of presidential succession – but in their attitude to all personnel decisions, which under Putin were generally unexpected and mysterious, their motivations a deep secret. His dismissal of Kasyanov as prime minister was more or less comprehensible – Kasyanov retained a close association with Yeltsin's circle and had protested the plan to arrest Khodorkovsky and break up Yukos. But only Putin knows what motivated Kasyanov's replacement with the unknown Fradkov, then Fradkov's replacement by the equally unknown Zubkov. Not only did these sudden personnel changes fail to arouse much resistance, but it seems even their underlying motivations were a subject of little interest. 'Such is the sovereign's will' – and nothing else was said.

Putin's immense power arises only slightly out of fear. Fear, of course, plays a meaningful role in disciplining the bureaucracy, the intelligentsia, and the business elite. Fear does not, however, achieve electoral results (at least, not fear of punishment for 'incorrect' voting). These results were no doubt subject to some degree of falsification, but not enough to determine their ultimate result. Nor can the effect of government propaganda explain Putin's power. Under Soviet rule, the entirety of the media was state run and propagandistic, and during elections to the First Duma, the television airwaves were flooded with propaganda for Russia's Choice, which proved a boon to neither Soviet power nor Russia's Choice itself. Propaganda sometimes falls on fertile ground and takes root; at other times it 'bounces off'. In this case, the ground on which propaganda landed was fertile. The notion of no-alternative power was not born from propaganda; rather, it came first, paving the way for propaganda to prove digestible.[2] The people went willingly to the polls and voted exactly as directed by their president, whom they trusted and even loved sincerely – and to whom they imagined no alternative.

In a 2006 poll, 51 per cent of respondents believed Putin should remain in office for a third term, with 23 per cent feeling 'completely positively' and 36 per cent simply 'positively' about the prospect of amending the Constitution to make it possible. Even more telling, 62 per cent said they would have supported a third term even if it violated the Constitution.[3] In 2008, 49 per cent expressed 'admiration' and 'fondness' for Putin; another 31 per cent 'did not have a bad word to say about him'; 58 per cent said they would be prepared to vote for him in 2012.[4]

---

2   Still, one cannot say the propaganda was 'totally' effective. In polling, many responses indicated a totally realistic, critical approach to social reality. For instance, in 2008, only 17% of respondents associated the relatively good economic situation with government policy; 50% associated it with rising global oil prices, and 16% did not agree the situation *was* relatively good (*2008 Yearbook*, 34). And 53% believed the gap between the rich and the poor had widened under Putin (p. 62). But none of this inhibited the recognition of the 'no-alternative' nature of power.

3   *2006 Yearbook*, 107–10.

4   *2008 Yearbook*, 62–3.

Putin's phenomenal popularity as a 'national leader', approaching the dimensions of a kind of miniature 'cult of personality', was undeniable and confirmed by numerous polls, including many outside Kremlin control. This popularity bears only a minimal (and indefinable) debt to the fortuitous aspects of the president's personality. Rather, it was a natural outgrowth of the stage in the system's development at which it arose.

A certain degree of popularity in the ruler stems from the particulars of Russian (and, to some extent, simply human) psychology. I speak of the 'monarchist' popularity that Yeltsin enjoyed even in the most terrible years of his rule, popularity that is indeed a consequence of the absence of alternatives. The fear of anarchy, power vacuums, and transfers of power drive people to 'love' the ruler, to seek out in him virtues that can justify their ready obedience and electoral support – when a society is faced with a power that leaves it no recourse, its only choice is to love that power. This is exactly why, however grotesque a figure Yeltsin may have been, his popularity continued to grow in every dichotomous vote, enabling him to win both the 1993 referendum and the 1996 elections. In *The History of a Town*,[5] Mikhail Saltykov-Shchedrin's satire on Russian political culture, the foolish denizens of Glupov adore every mayor sent their way, praising each one as 'handsome' and 'brilliant'. If it had been required of them not only to love these mayors but to express that love through voting, as became customary during the democratic era, they would undoubtedly have done so.

While Putin was many times more popular than Yeltsin, it is impossible to say whether he was more or less popular than those who ruled other post-Soviet imitation democracies – Nazarbayev, Aliyev, Karimov, Lukashenko, and so forth. Cults of personality, of one dimension or another, sprang up around all of them.

The significantly greater popularity of Russia's second president than its first owes primarily to the fact that under Putin, the country had emerged from the horrifying, transformational economic crisis

---

5   A highly regarded 1870 novel that offers the chronicle of a fictional small Russian town, whose name translates, roughly, to 'Dumbsville'. —Trans.

of the nineties and had finally achieved the stability and order it so urgently wanted. This, again, results not so much from Putin's wise decisions as the natural course of developments.

Sooner or later, that transformational economic crisis had to conclude with society psychologically and institutionally adapting to the new socio-economic conditions. Russia began recovering from the transitional recession before Putin even took office, back in 1997, and, with the exception of the 1998 crisis, which again interrupted things, GDP and standards of living continued to increase through-out the Putin era. In 2001, 22 per cent of respondents said they could not afford to put food on the table; by 2008 that number had shrunk to 12 per cent.[6]

Surviving the crisis was not Russia's achievement alone. Trans-formational crises were resolved and periods of growth begun in every post-Communist economy, even those that, rather than enjoy-ing the revenue from high energy prices as Russia did, suffered paying them. Of course, those whom conditions favoured enjoyed even greater growth. Thus, economic growth in Russia had no more to do with Putin personally than growth in Azerbaijan, for example, had to do with the Aliyev dynasty. But in Russians' general con-sciousness, the economic growth *was* personally connected with Putin, just as it was in Azerbaijan with Heydar Aliyev, and in Kazakhstan with Nazarbayev.

The political stabilization of society can likewise be understood as a natural outgrowth of comprehensible factors. After the bumpy period of the late eighties and early nineties, society was experienc-ing a kind of fatigue from its striving for stabilization and order, understood as the strong power of a no-alternative ruler. Measures toward the construction of a regime of personal power were greeted with happy readiness,[7] especially after the departure of the first

---

6   *2008 Yearbook*, 35

7   Those who agreed that the 'power vertical' – whereby all important decisions come by ukase from the Kremlin, and the influence of the govern-ment, the Duma, and the parties is kept to a minimum – 'is beneficial' factored at 38% in 2005, 43% in 2008; those who said it 'is harmful' comprised 32% in 2005 and 30% in 2008 (*2008 Yearbook*, 57).

president, who had been repudiated by the public. Under these conditions, strengthening the system of personal power did not require some kind of colossal effort – on the contrary, it mostly happened on its own, without overcoming any special resistance. But though the brunt of the work fell on Yeltsin, it was to Putin's rise to power that the much-desired return of order was tied in popular consciousness (just as, once again, the return of stability and order in Belarus was credited to Lukashenko, in Kazakhstan to Nazarbayev, and so forth).

Emergence from the transformational crises, and the attainment of acceptable levels of economic and political well-being and 'order', improved the public mood dramatically. People had become more confident in the future,[8] more satisfied with their political system, proud of their country again.[9] Naturally, they associated these feelings with Putin.

Another natural factor helps explain both the second president's popularity and the particularly 'nationwide' nature of this popularity. Yeltsin had been a revolutionary leader, and his support in all the elections where he ran was largely defined by social factors – it was always the younger, the better educated, the less precarious, and, most of all, the residents of the capitals [Moscow and St. Petersburg] and other large cities who turned out for him, the same people who had been the driving force in the 1991 revolution and who, at least in some crucial ways, had benefited from it the most. The poor, the uneducated, the aged, and those in the provinces tended rather to

---

8   Asked 'What feelings have grown stronger among the people around you in recent years?' the answer 'Hope' was chosen by 13% in 1990, 10% in 1999, 30% in 2003, and 41% in 2008. 'Fear' was given by 29% in 1990, 29% again in 1999, 15% in 2003, and 8% in 2008 (*2008 Yearbook*, 8). To the question 'Are you afraid of unemployment, poverty?' in 1994, 21% answered 'Not in the least', and in 2008, 45%. To the question 'Are you afraid of public humiliation, insults?' 21% in 1994, 44% in 2008. 'Are you afraid of a return of mass repressions?' – 26% in 1994, 47% in 2008.

9   To the question 'How proud are you to be a citizen of Russia?' the answer 'Extremely proud' was chosen by 32% in 2000 and 47% in 2008. The answer 'Not so proud' or 'not proud at all' was chosen by 20% in 2000 and 16% in 2008.

support the Communist opposition (though some of them inevitably supported Yeltsin in dichotomous voting). In analysing election results and polling on levels of trust for Putin, all correlations with socio-demographic factors basically disappear: Putin enjoyed the confidence and electoral support of overwhelming majorities in all strata of society.[10]

We can, I think, explain this by understanding the peculiar place of the second president in our national evolution. On the one hand, Putin was Yeltsin's hand-picked successor, and thus, by definition, the person charged with continuing and completing his work. He made no preparations for open dictatorship, instead talking about keeping up democratic development, continuing market reforms, and never reconsidering the outcomes of privatization. On the other hand, Putin can be seen as Yeltsin's opposite in terms of his place and role in the development of the country. Yeltsin was, most of all, the destroyer of the old system. However he may have endeavoured to fulfill the traditional role of the authoritarian Russian overlord, he ineluctably bore the stamp of his 'revolutionary imposture'. Putin, by contrast, was a 'creator', a restorer of order. His rise marked the end of the revolutionary period. Thus, without losing Yeltsin's old social base, Putin also added a new one – those strata for whom the revolutionary period was one of chaos, lawlessness, culture shock, immiseration, and the loss of 'Great Russia'.[11]

---

10   *See* Dmitrii Furman and Kimmo Kaariainen, 'I Believe the President', *Free Thought* [in Russian] 21, no. 5 (2003).

11   Clearly, Putin is playing a role somewhat comparable to Stalin's in the previous coil of the spiral. Stalin is something of a 'Janus' figure: he is a 'faithful disciple' and 'bearer of Lenin's legacy', and yet is at the same time the opposite of Lenin, a 'bearer of the legacy' of Ivan the Terrible and Peter the Great, a restorer of the traditional order after a period of chaos. One can hardly 'rate' Lenin or Stalin, but it is clear that under Stalin, a 'reconciliation' took place between the Soviet regime and many adherents of the 'old regime', convinced that another 'time of troubles' had at last been concluded, with Russia intact and risen from its knees. This similarity between second rulers flows from a deeper similarity among victorious revolutionary minorities: the need to create 'no-alternative' power, restoring Russia to its traditions of political autocracy. Of course, this comparison is by no means intended as an

In my view, it is no mystery that Yeltsin's successor should prove more popular than Yeltsin himself. Putin's popularity is a natural reflection of the fact that Russia's post-Soviet system is flourishing. It is in fact among the manifestations of this flourishing. His popularity resolves the contradiction between 'form' and 'content' intrinsic to systems of imitation democracy, the formal dependence of power on elections and the actual dependence of elections on power. Under Putin, power exerts tremendous control over society – evidently the most control it can under the present system – but in a relatively painless form that people need not constantly dream of escaping. Most people accept it without grumbling, even joyfully. The level of control corresponds to the condition of society and satisfies society.[12]

3.2 Achieving Power's Greatest Possible Control over Society and the 'Limits of the System's Growth'

The state of total safety from all discernible threats that power achieved under Putin – that is, the independence of power from society – made further movement along the path on which Russia had set out in 1991 unnecessary, even dangerous. The central motivation behind everything power did, the stimulus to all this immense evolution, was the striving to ensure no-alternative power. Power first had to deal with its actually dangerous enemies, then those who demonstrated the distant potential to become dangers, before it could finally eliminate the very possibility of all such threats. The 'optimal' state had been achieved.

---

equivalence. On the second coil of the spiral, everything is dramatically softer. If Putin is a kind of Stalin figure, he is 'Stalin Extra-Light'.

12   Characteristically, over the course of Putin's presidency, the proportion of the population that considered Russia's current system to be optimal increased. In 1998, 43% believed the Soviet system would be better, 32% the Western, with only 13% thinking the current, post-Soviet system was best. By 2008, the numbers had shifted to 24% Soviet, 15% Western, 36% current (*2008 Yearbook*, 21).

In theory, further movement along the same course was possible. Some media remained independent of the authorities, rivals to those in power continued to operate legally, and so on. In the next elections, the president could, with a little effort, receive not just 70 per cent of the vote, but 99 per cent. United Russia could develop from merely holding a majority of parliament to actually being the only permissible party, like the CPSU. Russian Orthodoxy could advance from being the primary religion of ethnic Russians to having the status of official state religion. And so forth. Still, the Soviet government had far greater control. Clearly, different levels of control are optimal for securing power under different systems. Since the Soviet system was based on a dogmatic ideology, it required a very high level of control – political loyalty alone did not suffice. Proclaiming and supporting Communist ideology – the worldview with which every Soviet citizen was inculcated from birth – were necessities. Denial of this ideology was tantamount to the revolutionary negation of the system it accompanied. This is why the publication of writing by figures like Trotsky and Solzhenitsyn posed a serious threat to power. But Russia's post-Soviet system is not based on a strict, dogmatic ideology. It can safely abide a relatively high degree of ideological freedom and pluralism, so long as these do not in turn incite meaningful political actions directed at the authorities on a scale that may threaten them. The level of control required here is dramatically lower. More importantly, like all systems of imitation democracy, this one requires a democratic 'façade', which must be preserved with a certain amount of pluralism and 'democraticness'.

As the system develops, establishing power's ever-greater control over society, there emerges a profound inertia that constantly pushes past the limit of optimal control. Power naturally strives to preserve itself, eliminating even the most remote possibilities of danger. It perceives danger where there is assuredly none. This move beyond the boundaries of optimal control happens regardless of supreme power's aspirations. For example, retaining power in elections requires the assurance of a certain minimal number of votes. But insofar as the success of local authorities is measured by supreme power, primarily according to their success delivering the required

ballots, those regional authorities will inevitably compete with one
another to provide better returns.[13] No governor can afford to be
seen as uncooperative. This in turn will predictably translate to
patently absurd numbers, like a 90 per cent vote for Putin in Chechnya. Once a certain level of electoral support has been established,
any drop in the numbers – even if they still exceed requirements –
can look like the start of a decline, the loss of support and control.
Inevitably, efforts will be made to inflate the numbers again, even to
the point of absurdity. Once we have gone from around 50 per cent
support for the president to seventy-something percent, returning to
50 per cent becomes quite difficult – whereas continuing to 80 per
cent seems only fitting and straightforward. In a manner of speaking, once we have started tightening the bolts, it becomes hard to
stop. But if we tighten them too intensely, we will strip their
threading.

In our evolution up to 2008, we reached a level of control that has
clearly already exceeded the optimal. It is excessive and dysfunctional. To some degree, this is beginning to annoy the people.[14] The
democratic façade has begun to collapse, and it is more and more
difficult to portray Russia as a democratic state, even one with a
distinctive character. There is a general sense that this is being felt by
power as well, disquieting it and driving changes in its behaviour,
away from the prior policy of endlessly tightening all available bolts.

This slowdown or even stoppage of the motion toward greater
control was reflected in many aspects of government activity during
Putin's second term. Here we must look not only at what power was

---

13   In this respect, the 2008 Belarusian parliamentary election is very
interesting. Lukashenko, tired of his geopolitical isolation and eager to
improve his 'image', voiced a desire – seemingly sincere – to see the opposition
sweep the parliament. It did not. The reason why is obvious – no local admin-
istrator anywhere in the country wanted it to be his district where support for
the ruling party had declined.

14   With respect to this, it is fascinating that for all the people's support
for the establishment of the 'power vertical', and all Putin's popularity, 61% of
respondents supported a return to direct elections of governors, and only 19%
opposed it (*2008 Yearbook*, 57).

doing, but also at what it could have been doing but was not. For instance, a certain necessary level of control had been established over the mass media, but it had not been carried to its logical conclusion – a number of opposition publications were still allowed to operate, and Medvedev went so far as to give his first interview with the Russian press to the liberal opposition paper *Novaya Gazeta*. Power created and promoted United Russia in a multitude of ways. There was nothing to stop it from becoming the sole party of power, and practically no danger that this party, itself a 'shadow of power', might try to limit that power. Yet Putin's own attitude toward his creation was clearly ambivalent. Putin never made himself the party's formal leader, and instead of a system with a single party under his control, he has sought to counterbalance it with Fair Russia – a party no less well controlled and no less loyal to him, but positioned as more 'leftist'. Next, work was initiated to create a loyal right-wing party – by this time, Medvedev was in office – and the authorities undertook some fairly meek efforts to burnish both parties. Instead of a simple, easily managed party system, those in power strove to create one far more complex, far less manageable, but more 'democratic'.[15]

All of this is explained by the authorities' awareness that continuing to increase control had become not only unnecessary but dangerous, deleterious to the façade of democracy. (Of course, it was never discussed in these terms.)

---

15 Again, we find many analogues to this in other post-Soviet states. Nowhere but in Turkmenistan and Uzbekistan has the opposition been completely liquidated. Everywhere else, the dominant, presidential party exists alongside a more marginal opposition. Experiments with managed, artificial multiparty systems are not a specifically Russian phenomenon. In Kazakhstan, Nazarbayev long carried out such experiments – until unmanageable Nazarbayev family conflicts erupted in the managed multiparty system and the parties degenerated into factions of support for individual members at war with one another. Nazarbayev then 'merged' these parties together to form the single party Nur Otan. The multiparty, controlled system now emerging in Russia even more closely resembles the one Karimov created in Uzbekistan, where a slate of parties are in competition to see who can demonstrate the greatest love for the president.

3.3 What Could Have Frightened the President?

We are beginning to approach an understanding of Putin's heretofore unexplained decision to leave the presidency at the end of his
second term. It was, manifestly, a decision Putin made freely – had
he wanted, he could easily have extended his rule without serious
resistance from the people or the ruling elite. (Yeltsin might have
done the same but for his health, though it would have required
significantly more effort.) Nonetheless, Putin decided to 'leave the
Constitution be', and seeing that he could not simply walk away (this
would truly have been difficult), he instead created the exceedingly
strange and inconstant situation of his own prime ministership
under President Medvedev, hardly comfortable for either of them.
By declining to renew his presidency, Putin did what no other leader
of a post-Soviet imitation democracy could (Yeltsin does not count;
his departure was obviously mandated by health concerns). As a
result, the Russian system deviated from the standard trajectory of
development, even managing to take a slightly more 'lawful' form in
the process.

What could Russia's second president have been 'afraid' of? It is
unlikely that he was showing any particular deference to the
Constitution – Putin understood quite clearly how that document
had come about, and in other circumstances he was hardly solici-
tous about its strictures. Something else was afoot. Amending the
Constitution so that Putin's power could be indefinitely extended
would once and for all have caused Russia's system to be lumped in
with the authoritarian countries of the 'third world', definitively
contradicting all claims that it was a variant on European democracy, if a rather quirky, particular, and 'sovereign' one. This would
require both determination and some kind of moral or conceptual
justification, none of which existed. Moreover, it would be to some
extent fraught with the possibility of destabilization, upsetting as it
would the established balance between the reality of no-alternative
power and formally democratic institutions. Putin walked up to the
line where 'normative' third world dictatorship begins, but did not

cross over.[16] Forward movement was halted and replaced by a kind of 'marking time' right at this invisible boundary, even a backing away.

For further evidence for this explanation, we can look to Putin's decision to nominate not one of his old KGB comrades, but rather Medvedev, a member of the intelligentsia with 'liberal' and 'legalistic' tendencies. Psychologically, Medvedev is almost as different from Putin as Putin was from Yeltsin. It is fascinating to observe that both Yeltsin and Putin, in choosing their successors, clearly sought out not people who resembled themselves, but rather those with psychological qualities well suited to the work that would surely arise at the current stage of the system's development.

For testament to this, we need look no further than the series of liberal and 'democratic' statements and symbolic gestures Medvedev offered immediately after his appointment-election.[17] Medvedev

16 The question arises of why the presidents of other post-Soviet states were not afraid to cross this line, why what was easy for Nazarbayev, Karimov, and Rahmon turned out to be difficult for Putin. Most likely, besides purely personal factors we cannot judge, certain cultural factors had a role to play here as well. For Russia (and, accordingly, for its president), it is very important that the country can feel it is a 'European' one. For us, comparison with Kazakhstan or Uzbekistan is a humiliation. There are also two further considerations. The regimes of central Asia have certain ideological justifications for authoritarianism that Russia does not share: Firstly, the highly exaggerated, but nonetheless real, threat from Islamic fundamentalism, compared to which 'secular' authoritarianism may be seen as a 'lesser evil'. (In Yeltsin's Russia, the 'red-browns' played a comparable role, but their threat is today a relic of the distant past.) Secondly, rulers in Asia have another available justification, a 'nationalist' one – democracy will arrive at some point later on, but what matters for now is that we are building the first modern Kazakh (or Uzbek, etc.) state. This makes it obvious that the optimal levels and forms of control, and the role of the democratic façade, will vary across imitation democracy systems, dependent on particular cultural factors. People kissed Türkmenbaşy Saparmurat Niyazov's hands, and this was 'functional', a strengthening of his authority. To kiss Putin's hands, or Lukashenko's, however, would be 'dysfunctional'.

17 Medvedev counterbalanced these liberal leanings with tough foreign policy, especially in Georgia. This seems only natural to me, lest Medvedev allow his 'liberalism' to be mistaken for weakness.

rejected the term 'sovereign democracy' and actively deployed a liberal vocabulary ('Freedom is better than unfreedom'), stigmatizing Russia's traditional vices in his writing and speeches[18] and speaking of actual democracy, with rotations of various political parties in power, as the goal of development[19] (albeit a distant goal that had to be approached slowly).[20] In truth, the steps Medvedev actually took toward liberalizing the system were paltry – he eased some of the restrictions on registering parties and on their participation in elections, slightly expanded the representation of minor opposition parties in the Duma, and reformed the Federation Council so that only deputies from legislative assemblies could now be elected-appointed, making it fractionally more representative. Others of Medvedev's acts, like the expansion of presidential terms to six years and the transition to actually appointing the chairman of the Constitutional Court, directly contradicted the goals he had elaborated (the motivations underlying these actions remain murky; it is possible that they reflected difficulties in the relationship at the heart of Medvedev and Putin's 'tandemocracy'). As far as Putin's replacement of the direct election of governors with their appointment, the new president remarked he could not see 'any conditions under which we

---

18   From the president's 2008 address to the Federal Assembly: 'Our state apparatus is also our largest employer, our most active publisher, our top producer, a court unto itself, a party unto itself, indeed, in the final tally, a people unto itself' ('Address to the Federal Assembly of the Russian Federation', 5 November 2008, kremlin.ru.).

19   'As in most democracies, the political struggle will be led by parliamentary parties, periodically replacing one another in power. The parties and their coalitions will form federal and regional bodies of executive power (and not vice versa), and will nominate candidates for head of state, regional director, and local government' (Dmitrii Medvedev, 'Forward, Russia!' [in Russian], 10 September 2009, gazeta.ru.).

20   Medvedev has pinned special hope on the development of the internet, which requires no drastic action or strenuous political activity. 'The proliferation of modern information technologies, which we will promote in every way possible, offers unprecedented opportunities for the realization of fundamental political liberties like freedom of speech and assembly, or for the detection and liquidation of nodes of corruption' (ibid.)

would abandon this decision, not now, not a hundred years from now'. But if the liberal measures undertaken by the new president meant little in themselves, they nonetheless spoke, along with a new style and a new, liberal vocabulary, to a change in vector. It is highly characteristic that among liberals who have pinned their hopes on Medvedev, those hopes are embodied in the word 'thaw', speaking as it does to an intuitive awareness of the parallels between Soviet and post-Soviet cycles of development.

To me, all of this suggests we have entered a new stage in the development of the post-Soviet system. If we again compare our system to a living organism (and the comparison is much more than mere poetic metaphor), we can say the organism has reached its full maturity, the point at which development is maximal and growth stops. Gradual motion toward ever-greater control over society ceases, with nowhere left to go. Once an organism has reached full maturity, the forces of self-destruction begin to act.

In the earlier developmental cycle of the Soviet system, a comparable stage of marking time and retreating after reaching and exceeding the maximum possible level of control (which had replaced the stage of gradual, single-vector development) stretched out for a long period, from the death of Stalin and the Khrushchev thaw to the start of Gorbachev's reforms. It is impossible to predict how long the same stage in the post-Soviet cycle will last. But it seems likely to be much briefer.

4

The Growth of Contradictions and the Movement toward a Crisis of the Political System

There are powerful contradictions intrinsic to the system of imitation democracy. Over time, they deepen until they precipitate a crisis of the system, in which it is destroyed. First is the contradiction between authoritarian 'content' and democratic 'form'. The system remains firmly in place so long as this contradiction continues unrecognized. But, unfolding within the framework of the system, the whole natural evolution of that system, like that of the society developing within the system's framework, is that the contradiction increasingly 'comes to the surface'.

The logic by which the system develops transforms the elections into a fiction, a ritual. The elections of 1991 were really free and really 'fateful'. The elections of 1996 too could be called 'fateful'. Although Yeltsin was objectively running as a no-alternative candidate, participants could see their own vote as the result of a free, even laboured decision. A certain spontaneity and incomplete predictability of results persisted even to 2000. But by 2004 and 2008, the elections were broadly understood not to be elections at all. Nobody could possibly doubt the outcome. They had never provoked protests, and no longer aroused any interest in anyone.[1]

---

1   In 2005, 30% of those polled reported believing Putin would 'appoint' a successor, as Yeltsin had, though only 18% approved of this. Only 18% believed the next president would be 'a new man who had defeated rivals in a fair contest'; 39% believed 'Putin and his circle would announce a successor, and it would fall on the people to support only him'; and 26% believed Putin would amend the Constitution to make a third term possible for himself (*2005 Yearbook*, 88–9). With the assertion that 'in the next presidential election, the appearance of a struggle will be manufactured, but the new

Psychologically, their significance approached that of Soviet electoral ritual.

At the peak of the system's development, the president's popularity camouflages the contradiction between the very idea of elections and the actual no-alternative nature of the results. To continue in this way indefinitely, however, is not possible. The 70 per cent of votes received by Putin in 2004 and by Medvedev in 2008 is, clearly, the most a candidate could possibly receive without massive, open fraud (this only happened in certain places, like Chechnya) on a scale impossible to hide.

But the solidity of any power depends on its society's recognition of its legitimacy, on the right of rulers to power. The senility that came over the USSR near its end grew precisely from a loss of faith in the ideology that had legitimized the Soviet system. In systems of imitation democracy, as in the democracies they imitate, power can be legitimized only through election by the people. To maintain the feeling of its legitimacy requires maintaining the illusion of election by the people. Therefore, the complete exclusion of society from the process of transferring supreme power, the ritualization of elections, and the falsification of their results inexorably lead to the delegitimization of power, and thus to the collapse of the system. It may seem to those in power that 70 per cent of the vote is better than 60 per cent and

president will nonetheless be whomever Putin points to', 57% agreed in April 2005, 53% in October 2005, and 51% in October 2006 (*2006 Yearbook*, 107).

In 2008, 38% agreed and 53% disagreed with the statement 'Since it is already clear who the winner in the next presidential election will be, it is a waste of my time to bother voting'; 13% described the atmosphere prevailing over the 3 March elections as one of 'overall indifference', 43% as one with 'no particular feeling', 33% as one of 'general enthusiasm'; 80% believed Medvedev had been made president 'by those already in power', and just 13% believed it had been 'ordinary voters' (*2008 Yearbook*, 76, 82).

Protests against reducing the elections to a mere formality began to be felt in a rising number of votes 'against everyone', which frightened those in power and led to the removal of this column from the ballot in 2006.

worse than 80 per cent, but the reality is that 80 per cent would mean an end was rapidly approaching.

The delegitimization process I am describing is one aspect of the system's evolution in the descending stage. The very logic of the system's development hastens its natural end. But this delegitimization is accelerated by processes of societal development taking place independently of the system's evolution. If the system's evolution leads to elections becoming ever more fictitious, then the society's evolution will be such that the ability to perceive this fictitiousness grows all the stronger. Russian society, for now, is mainly composed of people who lived under Soviet power and grew acclimated to totalitarian conditions, who may well see an imitation democracy system that is significantly freer than the Soviet system as authentically democratic (indeed, in many cases 'too democratic').[2] For many older Russians raised in the Soviet era, the ritual of voting for power has become normative, and voting for the opposition or to reapportion power is psychologically impossible. But that generation is on its way out, and the younger generations are growing up under different circumstances. They will not so readily as their parents perceive imitation democracy as real.[3]

---

2   In a study by the Levada Center, respondents in 2006 were asked to select the most democratic of a list of thirteen eras in Russian history: 2% said, 'Between February and October 1917'; another 2% said, 'From 1905 to 1916'; 4% said, 'The Gorbachev era'; and the most popular answer (22%) was 'The Putin era' (*2006 Yearbook*, 17). In 2008, 54% of respondents believed Russia was 'moving toward democracy', though 30% thought it 'had stalled' on its way (*2008 Yearbook*, 22).

3   Polling shows systematic differences between the attitudes of older and younger generations toward democratic values. Asked whether freedom of speech brought 'more good than harm', 65% of respondents from 16 to 25 years old answered 'yes' in 1994, and 69% in 2004; 39% of those over 55 answered 'yes' in 1994, and 31% in 2004. Asked whether multiparty elections did more good than harm, 28% of respondents from 16 to 25 years old answered 'yes' in 1994, and 36% in 2004; 21% of those over 55 answered 'yes' in 1994, and 19% in 2004. Freedom of international travel: for ages 16–25, 58% said it was more beneficial than harmful in 1994 and 69% in 2004; for those over 55, the equivalent figures were 28% in 1994 and 43% in 2004. Freedom of enterprise: for ages 16–25, 63% said it did more good than harm in 1994 and

Thus, there are two natural countercurrents. In one direction lies the ritualization of elections, the tearing down of the system's democratic façade, which has become less and less convincing. In the other direction lies the evolution of society to be less and less deceived by this façade. At some point, these two currents will inevitably collide, and the imitation democracy system will become impossible to maintain.

4.1 Atrophy of Feedback Mechanisms

Power's tightening control over society also means a gradual 'atrophying' of feedback from society. Power continually closes off all the channels through which it might receive information about what is really going on.

The elections cease to offer a realistic picture of public sentiment. The media offer an increasingly distorted view that eventually bears no resemblance to reality at all. Criticism of the authorities in mass media becomes exceptionally rare.[4] This has two consequences.

Firstly, the process of changing public consciousness does not immediately break the surface of public life; it takes place in the deeper layers of that consciousness, captured neither by elections nor by polls. Disappointments and irritations pile up imperceptibly, until at some point they inevitably break through the higher, 'conformist' layers of the consciousness – just as happened at the end of the Soviet era, when it only took a few years to transition from 99 per cent of the vote going to the 'bloc of Communists and non-partisans' and an overall 'support for the Party line' recorded in (authentic) surveys to the complete, bloodless liquidation of the CPSU and the USSR. Only

---

76% in 2004; for those over 55, the figures were 23% in 1994 and 41% in 2004. (Y. Levada, 'We Seek the Person' [in Russian] [Moscow, 2006], 305.)

4   This was on vivid display during the outbreak of the economic crisis. Those in power directly commanded the media not to use the word 'crisis'. There was almost no reporting on the spontaneous protests, even in Vladivostok where they grew quite large. There were even moves to prosecute for 'extremism' those who tried to warn the authorities.

a slight push is needed for a mass of individual, vague, suppressed negative feelings to suddenly find general and open expression. As the system evolves, the size of the push needed to do this continually decreases – a jolt the young organism barely feels can prove fatal for the older one.

Secondly, power is immersed in a world of illusion. All the real opponents with which it must reckon vanish (the only ones left are foreign powers, naturally increasing the sense of the outside world's hostility). Like their Soviet forebears, those in power begin to believe their own propaganda. They listen only to the experts who tell them what they want to hear, deepening the illusion. Warning signals no longer reach them (the ones from the special services do not count – Soviet history has already demonstrated their inability to register actual dangers in the late stages of the system's development). They can no longer anticipate the results of their own actions or sense when they may be leading toward unforeseen eruptions – like those caused by the 2005 monetization of social benefits, or the attempt in 2008 to ban right-hand-driving cars in Vladivostok – and to unanticipated international complications and economic losses, as in the gas conflict with Ukraine at the turn of 2008 and 2009. As the force needed to nudge them into disintegration decreases, the chance that those in power will produce it through their own actions accordingly rises.

Reality does manage to penetrate the minds of the rulers, but it does so in a distorted, mythological form. Power's vague fears about uncontrolled and incomprehensible processes being played out gets enveloped in the ramped-up struggle against foreign threats and 'subversive elements' – threats are always less intimidating when they are external and visible than invisible, mysterious, and vaguely felt. This adds to the inadequacy of power's response. In the Soviet period, power drowned out its fears of invisible, obscure forces by amassing missiles, waging war in Afghanistan, and ensuring it had hundreds, if not thousands, of KGB operatives for every dissident. Now power is assembling a massive OMON[5] force against a handful of 'dissenters',

---

5   OMON (an acronym of the Russian for 'Special Purpose Mobile Unit') is a well-known Russian special police force widely used for 'riot control'

stirring constant conflict with its neighbours, fighting in Georgia, and deploying warships to the Caribbean. Power cannot turn this natural process back, and its struggle against external apparitions and mythic threats only hastens it.

Outwardly, total control over society, the attainment of complete predictability in the sphere of formal public political activity, becomes its own opposite – a total lack of control and predictability. No one knows where or why local explosions of public protest like those in Kondopoga or Vladivostok[6] will break out, or how real is the danger of various private and local forms of protest merging into a broader kind of 'trouble'. No one knows what will happen in the North Caucasus. No one, including the members of the tandem themselves, knows how long it will last or what its end will be.

4.2 Social Mobility 'in the Bureaucratic Style'

Another natural process that weakens power and, in the end, leads to the destruction of the system is the establishment, and eventual dominance, of a specifically bureaucratic form of social mobility.

The era of 'chaos' from the late eighties to the early nineties was also one of new elevators of social mobility, an age of quicksilver careers and the emergence in public life of people who made it to the top neither through bureaucratic means nor at the will of the 'bosses' – parvenus of the most varied kinds and sensibilities (from

---

(including against peaceful protests) and in paramilitary operations. OMON forces were involved in street fighting during the 1993 constitutional crisis and were accused of human rights abuses for their conduct in the two Chechen Wars. —Trans.

6   In 2006, the northern Russian town of Kondopoga saw several days of vigorous protest, eventually giving way to ethnic rioting, in the aftermath of a fight in which two ethnic Russians were killed by Chechens at an Azeri-owned bar. Migrants from several regions – including Azeris, Chechens, Georgians, and Dagestanis – were targets of the violence. The same year saw protests in the far eastern Russian city of Vladivostok after nine employees died in a fire at a Sberbank office that many alleged had been mishandled. —Trans.

Sakharov to Zhirinovsky, Lebed to Berezovsky). It was an era of
personalities who were not always appealing, but were strong and
colourful – of personalities like those on Viktor Shenderovich's TV
show, *Kukly* (Puppets). But it is now long past.

The establishment of power's ever-stronger control over society
is at the same time a widening of the range of responsibilities and
social positions whose allocation will be determined by the higher-
ups, ultimately by the president. Under Putin, the size of Russia's
bureaucratic apparatus eclipses that of the entire USSR. This is
about more than just the number of officials – crucially, the
mechanisms of bureaucratic mobility extend to spheres not formally related to the apparatus of the bureaucracy itself. The
rectors of large universities started to be appointed by the president, as was the president of the Russian Academy of Sciences.
Formally elected posts, like parliamentary seats, came to be de
facto appointments.

Mechanisms of selection, 'career filters', and 'career elevators'
under the bureaucratic system of mobility were set up quite differently than under other systems of mobility (based on the market,
science, and so on) or in the system of political mobility defined by
democratic competition for votes. Pleasing the bosses demands a
totally different set of qualities than pleasing the people. When the
sphere of public democratic politics contracts, people capable of such
politics disappear from the elite. On its own, this kind of change in
the elite's dominant personalities does not always mean their deter-
ioration in quality. Demagogue-populists, who rise high in huge
numbers in young, 'unestablished' democracies (and in young imitation democracies), as happened here at the turn of the nineties, differ
totally from bureaucratic careerists – though they are hardly better
or smarter. The democratic mobility model does not presuppose the
systematic elevation of increasingly intellectually and morally weak
people. The demagogues and madmen that are characteristic of
young, unestablished democracies and 'periods of transition' often
disappear. But in an authoritarian society with a corresponding
bureaucratic system of mobility, the principle of 'survival of the
weakest' is constantly at work.

Bosses making appointments can never really escape the fear that their subordinates might 'steal their jobs' by appealing over their heads. They aim to be surrounded by compliant and controllable people, the kind who will make them look smarter and more capable by comparison. Bureaucratic social mobility therefore tends to promote more and more faceless drones to the top. The quality of the bureaucratically recruited elite steadily deteriorates, and the continued action of the mechanisms of bureaucracy has disastrous consequences for the quality of the elite overall.

This thesis beautifully illustrates the gradual intellectual and moral decline of the Soviet elite from Lenin to Chernenko.

This natural process took place again on the post-Soviet coil of the spiral under Yeltsin, who constantly 'eliminated' every rival or anyone capable of becoming one, or simply anyone whose personality made them uncontrollable and capable of offering resistance to any of his decisions (this was a hugely varied group – Rutskoy, Khasbulatov, Burbulis, Gaidar, Lebed, Chernomyrdin). Under Putin, this process continued at an accelerated pace, to the point where it became apparent even to the mass television audience, sparking jokes about 'Putin's vegetables' – and quite possibly stoking some anxiety for Putin and his successor.[7] It clearly happens faster in our current system than it did under the Soviet one. This is true for two reasons: firstly, because the contemporary elite has been tremendously continuous with the late Soviet elite, leading to the inheritance of many who were already highly 'degenerated' by years of Soviet bureaucratic selection; and secondly, because through the Soviet period, even the late Soviet period, there remained at least some ideological motivation behind appointments and career trajectories – a motivation now almost completely absent.

---

7 It may in part have been the realization that talented people could no longer rise through the accustomed paths of political mobility, and the experience of the low quality of the elite, that animated the creation of bodies like the Civic Chamber and the Presidential Council for Civil Society and Human Rights, to which members can be appointed through non-political, non-bureaucratic paths. Of course, these bodies also perform the function of neutralizing, or 'domesticating', potentially dangerous figures.

The elite are deteriorating in quality not only because of the particular nature of bureaucratic mobility, but also because of the corruption that always abounds in systems of imitation democracy. Corruption plays a role in these systems different from the one it plays in real democracies and various kinds of nondemocracies (open military dictatorships, traditional monarchies, and so on) that are less marked by the gulf between legal form and illegal content. Departures from the law by those in power pursuing personal ambitions are closely tied to the very essence of the system, insofar as no-alternative power under the operation of formally democratic norms can be achieved only illegally or, at most, quasi-legally. The key form of corruption is control over the elections. But clearly, if the violation of the highest constitutional norms is in principle required for the system to function, the possibilities for limiting corruption will be minimal. It is no coincidence that corruption was steadily on the rise throughout the Putin era – it developed in parallel with the expansion of power's control over society. The same force has driven his successor to worriedly pursue anti-corruption measures.[8]

A docile, faceless, corrupt elite without initiative is ideal for authoritarian power acting in conditions of stability-'stagnation'.[9] An elite of this kind cannot become ideologically oppositional. It knows solidarity only in a weakened form. Power will always keep its individual members in check when they rebel, whatever the reason. The elite will never fail to pay their 'tribute' in good order (for local authorities, this means the 'correct' distribution of electoral results; for the owners of major media outlets, the 'correct' coverage of events; for judges, the 'correct' judicial decisions; for oligarchs, it simply means money), receiving 'indulgences' in return for their corruption. It is highly characteristic that Putin, having become

---

8   According to Transparency International's 'Corruption Perceptions Index', on a scale of zero to ten, where ten is the complete absence of corruption and zero is the most corrupt system imaginable, Russia scored a 2.5 in 1996, a 2.4 in 2005, a 2.3 in 2007, and a 2.1 in 2008. Among 180 countries, it ranked 147th (lenta.ru/news/2008/09/23/Transparency/).

9   Furman uses of the term *zastoi* for stagnation – this is what Russians call the Brezhnev era.

prime minister, promptly warned his young president against making changes in personnel too quickly. However little the current elite may be to his liking, they are optimal for maintaining stability and control. And yet they are ill suited to any purpose that requires ideological motivation, dedication, discipline coupled with independent decision-making, or persuasiveness. In a crisis, such an elite is useless, eager to flee the sinking ship – to which it is bound by nothing but personal interests – as fast as it can. At the end of the Soviet period, the de-ideologized and degraded late Soviet elite mounted only the most pitiful resistance to the anti-Communist revolution and fled quickly to the camp of the democrats. The even more de-ideologized and degraded post-Soviet elite, when power faces a real threat again, will surely put up even less resistance.

4.3 The Only Ideology Is Guaranteeing Loyalty

Unlike the Soviet system, the current, post-Soviet system has no ideological (or mythological) goals of its own, like building Communism or assuring the victory of socialism around the globe. The goals that felt real at the start of Soviet development, spurring both the authorities and millions of everyday people to action, had lost their motivating significance by the end of the Soviet period. But even during this period, through sheer inertia, those same ideals gave a certain consistency and logic to the authorities' conduct, both internally and internationally.

In the early days of the post-Soviet system, a somewhat similar role was fulfilled by the notion of building an advanced democratic market society and 'returning to global civilization'. But the actual course of development did not lead in the direction of democracy at all, and this goal quickly fell away. The behaviour of those in power, and the course of the system's development, were driven in practice by the pursuit of no-alternative power and the return of the order and controllability that had been lost at the start of the nineties. But once these goals were achieved, it turned out, they disappeared from the system altogether, like the prospect of development itself. There was no clear image of Russia's political future, let alone a clear plan of action for achieving it.[10] Power could neither claim that the system of no-alternative presidents transferring power to chosen successors was ideal for Russia (or ideal as such) nor admit that it was a faulty system careening toward inevitable crisis and fated someday to collapse and give way to actual democracy. It was doomed to inconsistency and incoherence in words and thoughts. The absence of any electoral platforms from Putin or Medvedev, along with their refusal to debate policy with rivals (or quasi rivals), symbolized not only their preference for traditional, monarchic loyalty (the tsar does not debate policy with his subjects) but also the fact that they truly had no plans for the future more concrete than warm wishes for an advanced, prosperous, strong Russia. All that motivated their actions was the simple desire for the preservation of the system, for 'stability', for the assurance that the future would be just like the present. This declaration of stability as a goal unto itself is what 'stagnation' consists of, and it emerged much earlier in the history of the post-Soviet state than in that of its Soviet antecedent.

Politics boiled down to ensuring and testing the loyalty of bureaucrats and oligarchs. The only other thing required of those groups was the suppression of any spontaneous public actions that might lead to destabilization. The president (or, now, the tandem of president and prime minister) found himself at the head of a massive 'clan'-like system of patron-client relations covering the entire society, and his primary job was looking after its stability.

But whenever the purpose of control is to ensure stability and loyalty, it inevitably gets reduced to mere form, as happened in the late Soviet period. We see this very clearly, for example, in the Kremlin's attitude toward regional authorities. In the late Soviet period, supreme power was totally content with the unconditional loyalty offered by the leaders of the republics, whom it thus allowed to freely build their own systems of clientelistic hierarchy. Internally independent,

---

10   In Medvedev's writings, democratic images of the future have a dreamy quality, reminding one of Manilov in Gogol's *Dead Souls*. They have nothing to do with his actual conduct in office.

'autonomous' systems of power arose, headed by the Rashidovs, Kunayevs, Bodiuls,[11] and so forth. Moscow was too afraid to touch them, lest they 'destabilize' the situation. Precisely the same thing is happening now. Outwardly, extreme centralism is being combined with the impossibility of actual change and the no-alternative systems of Luzhkov, Rakhimov, Shaimiev, and Ilyumzhinov.[12] Of the completely self-reliant power of the Kadyrov dynasty, which totally disregards Russian law but pledges its loyalty as Moscow's vassal, there is nothing to be said. The position of the loyal oligarchs, who can count on the authorities to come to their rescue whenever things get difficult, is also stable – because they are already under control, and because if any of them were to fall and be replaced by someone new, there would be a risk of 'destabilization' and other dangers. Power is fettered by its fear of destabilizing the situation. This can be seen especially clearly now in the 'tandem', where Medvedev, who is working to liberalize the system somewhat, has decided he can do so only by baby steps. The total centralization and near omnipotence of presidential power, absent other goals, turns into powerlessness.

---

11   Sharof Rashidov was the notoriously corrupt first secretary of the Uzbek Communist Party from 1959 until his death in 1983, in which capacity he oversaw the transfer of significant wealth from Soviet funds to Uzbekistan. Dinmukhamed Kunayev was the first secretary of the Kazakh Communist Party from 1964 to 1986, and a close associate of Leonid Brezhnev (who had held the same post a few years earlier). He was responsible for the promotion of a number of ethnic Kazakhs into government positions. When Gorbachev removed him from the role, replacing him with an ethnic Russian who had never lived in Kazakhstan, rioting broke out in several Kazakh cities, including the capital. Ivan Bodiul was first secretary of the Moldavian Communist Party from 1961 to 1980, rising, like Kunayev, under the patronage of Leonid Brezhnev, who had also held this job earlier. —Trans.

12   These so-called heavyweight governors would all leave office in 2010, either dismissed by, or citing the wishes of, Dmitry Medvedev. Yuri Luzhkov, discussed in earlier chapters, had been mayor of Moscow since 1992. Murtaza Rakhimov had served as president of Bashkortostan, a republic within the Russian Federation, since 1993. Mintimer Shaimiev had been president of Tatarstan, another of the Russian Federation's republics, since 1991. The eccentric Kirsan Ilyumzhinov had been president of the Republic of Kalmykia since 1993. —Trans.

Having progressed swiftly through a romantic period of revolutionary formation, outrunning chaos, constructing an authoritarian order, and reaching maturity – that is, the state of maximum possible control – the system plunged into a period of purely inert existence, similar to the period of stagnation in the Soviet development cycle. In the second 'coil of the spiral', this happened much faster than it did in the first. The mature stage is followed by sclerotic senescence and the approach of the 'final crisis'.

4.4 The Crisis Is Sure to Come as a Surprise

As it 'grows old', an organism becomes increasingly fragile, less and less capable of resistance. Considering this, we can predict a future crisis with 100 per cent certainty. The idea that our quasi dynasty can continue indefinitely – A names B as a successor, B gets a majority of votes in the elections, B names C as a successor, and so on – can be rejected out of hand.

But it is impossible to predict the form this crisis will take or when it will begin. It depends on many factors we cannot calculate. There is no telling how the current economic crisis will end, or how it will impact us. (To some degree, of course, we can assume it will hasten a systemic crisis, but there is no direct connection here.) A great deal will depend on how unpredictable events unfold in the unstable sphere of Medvedev and Putin's relations, totally concealed from the public and confined to a narrow stratum within the Kremlin elite.

The experience of other systems of this 'species' speaks to the eventuality of a lethal crisis that always seems to 'creep up unnoticed'. Its unexpectedness is intrinsic to systems where power gets no feedback from the public, where false alarms ring out constantly but warnings of real danger never arrive. Nonetheless, we can say something about this future crisis and the forms the fall of this system is likely to take.

The most desirable form of development, of course, would be a 'revolution from above' – a deliberate dismantling of the system and a managed transition to democracy similar to what Gorbachev attempted in the USSR. Hopes for such a process have been awakened by the democratic statements the new president has made. Gorbachev's reforms by no means represented the vision of Soviet societal development likeliest to be realized, and the 'Gorbachev model' cannot be called a success. All the same, if Gorbachev was unable to forestall revolutionary chaos, his reforms clearly helped minimize that chaos, and saved us from more frightening possibilities. Even in the most optimistic vision of the successful and conscientious implementation of Gorbachev's reforms, crises relating to the first rotation of power and the centrifugal processes of the USSR would have lain ahead. But Gorbachevian dismantling of the system 'from above' seems even less likely in contemporary Russia than it was in the late Soviet period.

The task of transition from a system of imitation democracy to one of actual democracy seems relatively simple – certainly far simpler than the transition from Communism to democracy. It requires dismantling and restructuring on a far smaller scale – the market and private property already exist (albeit in limited and inferior form), there is no totalitarian ideology to be reckoned with, and even the Constitution can be let alone at first. But we also face specific challenges here. Precisely because the task before Gorbachev was such a complex one, he could take his time dismantling and 'restructuring' the system, achieving and preserving tremendous personal popularity and support and encountering little in the way of active opposition. For a long time, Gorbachev's liberalizations meant not a weakening but a fortification of his personal popularity and power (he had liberated himself from the ideological and personnel ties that had bound him), and the opposition he could not face down arose only at a very late stage in his reforms. But in the post-Soviet system, the tasks faced by a president actually trying to lead the country toward democracy would, paradoxically, be more complex than those faced by Gorbachev. In fact, the transition from a system of imitation democracy to one of actual democracy essentially boils down to the creation of, and transfer of power to, an active opposition; once the first democratic rotation of power has been implemented, the path to a system in which such rotations are the norm is clear. But the task of creating an opposition capable of taking power while wielding the very power they would take is psychologically unnatural. No president can create his own opposition and prepare his own electoral defeat – this runs counter to all basic human instinct. Some liberal measures, like the timid steps Medvedev has recently tried to take, or even somewhat more radical ones, are, of course, possible, and these may to some degree mitigate the severity of the future crisis. But it is tremendously difficult to imagine an imitation democracy being dismantled from above, in accordance with a 'presidential plan' – personally, I am unaware of any historical precedents.[13] The most that can be expected from the president in such a system is that in a situation arising against his will and promising to threaten his hold on power, if he does put up a fight, he will not 'go too far' and will surrender as readily as, for example, Shevardnadze did in Georgia.

A relatively soft and orderly version of a transition to democracy may also be imagined in connection with a split at the top of the kind that was foreshadowed in 1999, when we were not so far from elections offering actual alternatives. Such a situation could, theoretically, recur. Now, for example, we've seen the emergence, generated by the tandem, of something like two top 'parties', the Putinite and Medvedevian. But it is hard to imagine the series of events that would relocate their clandestine and symbolic struggles to the public sphere, let alone electoral politics. The situation in

---

13   There do exist examples of successful transitions to democracy from traditional monarchic systems, in which the monarch proposes a constitution. There are also examples from military dictatorships, in which the generals send the army to barracks and then organize elections. But these systems lack the misalignment between form and content that characterizes imitation democracy, and as such they can much more easily resolve the question of their rulers' ultimate fates. The monarch can remain a monarch. The military, if they are not guilty of any serious atrocities and the events that brought them to power can be recognized as an extraordinary measure demanded by a unique moment, can remain the military. The position of presidents and ruling elites in imitation democracy is trickier – they simply cannot avoid systemically violating the law.

1999, too, arose from a rather random series of events, and its escalation to elections with real alternatives, transcending the limits of our system, would have been possible only if even less likely events had taken place. In any case, Putin has categorically denied the possibility of his running against Medvedev, clarifying that the two would decide on the next president together, with no participation by the public.

As unlikely, as practically unthinkable, as a 'revolution from above' or a 'split at the top' may be, for Russia the crises that have dismantled softer versions of comparable systems, like the colour revolutions in Ukraine, Georgia, and Serbia, are no likelier (as, indeed, colour revolutions are basically unthinkable for countries like Uzbekistan, Turkmenistan, Tajikistan, Kazakhstan). The panicked fear of colour revolutions that gripped power at the start of this decade was quite neurotic and pathological. It compelled the creation of Nashi, a sort of post-Soviet parody of Komsomol or China's Red Guards, to fight revolutionaries in the streets. Such a revolution requires a strong and well-organized legal opposition that can receive a majority of votes in the elections and also lead people into the streets when election fraud robs them of their victory. Back in 1996, it was theoretically possible that events would develop in this way. Now not only do we have no such opposition, but there is no chance for one to arise. Elections have essentially lost the air they once conveyed of being an important event. Our evolution toward power's establishment of ever-greater control over society has progressed too far.

All scenarios involving a 'gentle', organized dismantling of the system here are thus either out of the question or profoundly unlikely. This can only mean the crisis that inevitably approaches our country will take on more unexpected, spontaneous, and unorganized forms.

In the Russian consciousness, there is a neurotic fear of anarchy and chaos that comes from our history and prompts the public to agree readily to the establishment of authoritarian power (any power seems a lesser evil compared to a power vacuum). But outwardly stable authoritarian systems lead in their natural evolution to precisely those periods of chaos Russia so wishes to avoid. We paid for the stability enjoyed by Russia's nineteenth-century autocracy, contrasting so starkly with the turbulent history of Western Europe, with the catastrophic events of 1917. It is very likely that the cost of the Putin era's stability and manageability will similarly be repaid through a coming period of chaos and collapse.

5

In Place of a Conclusion: Possible Outcomes of the Coming Crisis

The end of the present system's life cycle, as I have tried to demonstrate, is the no-alternative result of its development. It is not only likely, but inevitable. With every year it draws nearer. But the timing and shape of this future crisis cannot be foretold. Such crises always arrive unexpectedly. The autocracy fell suddenly, the USSR fell suddenly, the colour revolutions sprang up suddenly.

It also seems quite likely that this future crisis – like the twilight of the Soviet system and even the collapse of the tsarist system, indeed the ends of all such systems – will again see appeals to democratic principles and attempts to establish a true democracy. One is hard pressed to imagine the crisis taking any other ideological form. As the preceding analysis should make clear, however, in my view neither appeals to democracy nor even the sincere desire to establish it are enough to carry such a movement to victory. Thus, the outcome of the future crisis is not predetermined – there are several possible alternatives. Logically, we can imagine the outcome in two distinct ways: as a transition to democracy, or as a new cycle isomorphically resembling the last.[1]

---

1   In the Russian mass consciousness, there lurks another future Russia – one that has disintegrated into many states. I think that those who describe Russia's disintegration combine two different ideas of what Russia is: on the one hand, a political state with defined borders, and on the other, the ethnic territory of the Russians. Russia the state and Russia the ethnic territory are two very different things. The Russian state includes countries dominated by cultures extremely different from the Russians' (remnants of empire). The possibility of one or more of them 'breaking off' in some acute crisis cannot be ruled out – indeed, it nearly happened in Chechnya. But this would be

5.1 The First Alternative: A Successful Transition to Democracy

The first alternative is a successful transition to democracy that takes place immediately after the collapse of the present system.

In Russia, democracy was proclaimed in 1917 and again in 1991. In neither case was the attempted transition to democracy successful. The failure of 1917 was many times more terrible than the failure of 1991. The post-Soviet system is significantly 'softer' than the Soviet one, retaining elements of democracy far longer, and the façade of legality and democracy plays a far greater role. I write eighteen years after the collapse of Soviet power. Eighteen years after the collapse of tsarism, it was 1935. Within both cycles, the development was toward power's ever-greater control over society, but it should suffice to compare the degree of control exerted in 2009 with that exerted in 1935 to demonstrate the colossal difference between the two systems and their cycles of development.

The difference in these cycles is, first of all, a result of the modernization our society underwent during the Soviet period. If public life during the Soviet era was marked by the cyclical process of the Soviet system's development and decline, then 'deep below the surface', steady processes of modernization were nonetheless unfolding.[2] And if Russian society was not yet ready to live under democracy

---

Russia's collapse only 'in a narrow sense of the word'. The disintegration of ethnic Russia into a multitude of viable Russian ethnic states is all but inconceivable (though one can easily imagine a chaotic situation in which many Russian republics are separately proclaimed). It is exceptionally difficult to find examples of the disintegration of an ethnically homogenous territory. The fear of Russia's disintegration seems to me neurotic.

2 Not just Russia, but all the post-Soviet countries, having 'come through' the USSR, 'emerged' from it immeasurably more modern and closer to democracy than they had 'gone in'. This goes not only for societies like those of Kazakhstan or Tajikistan, which carved trails through the USSR that cannot but be called astonishing, but also to developed states that were relatively late to join the USSR, like the Baltics. In its first, interwar period of independence, Lithuania managed to preserve democracy only until 1926,

by the end of the Soviet period, it was immeasurably closer than it had been in 1917. In 1991, as in 1917, we proved unable to 'clear the bar', but this time we got much closer to the bar and created a system that was not totalitarian, but merely imitation democratic. It is clear that within the framework of the post-Soviet system, too, there is a cycle of the system's development on the surface, while processes creating the grounds for democracy are working, not always visibly, deep below.

The structure of society is changing. For one thing, the more traditionalist strata are disappearing – starting with the traditional peasantry, whose psychology, shaped by communality, serfdom, and then Soviet collective farming, is undoubtedly the most important force that has shaped our political culture. There is also an expansion of new strata, whose living conditions presuppose less routine, greater personal self-sufficiency, more freedom of choice. An ever-increasing number of people are becoming economically independent of, or less dependent on, the state. Relations and habits formed around 'the market' and private property are taking root. Russian society is increasingly included in the global system. People are growing more accustomed to the relative freedom ushered in by the 1991 revolution, which was never completely eradicated – and in some ways was even consolidated – by the regime of imitation democracy that followed.[3]

Estonia and Latvia until 1933–4. A period of dictatorships swiftly followed. If we compare the development of the Baltic countries in the interwar and post-Soviet periods, we cannot but conclude that Soviet development, for all its nightmares, nonetheless represented forward motion.

3 Polls show that many democratic freedoms have already been deeply internalized in Russia. For example, presented with the statement 'In exchange for a guaranteed decent salary and pension, I would relinquish my freedom of speech and the right to travel abroad', in 2002, 43% agreed and 48% disagreed; in 2008, 38% agreed and 52% disagreed (*2008 Yearbook*, 103). In 2008, 32% agreed that 'we need a single, strong ruling party'; 45% that we need two or three large parties; 8%, many small parties; and 6% that we do not need parties at all (p. 72). Further, 61% agreed that Russia needs a political opposition to power, and only 21% that it does not need one (p. 85), and 60% agreed with the necessity of TV channels outside state control (p. 99).

A generation raised under Soviet power, its psychology characterized by a fear of power and an even greater fear of free choice, which
it sees as coming tinged with the threat of anarchy, is on its way out
due to natural causes. That old woman who said that she would vote
for Zyuganov once he was president is likely in the grave. The new
generation has had a very different experience, growing up under
dramatically different circumstances. For the post-Stalin generation,
the vaunted 'children of the sixties', the absence of mass terror
became normative, which is exactly why they were able to strive for
more – more political liberties, more socio-economic freedoms. In
just the same way, for the generation now coming of age, private
property, freedom of information, a life free of totalitarian ideology
and all-encompassing ideological control, the possibility of travel
abroad, even a multiparty system – all of these are 'normal' aspects of
life, familiar since childhood, and broadly expected. The transition
of this generation to political activity amid a systemic crisis should,
of course, be driven by a desire for more: an actual democracy, based
on honest and meaningful elections with alternatives. It is quite
reasonable to imagine that Russia's third attempt at a transition to
democracy, in the year two thousand something, may at last succeed
(as the Russian idiom has it, 'God loves a trinity').

This would mean that after a deep political crisis, the first actually free, unmanipulated elections to supreme power in the history
of Russia would take place, and that the winners would not then
work to tighten their hold on power by fixing the next elections (or
they might try, but would be thwarted by the opposition and the
public). After a few rotations, the system of real elections would have
been consolidated. Fear of free choice and of the transfer of power
would be a thing of the past. Russia would emerge from its systemic
cycles of no-alternative power and anarchic 'times of troubles'.
From the vantage of the present, this sounds utterly utopian – as it
has seemed in many countries that subsequently became stable
democracies.

Still, this is just a possible scenario – not an inevitable one. The
deep cultural and psychological peculiarities of Russian society that
make the establishment of democracy so challenging here are also

reproduced in the younger generations, interacting in complex ways with 'modern' sensibilities. Nashi, of course, are neither the Komsomol nor the Red Guards, but they do demonstrate that a traditionalist sensibility continues to be reproduced, albeit in a weakened and more farcical form. And for the next generation, a transition to democracy will prove very challenging – much harder than just reining in the ruling presidential quasi dynasty and bringing some democratic forces to power. There will arise anarchic elements, and accordingly a desire to escape them under the shelter of 'strong power'.

Those who come to power may well do all they can to buttress that power and prevent future rotations, as the victors of 1991 did, and as has happened many times in the histories of the most varied peoples.[4] There is no reason to assume they will be stopped. Indeed, democracy requires not just the victory of democratic forces, but also the presence of a strong democratic opposition that accepts the rules of the game. The undeniable weakness of the efforts at resistance on the part of the current elite (if one agrees they have resisted at all) will do nothing to make the establishment of democracy likelier, just as the weakness of resistance by the Soviet elite in 1991 did not. The total switch of the old elite to the side of the victors will tend to increase the chances that the old order will be resurrected in a new form.

Thus, we cannot assume this third attempt will inevitably be successful.

---

4   For an example of a similar development in the post-Soviet space, we need look no further than Belarus, where Lukashenko rose to power democratically, in a spontaneous 'electoral revolution', but then created an imposing regime of no-alternative presidential power. In Kyrgyzstan, we find a similar cycle, even starker in form – the Tulip Revolution's ouster of Akayev loosed anarchy on the country, which plunged directly into the even harsher Bakiyev regime. Another example is Georgia, where two weak regimes of imitation democracy (Gamsakhurdia and Shevardnadze) were toppled in popular uprisings (the first one violent, the second a 'colour revolution'), but the strong tendencies of those in power toward authoritarian transformation make it seem unlikely they will be dislodged by electoral defeat.

5.2 The Second Alternative: A Return to No-Alternative Power and the Start of a New Cycle

The second possible outcome of the future crisis that we cannot rule out is the failure of the third attempt, and a return to no-alternative power. In this scenario, after two cycles of transition from unsuccessful attempts at establishing democracy to temporary pacification under an authoritarian system, followed by a new crisis and the start of a new attempt, there will be a third. Historically, many countries of the 'third world' have been stuck in such cycles repeated over many iterations. In a number of Latin American countries, for example, it has happened dozens of times.

Still, the objective task of the transition to democracy remains unchanged, even as its completion is again consigned to an uncertain future, awaiting the next attempt. It is a task that cannot really be 'cancelled'. Democracy is a facet of the modern world. The transition to it is a necessary part of contemporary development, of modernization. This is part of what is meant by the 'adulthood' or 'maturity' of a society. The zone of democracies is gradually expanding; new countries are continuously transitioning, including many whose traditional cultures would seem a world apart from the Western countries where modern democracy was born.[5] In Europe, Russia and Belarus are the last unfree countries.[6] And however difficult

---

5   According to estimates by the American NGO Freedom House, in 2009, out of the world's 193 countries, 46% were 'free'; 32% were 'partially free'; 22% were 'not free'. In 1977, 28% of countries were free; in 1985, 35%; in 1997, 42%. Twenty-four out of the twenty-five countries of Western and Southern Europe are considered free; thirteen out of the twenty-eight in Eastern Europe and the former USSR; twenty-five out of thirty-five in the Americas; sixteen out of thirty-nine in the Asian Pacific; ten out of forty-eight in sub-Saharan Africa; one out of eighteen in the Middle East and North Africa. Russia is counted as 'not free'.

6   If we were to include the Transcaucasian republics in Europe, there would be three nonfree ones, because this group includes Azerbaijan.

the forces of Russia's cultural traditions and historic experience make a transition to true democracy here, eventually, whether after the crisis of the present system or the crisis of the one that follows it, it is inevitable. Today, the task of transitioning to democracy seems incredibly difficult, if not impracticable. Until relatively recently, the task of eliminating the Communist system seemed impracticable, too.

Democracy is not 'happiness'; it is the contemporary norm. A feeling of happiness may accompany the transition to democracy, as it may accompany the completion of a university degree, or the achievement of any high standard. But after a brief burst of euphoria, the harsh reality of daily life takes over. Time passes. People may long for the time they once hurried to leave behind, but to which they now cannot return. The problems Russia will face in the middle and end of this century may be much more difficult than the problem of the transition to democracy. But that is the problem we have been considering here. And by that time, it will already have been solved, a forgotten relic of the distant past.

'Partially free' European countries include Albania, Armenia, Bosnia and Herzegovina, Macedonia, Moldova, Montenegro, and Turkey.

Afterword

Tony Wood

The book you have just finished reading was written in the late 2000s, synthesizing the remarkable analysis of the post-Soviet political order that Dmitrii Furman had developed over the previous few years. It was first published in Russian in 2010, just after the high point of what Furman called the 'imitation-democratic' system. By the time it came out, Vladimir Putin had served two terms as president (2000–2004 and 2004–2008) and handed power to his appointed successor, Dmitrii Medvedev – a seamless transition, validated by apparently democratic elections, that displayed the system's confidence and solidity. But as Furman argued back in 2010, the very nature of the system meant that it was headed for a period of crisis sooner or later.

Twelve years on, Russia's imitation-democratic regime remains in place, having survived a series of upheavals – including nationwide demonstrations against electoral fraud in 2011–12, and regular outbursts of protest thereafter. But in February 2022, the Kremlin plunged Russia and its neighbors into catastrophe through the criminal invasion of Ukraine. Whatever the eventual outcome of the war, the post-Soviet world seems to have entered a new era. In this very different context, how should we situate Furman's work within the wider field of commentary about Russia? What light does his analysis of the origins and evolution of Russia's ruling regime shed on its present actions, and how does it help us to understand its possible futures?

As Keith Gessen notes in his foreword to this volume, Furman's analysis stands out sharply from the general run of commentary on Russia in several key respects. Written with a distinctive combination of critical force and cool detachment, it notably breaks with all the core tenets of the standard Western view and goes against most of the cherished beliefs of the Russian liberals who were Furman's immediate peers. For much of the 1990s, discussions of Russian politics framed developments in terms of a twofold 'transition' to capitalism and liberal democracy. A burgeoning literature emerged devoted to measuring Russia's progress along a normative track whose endpoint was convergence with the West. But in the 2000s, as Putin's grip on power tightened, the optimism of the previous decade dissipated. The framing question now became that of how to explain Russia's apparent regression, and the tropes of transition gave way to a new emphasis on the lingering pathologies of the Soviet past. In the West, this meant a return to something much closer to the Kremlinology of the Cold War era, accompanied by a fixation on the persona of Putin that was also matched in much Russian commentary. If Yeltsin had for a time represented Russia's fragile democratic present, Putin incarnated the return of its autocratic past. Common to most mainstream interpretations, indeed, was an insistence on an almost Manichean contrast between the two men's rule, as embodiments of the drastic turn Russia's political history had seemingly taken at the turn of the twenty-first century.

Furman's account, as readers will have seen, goes against each of the assumptions underpinning the conventional view. Firstly, he undoes the idea that Yeltsin represented any kind of democratizing momentum in Russia. On the contrary, the 1991 triumph of the 'democratic' movement headed by Yeltsin was the first step in the construction of a fundamentally different species of regime, in which the opposition would never be allowed to take office. While Yeltsin's administration received the fulsome backing of Western governments and pundits as a paragon of democracy, it went about the task of perpetuating its hold on power by rigging elections and empowering a new capitalist class. Secondly, Furman dismissed the idea of any fundamental rupture between Yeltsin and Putin, instead depicting the two men as representing successive phases in the construction of a single system. Putin inherited and consolidated in the 2000s what Yeltsin had built in the 1990s – a relationship symbolized by the handover from Yeltsin to Putin on New Year's Eve of 1999. (Underscoring the bonds of complicity between the two, Putin's first act was to exempt his predecessor from prosecution.) Thirdly, and following on from this, Furman did not see Putin's regime as any kind of sinister regression to Soviet habits or deviation from a democratic path along which Yeltsin had been leading Russia. Rather, Putinism was a natural outgrowth of the imitation-democratic system Yeltsin had founded. It was therefore not the Soviet past that best explained the features of Putin's rule, but the internal logic of this new, post-Soviet system.

In offering this alternative view of Russia's post-Soviet political evolution, Furman did more than break with the profoundly normative character of Kremlinology and the teleological narratives of 'transition'. He also shifted the entire axis of comparisons for Russia. Most coverage of the country had tended to set Russia alongside one or more Western states, with occasional provocative exceptions comparing it to other middle-income countries. Furman, by contrast, placed Russia in the company of the states that in fact most closely resembled it: the fourteen other republics that had emerged from the disintegration of the USSR.[1] From 1991 until his death in 2011, he produced a series of studies of the political systems of post-Soviet countries, often in co-authorship with scholars from the country in question. These ranged from early works on national movements in Estonia (1991) and Armenia (1993) to a co-authored volume on Kyrgyzstan's political cycles, which appeared in 2012.[2] In between

---

1   For an English-language overview of Furman's analysis of commonalities and contrasts between the fifteen republics, see the interview 'Imitation Democracies: The Post-Soviet Penumbra', New Left Review 54 (November–December 2008).

2   Furman, *Stanovlenie politicheskikh organizatsii v sovremennoi Estonii* (Moscow, 1991); *Kul'turnye i sotsial'no-psikhologicheskie osnovy sovremennogo armianskogo natsional'nogo dvizheniia* (Moscow, 1993); and, with Sanobar Shermatova, *Kirgizskie tsikly: Kak rushatsia rezhimy* (Moscow, 2012).

came comparative volumes he edited or co-edited on Ukraine (1997), Belarus (1998), Chechnya (1999), Azerbaijan (2001), the Baltic states (2002), Kazakhstan (2004), Moldova (2007), as well as on the Commonwealth of Independent States (2006).[3]

This impressive and systematic comparative scholarship provided the basis for the parallels and contrasts Furman so masterfully draws in this volume. It also made Furman a genuine outlier: since the end of the Cold War, there had been a surprising lack of comparative work looking at the post-Soviet states as a bloc. To some extent, this reflected Western research agendas and the nation-building priorities of the new states themselves: in both cases, there was a rush to determine what was most distinctive about each country, rather than what united them. In Russia, the question of comparison was freighted with status anxieties. Parallels with Western countries, however unflattering in the present, at least implied that this was the relevant peer group. To find similarities between Russia and Kazakhstan or Azerbaijan, conversely, would place Russia in the wrong company.

Furman cut through such prejudices with a characteristic calm and clarity: it stood to reason that these states would resemble each other initially, since they emerged from the same Soviet carapace, and their rulers confronted similar political dilemmas. Together they established a type of regime common not just across the post-Soviet space but also beyond – a 'species', as Furman terms it, with a life cycle and behaviors peculiar to it. The question was how and why the trajectories of these countries diverged after 1991. Here Furman drew on his prior formation as a scholar of comparative religion, finding

---

3   Respectively: Ukraina i Rossiia: obshchestva i gosudarstva (Moscow, 1997); Belorussiia i Rossiia: obshchestva i gosudarstva (Moscow 1998); Chechnia I Rossiia: obshchestva i gosudarstva (Moscow 1999); Azerbaidzhan i Rossiia: obshchestva i gosudarstva (Moscow 2001); Strany Baltii i Rossiia: obshchestva I gosudarstva (Moscow 2002); Kazakhstan i Rossiia: obshchestva i gosudarstva (Moscow 2004); Moldavskie moldavane I moldavskie rumyny: Vliianie osobennostei natsional'nogo soznaniia Moldavan na politicheskoe razvitie Respubliki Moldova (Moscow 2007); and SNG: Problemy integratsii i dezintegratsii (Moscow 2006).

deep cultural roots for the different political systems that would emerge during the 1990s.[4] But he also ascribed many of the gaps that began to open up between former Soviet states to their differing endowments: their degrees of regional and ethnolinguistic diversity, their confessional divisions, the extent to which their social structures tended towards hierarchy or rough egalitarianism. All of these were enabling, though not in themselves sufficient, conditions for a given country to break from the 'imitation-democratic' pattern with which they had all begun.

An astute commentator on current affairs, Furman was alert from early on to the speed with which post-Soviet states were diverging from each other. Through the 1990s and 2000s, his writings for wider audiences – gathered in two volumes, one for each decade – often turn to developments elsewhere in the former USSR.[5] Both there and in the present volume, Furman highlights the degree to which countries such as Ukraine, Georgia, and Kyrgyzstan were able to establish more genuinely competitive political systems than that in Russia. (In this respect, too, he was engaging in a comparison many of his fellow Russian liberals would find uncomfortable: in the march towards democracy, had Russia fallen behind Kyrgyzstan?) Yet the Colour Revolutions that took place in these countries – Rose in Georgia in 2003–04, Orange in Ukraine in 2004, Tulip in Kyrgyzstan in 2005 – were the exceptions: the imitation-democratic regime type remained dominant across most of the post-Soviet space through the 2000s. Within that species, Russia's was the most stable and successful of all, reaching an undisturbed maturity – what Furman calls its 'golden age' – in Putin's second presidential term, from 2004–2008.

---

4   Furman's first book was on *Religion and Social Conflicts in the USA*, Moscow 1981; thereafter he published and edited books on Sikhism and Hinduism, the Islamic reformation, religion in Russia. A selection of his writings on the religion was published in Russian shortly after his death: *Izbrannoe*, Moscow 2011. For the most substantive engagement with Furman's work on religion, see the first part of Perry Anderson's intellectual portrait: 'One Exceptional Figure Stood Out,' *London Review of Books*, 30 July 2015.

5   Furman, *Nashi desiat' let: Politicheskii protsess v Rossii s 1991 po 2001 god* (Moscow 2001); and Publitsistika 'nulevykh': Stat'i 2001–2011 gg. (Moscow 2011).

But even as the system reached its peak, some of its limitations were already becoming apparent. Furman wrote this book halfway through the Medvedev presidency (2008–12), at a moment he saw as marking the imitation-democratic system's entry into a phase of stagnation. Beyond this standstill, he argues in the final chapters of this book, a period of crisis awaited, in which the contradictions of the system would multiply. These included not only a widening gap between democratic 'form' and authoritarian 'content', but also an atrophying of 'feedback mechanisms' – a loss of contact between rulers and ruled, rendering it ever more difficult for the regime to get an accurate read on society. At this point, the very impulses to control society and eliminate political challenges that had enabled its consolidation would turn from assets to liabilities. For Furman, this was not so much a matter of individual failings as of systemic evolution. In his biological metaphor, after reaching maturity imitation democracies inevitably enter a period of senescence and decline. Either their grip on power is loosened, or the very tightening of that grip produces crises of rule. The question then becomes one of whether the system is swept away by those crises, or whether it can survive them by adapting or renewing itself.

To what extent do events since 2010 bear out Furman's prognoses? His final chapters were predictive only in a broad sense, but despite the wealth of circumstances he could not have foreseen, the evolution of Russia's imitation-democratic regime has in many ways conformed to the pattern he laid out then. Furman clearly did not imagine Putin would return to power in 2012, let alone that he would remain there a decade later, his grip on power extended indefinitely thanks to a 2020 constitutional amendment. But this in itself arguably confirms Furman's diagnosis of senescence. Faced with multiplying dangers – the fallout from the global economic crisis after 2008, the sudden upsurge of popular protest at home in 2011 – Russia's ruling system responded by returning Putin to power and heightening its use of repressive methods. An imitation democracy still in the process of growth would have been able to find another leader, would have imagined other options for its prolongation beyond simply insisting on more of the same. While the constitutional amendment of 2020

might be taken as a sign of flourishing authoritarianism, by perpetuating the system's reliance on Putin it also signals the increasingly
illusory character of its democratic façade, codifying the system's
slow-burning crisis rather than resolving it.

Of course, the major development that Furman could not have
foreseen was the drastic escalation of hostilities between Russia and
Ukraine, culminating in the Russian invasion of February 2022. Few
would have predicted this outcome even one or two years ago, let
alone in 2010. When Furman was writing, many of the events that
would prepare the ground for the present disaster still lay in the
future: the Maidan protests and fall of Yanukovych in 2013–14,
Russia's annexation of Crimea and its support for separatist militias
in the Donbas over the following years, and the establishment of
sanctions against the Russian regime by the US and its allies. Even
in the wake of all this, the Kremlin's decision to invade Ukraine in
February 2022 took well-informed observers by surprise, their shock
compounded by the seemingly impulsive or even irrational nature of
this course of action. Yet the decision was also indicative of precisely
the kinds of pathology Furman identified as likely in an imitation-
democratic regime in its senescence: a narrowing of decision-making
circles, a lack of feedback mechanisms, and above all a growing insu-
lation of those at the top from reality.

Nevertheless, the appalling developments of 2022, coming in the
wake of more than a decade of mounting tensions between Russia
and the West, do point to one major absence in Furman's analysis,
highlighted by Perry Anderson in the most perceptive and thorough
English-language engagement with Furman's work.[6] Geopolitics
plays little role in his anatomization of 'imitation democracy', which
remains focused on the internal evolution of each regime, and the
prospects for a genuine democratization within each. While Furman
provided an unrivalled comparative analysis of the family of post-
Soviet regimes, the dynamic interactions between them remained
largely outside his frame. So, too, did the question of how they were

6 See Anderson, 'Imitation Democracy', *London Review of Books*, 27
August 2015.

jointly and separately affected by the larger force field of inter-state power relations.

Above all, Furman allows little room for the possibility that this geopolitical context could itself reshape imitation-democratic regimes – whether by speeding their downfall from without or by artificially extending their lifespan. In the post–Cold War period Furman analyzed, these external factors had considerable weight. The lopsided geopolitical balance of the 1990s brought the global dominance of the US and a drive to extend its sway over the former Soviet satellites in Eastern Europe. The 2000s were marked by the expansion of NATO into former Soviet republics, and by Russia's growing resentment of its choice between subordination or exclusion from the post–Cold War order. The Russo-Georgian War of 2008 was the first in a series of Russian attempts over the next decade to unsettle the existing balance of global forces, the failure of which only diminished Russia's influence and at the same time heightened the Kremlin's determination not to cede further strategic terrain. These geopolitical factors not only drove Russian policy in Ukraine in 2013–14; they also played a central role in the regime's internal ideological reconfiguration through the 2010s, as the imitation democratic system took on an increasingly nationalist coloration. These considerations fall outside the analysis Furman lays out in this volume, in which ideology is ultimately a secondary feature of imitation-democratic systems, which are cynically pragmatic. They can be nationalist just as easily as they can be anything else, switching philosophies depending on the circumstances. The decisive factor is simply their need to maintain their hold on power.

Yet elsewhere in his writings, Furman did draw a connection between the fate of Russia's imitation democracy and its external policies. In 2007, he wrote on essay on the Commonwealth of Independent States (CIS), the loose association of post-Soviet states formed in late 1991 as the USSR disintegrated.[7] Even at the time, its founding members treated the CIS as the means for a 'civilized

---

7   Furman, 'SNG kak posledniaia forma Rossiiskoi imperii', in I. M. Kliamkin, ed., Posle imperii, ed. I. M. Kliamkin (Moscow, 2007), 79–102.

divorce', in the famous words of then-Ukrainian president Leonid Kravchuk. Furman situated it in a longer historical arc, identifying it as the 'final form of the Russian empire', which was now reaching the end of a century-long process of dissolution. Made fifteen years ago, his arguments about Russian nationalism and imperialism seem especially worth returning to in the light of current events.

Furman identified three distinct avatars of the Russian empire, each embodying a distinct stage of its entropic decline. The first, of course, was the vast domain of the Romanov dynasty, which was different from its European peers in lacking a distinction between metropole and colony. For much of the empire's existence, Russian ethnicity also conferred little advantage on its citizens (indeed in many cases the reverse applied: Poles and Finns could exercise more liberties than Russian serfs). Yet in the second half of the nineteenth century, a combination of top-down Russification policies and an expansion of literacy fostered a growth of national consciousness across the empire, leading to mounting centrifugal tensions.

In 1917, the empire fell apart under the pressure of world war and popular revolt. It could only be knitted back together by shifting its foundations: in the wake of the Civil War, the Bolsheviks created a nominally federal union that enshrined the rights of national minorities, while remaining strictly unitary and centralized in practice. This was a second incarnation of the empire, but a highly contradictory one. For Furman, while the USSR replicated the tsarist empire in territorial outline, it was distinct from it in its deliberate submergence of Russian nationalism. The price of continued de facto Russian dominance was its de jure denial. At the same time, the construction of the Soviet system paradoxically assisted in the creation of non-Russian national structures that, by the end of the 1980s, were poised to emerge as the governing organs of newly independent countries. The anomaly, Furman observes, was Russia itself, which lacked such national institutions. As a result, at the end of the Soviet era Russian nationalism adopted conflicting goals: it 'strove not for the disintegration of the USSR but for it [the USSR] to become a state where Russian dominance could be overt and unconditional'. Under

Yeltsin's leadership, Russian democrats furthered Russia's sovereignty at the expense of Gorbachev's all-Union government. Yet their very success brought failure: 'the struggle for "Russian greatness" led to the destruction of the state within whose framework alone Russia could be "great".'[8]

For Furman, the abruptness of the USSR's collapse crucially conditioned the character of Russia's 'post-imperial syndrome'. In a March 1991 referendum held across most of the Union – the exceptions were the Baltic states, Armenia, Georgia, and Moldova – an overwhelming majority of voters, some 78 percent, supported the preservation of the USSR. Nine months later, however, the Union was dissolved by the presidents of only three of its constituent republics. (As Furman put it, 'somewhere in the Belovezha forest [in Belarus], three men got together and overnight, "over a half-litre" [bottle of vodka], decided everything.') The speed and furtiveness of this decision would have far-reaching consequences. Not only was Russian society 'not prepared for non-imperial existence and non-imperial politics'; on a more basic level, 'the collapse of the USSR was not understood as the emergence of fundamentally new relations between truly independent states.'[9]

This was why, for Furman, the CIS that emerged from the USSR's ruins was such an ambiguous construct: at once an association of free and sovereign states, and a fictive container for an imperial politics Russia had yet to relinquish – a privileged zone of influence that it termed its 'near abroad'. Yet this third avatar of the Russian empire was an extremely weak, diluted one, offering only a 'phantom unity' across what used to be the imperial space.[10] The newly independent states would inevitably diverge. For Furman, indeed, the main thing holding the CIS together was not a shared supra-national heritage or deeply held common interests, but something much narrower and altogether frailer: the desire for self-preservation of the imitation democratic regimes that ruled most of the former Soviet states. The

---

8   Furman, 'SNG kak posledniaia forma Rossiiskoi imperii,' p. 89.
9   Ibid., 90, 91, 93.
10 Ibid., 98.

similarities between ruling systems bound them to each other in a kind of authoritarian compact, as Furman saw it, with Russia at the centre of an imitation-democratic bloc. Yet these ties in themselves obstructed the development of any more genuine political or economic integration: the same logic that prevented these regimes from loosening their grip on power precluded the loss of control that such processes would entail. As a result, Furman argued, the fate of the CIS was ultimately tied to that of imitation-democratic regimes themselves – which in his view were slated for disappearance, sooner or later. In line with this, it is not coincidentally the countries that have diverged most from Russia in terms both of their internal politics and above all their geopolitical alignment that have peeled away from the CIS: Georgia withdrew in 2008, and Ukraine from 2014 onwards.

As of this writing, the war in Ukraine continues to rage, and Furman's optimism about the inevitable vanishing of Russian imperial politics may ring somewhat hollow. But analytically, he was surely right to link the fate of the imperial worldview to that of the country's political regime. As he put it, 'Russia's return to the path of recreating an authoritarian system and its return to an imperial [foreign] policy are two aspects of the same process'; these aspects are, moreover, 'functionally interconnected'.[11] The prolongation of the imitation-democratic regime for over a decade since this book was written has also involved an extension – and deepening – of Moscow's commitment to an imperial path. Conversely, the rise of an increasingly assertive nationalism within Russia itself has undoubtedly provided a solid foundation for the regime's continuation. In this altered context, it may make more sense to take Furman's analysis of Russian imperial decline less as a prediction than as a diagnosis, identifying some of the conditions that will be required for Russia to be at peace with its neighbours and with its post-imperial role. A decrease in geopolitical tensions is obviously prominent among those conditions. But if imperial politics and imitation democracy are functionally interlinked, then bringing about such a shift will also

---

11   Ibid., 100.

require a democratization from within that is accompanied by a rejection of the imperial worldview – a rethinking of Russia's place in the world, and of its purposes and possibilities at home.

Furman's metaphor of the spiral, which gave this book its original Russian title – *Dvizhenie po spirali*, 'Spiral Motion' – suggests both repetition and progression, both the recurrence of imitation-democratic regimes over time and their eventual decay and disappearance. Reading his analysis today, it may be tempting to think that its original object is no longer present – that the developments of the intervening years have produced a mutation in the imitation-democratic regime's genetic code, transforming it into a different type of system altogether. But from Furman's point of view, these mutations themselves would represent at most another coil in the same spiral, a replication of substantively the same power relations in outwardly new forms. This kind of repetition was the second of the two scenarios he laid out in the book's brief final chapter, the first being a successful transition to genuine democracy in Russia. It is perhaps difficult, in the present moment, to share Furman's certainty that this first scenario will take place – not least because the contours and substantive content of democracy will themselves surely be the object of intense struggles. But in the meantime, we would do well to absorb some of Furman's calm conviction that political systems are repeatedly vulnerable and always finite, and to take on some of the historical optimism with which he concludes his essay on Russian empire: 'compared to the distance we have already travelled, there is not so far to go at all.'[12]

26 May 2022

---

12   Furman, "SNG kak posledniaia forma Rossiiskoi imperii," p. 102.

Index

A

Abdildin, Serikbolsyn, 49n4
Ablyazov, Mukhtar, 96n56, 115
Abramovich, Roman, 78, 93
Agin-Buryat Autonomous Okrug,
    90n48
A Just Russia, 100
Akayev, Askar, 22n32, 47n1, 49n4,
    96n56, 110, 155n4
Akhedzhakova, Liya, 61
Akhmadulina, Bella, 61
Aksyonenko, Nikolai, 83, 118
Albania, 157n6
Alexander I, 77
Aliyev, Heyar, 49n4, 112n74,
    123
'All power to the Soviets,' 48, 52
Amalrik, Andrei, 26
Anderson, Perry, 165
anti-Communists, 3
antidemocratic state, 117n75
antisemitism, 24
Armenia, xviiin6, 6n5, 16–17,
    22n32, 112n74, 113, 157n6, 168

Article 104 (Constitution), 48
Asanbayev, Yerik, 49n4
Assad dynasty, 78n37
Astafyev, Viktor, 61
Ataýew, Öwezgeldi, 78–79n38
authentic separation of powers,
    82
authoritarianism, 57, 77
autonomism, 56
Azerbaijan
    conflicts within, 112–13
    coup within, xviiin6
    defining of, 6n5
    democracy within, 7n8
    economic status of, 123
    leadership regime within, 22n32,
        96n56, 112n74
    political conflicts within, 49n4
    political history within, 16–17
    succession of power within, 78,
        78n37, 78n38
    as Transcaucasian republic,
        156n6

B

Bakiyev, Kurmanbek, 113

Bakiyev regime, 155n4

Baltic States, 16, 168. *See also specific states*

Barkashov, Alexsandr, 54

Barsukov, Mikhail, 94n52

Belarus

defining of, 6n5

democracy within, 7n7

imitation democracy within, 113

integration game with, 70

leadership within, 96n56, 112n74

murders within, 103

no-alternative power within, 156

opposition within, 116

parliament dissolution within, 47n1

peaceful transition of power within, xvii–xviii

political climate of, 155n4

political conflicts within, 49n4

Belovezh Accords, 39, 40–41, 42, 112n74

Berdymukhammedov, Gurbanguly, 79n38

Berezovsky, Boris, 78, 94, 94n52, 95, 97

Beslan hostage crisis, 91

biological organism, development of, 45

Bodiul, Ivan, 145n11

Boiko, Maxim, 57–58n17

Bolsheviks/Bolshevism, 167

Bonner, Yelena, 27, 35, 52–53, 53n10

Bosnia, 157n6

Brazauskas, Algirdas, 44n63

Brezhnev, Leonid, 145n11

Burbulis, Gennady, 32

C

capitalism, 31, 31n46, 160

career filters/career elevators, 140

centralism, 145

Chávez, Hugo, 111

Chechen War, 72–73, 85

Chechnya/Chechens, 55, 56n16, 70, 89, 92, 118

Chernomyrdin, Viktor, 59, 80, 81

Chubais, Anatoly, 68, 92–93

Civic Chamber, 141n7

Clinton, Bill, 32

Cold War, 115

Color Revolution, xvii, xviiin6, 110, 114, 155n4, 163

Commonwealth of Independent States (CIS), 112, 166–67, 168

Communism, xv, xvi, 1, 2–3, 44n63

Communist Party

election results of, 63, 66, 100

opposition to, 69–70

quasi extremism of, 72

succession of power within, 77

superficial radicalism of, 71–72

Communist Party of the Russian Federation (CPRF), 3, 71, 86

Communist Party of the Soviet Union (CPSU), 39

Congress of People's Deputies, 36, 48, 48n3, 50–51

consciousness, public, changing of, 137–38

Constitution, 47–48, 62, 63–65
Constitutional Court, 46–50, 59n19, 62
corruption, 142
coups, 38–39, 112n74, xviiin6
Cranston, Alan, xviin3
Crimea, 165
crisis, final, 146–50, 151–57
Czech Republic, xv

D

Dagestan, 85
The Day of the Oprichnik, 106
Declaration of State Sovereignty of the Russian SFSR, 36
delegitimization process, 136
Delyagin, Mikhail, 75n36
demagogue-populists, 140
democracy
    challenges of, 13
    as contemporary norm, 157
    defined, xvii
    expansion of, 156
    expectations of, xvin2
    failed attempts regarding, 152, 154
    freedoms from, 153, 153n3
    liberal, 160
    locations of, xxn7
    as norm, 5–6
    public opinions regarding (Russia), 9n20
    requirements for, 12–13
    statistics regarding, 156n5
    strengths and weaknesses within, 23–41
    successful transition to, 152–55
    tool for, 11–12
    unwalkable path to, 10–14
    in the West, xxin10, 15n26, 17, 18–19n29, 31, 104, 109–10
Democratic Choice of Russia-United Democrats bloc, 63
democratic mobility model, 140
Democratic Russia, 99–100
democrats (Russia), 26–27, 34–35, 98
demshiza (democracy schizophrenia), 3–4
dictatorship, 43n62, 131n16, 153n2
Duma, 62–63, 64, 66, 80–81, 99
Dyachenko, Tatyana, 78n37

E

economic determinism, 29
economy, within Russia, 118–19
Egypt, 78n37
Elchibey, Abulfaz, xviiin6, 22n32, 112n74
elections
    corruption within, 70, 74, 75n36, 142
    early voting within, 59, 59n19
    as fateful, 134
    fraud within, 159
    legitimacy question regarding, 135–36
    post-Soviet, 66–76
    power retaining through, 127–28
    public opinion regarding, 136–37n3
    results of, 63

within Russia, 37–38, 119–20, 121
statistical declines within, 128
elite, 77, 141–42
energy, within Russia, 119
Estonia, 7n5, 14, 20, 153n2
European Union (EU), 108–9

F
Fatherland - All Russia, 86, 87, 99
fear, 121, 138–39, 141
federalism, 55n13
Federation Council, 64, 90, 91
Federation Treaty, 56
feedback mechanisms, atrophy of, 137–39
Fifth Duma, 100
final crisis, 146–50, 151–57
First Chechen War, 85
Fourth Duma, 100
freedom, public opinion regarding, 153n3
Furman, Dmitrii, 159, 160–63, 166–67

G
Gaddafi dynasty, 78n37
Gaidar, Yegor, 28, 51, 51–52n8
Gamsakhurdia, Zviad, xviiin6, 22n32, 112n74
geopolitics, 165
Georgia
colour revolution within, 110
conflicts within, 112–13
coup within, xviiin6
defining of, 6n5

imitation democracy failure within, 113
leadership regime within, 22n32, 112n74
political climate of, 155n4
political history within, 16–17, 163
referendum exception of, 168
Gessen, Keith, 160
Glinski, Dmitri, 65–66
God Forbid! (newspaper), 74
Gorbachev, Mikhail, 1–2, 23, 32n50, 50, 147
Granin, Daniil, 61
Gryzlov, Boris, 116
gubernatorial term limits, 91
Gusinsky, Vladimir, 95, 118

H
habituation to sovereignty, 114
Herzegovina, 157n6
The History of a Town, 122
Huntington, Samuel P., xvii

I
Ilyin, Ivan, 107
Ilyumzhinov, Kirsan, 92, 145n12
imitation democracies
contradictions to, 134
defined, xxii
geopolitics within, 165
growth process within, 164
process scenarios regarding, 21–22, 22n32
succession within, 78
uniqueness of, xxii–xxiii

impeachment, 64
intelligentsia elite, 30–31
In the First Person (Putin), 88–89
Isayev, Maksim, 11n21
isomorphic conflicts, 49n4
Ivan Rybkin bloc, 99, 100

J
Jews, 24, 24–25n33, 93

K
Kadyrov, Ramzan, 92, 145
Karimov, Islam, 49n4
Karyakin, Yuri, 63
Kasyanov, Mikhail, 74, 102n62, 118,
    120n1
Kazakhstan
    defining of, 6n5, 7n6
    economic status of, 123
    leadership within, 79n38, 96n56
    murders within, 103, 115–16
    Nur Otan party within, 129n15
    opposition within, 129n15
    parliament dissolution within,
        47n1
    political conflicts within, 49n4
    political history within, 17
    public opinion within, 16n28
    rioting within, 145n11
    Transition of, xv
    trials within, 115
Kazakov, Aleksandr, 51
Kazhegeldin, Akezhan, 29n44,
    96n56
KGB, x, 1, 84, 86, 102, 103, 138
Khasavyurt Accord, 89

Khasbulatov, Ruslan, 8, 8n16, 35–36,
    50, 54, 54n12
Khodorkovsky, Mikhail, 95,
    95–96n55
Khrushchev, Nikita, 77
Khudonazarov, Davlat, 28n43
Kim dynasty, 78n37
Kiriyenko, Sergei, 80–81
Komi-Permyak Autonomous
    Okrug, 90n48
Kondopoga, Russia, 139n6
Korzhakov, Alexsandr, 67, 78, 102n61
Kostikov, Vyacheslav, 60
Krasnodar Krai, 90n48
Kravchuk, Leonid, 40n61, 112n74,
    166–67
Kremlin, 39
Kuchma, Leonid, 110
Kulov, Felix, 49n4, 96n56
Kunayev, Dinmukhamed, 145n11
Kwaśniewski, Aleksander, 44n63
Kyrgyzstan/Kyrgyz Republic
    colour revolution within, 110
    coup in, xviiin6
    defining of, 6n5
    leadership within, 22n32, 96n56,
        113
    parliament dissolution within, 47n1
    political climate of, 155n4
    political conflicts within, 49n4
    political history within, 17, 163
Kyrgyz-Tajik conflict, 4

L
Landsbergis, Vytautas, 28n43
Latvia, 6n5, 14, 153n2

Lebed, Alexsandr, 74, 75
legitimacy, importance of, 135–36
Leningrad, 30–31
liberal democracy, Transition to,
    160
Liberal Democratic Party of Russia
    (LDPR), 63, 66, 100
Libya, 78n37
Lithuania, 6–7n5, 14, 44n63,
    152–53n2
Litvinenko, Alexander, 116
loyalty, 91–92, 143–46
Lucinschi, Petru, 47n1
Lukashenko, Alexander
    conflict of, 49n4
    dictatorship actions of, 96n56,
        112n74, 114
    election of, xviii
    parliament and, 47n1
    Yeltsin and, 70
Luzhkov, Yuri, 87, 145n12

M
Macedonia, 157n6
Maidan protests, 165
Major, John, 62
managed democracies, xxii
market mythology, 28–29
market reforms, 51, 98
market romanticism, 28–29, 50, 52
Marx, Karl, 29
Marxist-Leninist reformation, 2n1
Maslyukov, Yuri, 81
mass media
    control of, 60, 129
    distortion by, 137

economic crisis response within,
    137n4
    submission of, 97
materialism, 19–20, 29
Medvedev, Dmitry
    characteristics of, 131
    election of, 119, 120
    leadership of, 129, 132–33, 145n12
    quote of, 9n19, 132, 132n19
    viewpoint of, 9
Milošević regime, 111
Mirsaidov, Shukrullo, 49n4
Mitchell, George, 61
Moldavian Communist Party,
    145n11
Moldova
    conflicts within, 113
    defining of, 6n5
    imitation democracy failure
        within, 113
    leadership regime within, 22n32,
        112n74
    parliament within, 47n1
    peaceful transition of power
        within, xvii
    referendum exception of, 168
    as Transcaucasian republic, 157n6
Montenegro, 157n6
Moscow, intelligentsia within, 30–31
Mubarak, Hosni, xxin10
Mubarak dynasty, 78n37
murders, 103

N
Nagorno-Karabakh war, 4
Nashi, 149, 155

nationalism, 25–26, 167, 168
Nazarbayev, Nursultan, 47n1, 49n4,
    79n38, 123, 129n15
NDR (Our Home is Russia), 99
New Azerbaijan Party, 115
Nicaragua, 78n37
Nicholas II, 66
Nikolai I, 77
1917 Transition (Russia), 18
1991 revolution within, 32n47,
    37–38n57, 41
no-alternative power, 58, 65, 88, 92,
    143–44, 156–57
nomenklatura elite, 31–32, 55, 57–58
North Atlantic Treaty Organization
    (NATO), 108–9, 166
North Korea, 78n37
Novaya Gazeta, 129
NTV, 97
Nurkadilov, Zamanbek, 115–16
Nur Otan (Kazakhstan), 115,
    129n15

O
Okudzhava, Bulat, 61
oligarchs, 92–97
OMON (Special Purpose Mobile
    Unit), 138–39, 138–39n5
Orange Revolution, xvii, 163
ORT, 97
Ortega, Daniel, 111
Orthodox Christianity, 106
OSCE Ministerial Council, 62
Ossetian-Ingush conflict, 4
Ostrovsky, Alexsandr, 69n30
Our Home is Russia (NDR), 99

P
Pamyat, 24
parliament/parliamentary party
    characteristics of, 53–54
    control over, 98–101
    dissolving of, 47n1, 59, 64
    international climate and, 58
    presidential conflict and, 46–50
    United Russia and, 100–101
Paul I, 77
peasantry, 153
People's Democratic Party of
    Tajikistan, 115
Peter I, 17, 66
Poland, xv, 44n63
Politburo, 77, 78
political mobility, 141, 141n7
political stabilization of society,
    123–24
political system
    'All power to the Soviets,' 48, 52
    characteristics of, 63–66
    Constitutional Court *versus*
        president within, 46–50
    ideological quests within, 104–8
    ideological traditions within, 48
    of Kazakhstan, 49n4
    mass media submission within,
        97
    1993 crisis of, 57–66
    oligarchs submission within,
        92–97
    post-Soviet elections within,
        66–76
    of post-Soviet Russia, 104–8
    privatization and, 50–51

public opinion regarding, 58n18
special operations within, 101–4
special services within, 101–4
struggle for power within, 48
subordinating regional power
within, 88–92
succession crisis of, 76–88
suppressing separatism within,
88–92
threat elimination within, 45
United Russia creation within,
98–101
Politkovskaya, Anna, 103, 116
Popular Front Party, xviiin6
post-imperial syndrome, 168
post-Soviet states, 161–62, 163.
See also specific countries
power
atrophying of feedback and,
137–39
control over society through,
126–29
destabilization and, 145
fears of, 138–39
illusion within, 138
political destabilization of, 107
Presidential Council for Civil
Society and Human Rights,
141n7
Presidential Security Service, 102–3
presidents
authority expansion of, 63–64
conflicts of, 46–50, 49–50n4
Constitutional Court conflict
and, 46–50
post-Soviet elections of, 66–76

succession power of, 78
war of position of, 59. *See also
specific people*
Primakov, Yevgeny, 81–83, 82n41,
87
prime minister, role of, 80. *See also
specific people*
privatization, 50–51, 57–58n17, 92
propaganda, 74, 121, 121n2
property ownership, 57–58, 96
protests
election, 63
within Kazakhstan, 145n11
within Kondopoga, Russia, 139n6
Maidan, 165
parliamentary party and, 58
rise of, 51
within Vladivostok, Russia,
139n6
White House siege as, 60–62
public consciousness, changing of,
137–38
Putin, Vladimir
bureaucratic social mobility
under, 141
characteristics of, 84–85, 125
control of, 96–97
decree from, 87
election of, 87–88, 119, 121
elites and, 143
fear and, 121, 130–33
In the First Person, 88–89
golden age of, 118, 163
influence of, 160
lack of plans by, 144
leadership of, 9, 161

legislation by, 91
loyalty of, 84
motivations of, 144
as national leader, 107
popularity of, 122–23, 124–26,
   135
presidential abandonment of,
   119–20, 130–33
as prime minister, 83–86
public image of, 86
public opinion regarding,
   134–35n1
quote of, 9n18, 14, 27n39, 86–87,
   89, 95n54, 103, xxin10
return to power by, 164
second term of, 120–26
as successor, 125
support for, 86
viewpoint of, 12

Q
quasi-one-party system, 98–101,
   101n58
Quliyev, Rasul, 49n4, 96n56

R
Rahmon, Emomali, 7n10, 112n74
Rakhimov, Murtaza, 92
Rashidov, Sharof, 145n11
Rasputin, Valentin, 26n36
reality, distortion of, 138–39
Reddaway, Peter, 65–66
regional authorities, Kremlin's
   attitude toward, 144–45
regional chiefs, election process of,
   64–65

regional power, subordinating,
   88–92
Republic of Adygea, 90n48
revolution, requirements for, 149.
   See also specific revolutions
Rodina, 100
Romanov dynasty, 167
'roof,' defined, 93
Rose Revolution, xviiin6, 163
Russia
   antisemitism within, 24
   avatars of, 167–68
   as centre of gravity, 111
   as Christian dictatorship, 107
   comparison to, 161–62
   confrontations of, 108–17
   cultural development within, 15
   cultural orientation of, 14
   defining of, 6n5
   democracy weakness within, 24
   democracy within, 8, 17
   democratic deputies within,
      30n45
   democrats within, 26–27, 34–35,
      98
   economic status of, 118–19,
      122–23
   election within, 37–38, 119–20,
      121
   energy supply within, 119
   ethnic bloodshed within, 4–5
   ethnic concerns within, 24
   European orientation of, 14–15,
      14–15n25
   federal okrugs within, 90
   ideals regarding, 151–52n1

intelligentsia elite within, 30–31
limitations within, 164
living standards within, 37–38n57
market mythology within, 28–29
materialism within, 19–20, 29
media control within, 129
nationalism within, 25–26, 167,
    168
1917 Transition of, 18
1991 revolution within, 32n47,
    37–38n57, 41
no-alternative ideal within,
    143–44
nomenklatura elite within, 31–32
political history within, 16, 17–18, 21
political system development
    within, xix–xx, xviii
post-imperial syndrome of, 168
post-Soviet system within, 116
power control within, 126–29
preventive dread within, 28
psychology within, 122
public opinion within, 9n20, 18,
    18–19n29, 36–37, 52n8, 58n18,
    109n71, 124n8, 124n9, 126n12,
    134–35n1, 136–37n3, 136n2
regional authorities attitude
    within, 144–45
repression within, 164
rise of, 108–17
scandals within, 115
society atomization within, 20–21
solidarity of, 111
Time of Troubles within, 17–18
Transition hypotheticals within,
    21

Transition within, xv, 14–22
2020 constitutional amendment
    within, 164–65
unified culture within, 23
United, 98–101
upheavals within, 159
Western neglect of, 109–10
Russia Day, 36
Russian Central Bank, 81
Russian National Unity movement,
    54
Russian Soviet Federative Socialist
    Republic (RSFSR), 35,
    54–55n13
Russia's Choice, 62–63
Russo-Georgian War, 166
Rutskoy, Aleksandr, 8, 37, 50, 54

S
Saakashvili, Mikheil, 22n32
Sakharov, Andrei, 48n3, 56
Salih, Muhammad, 28n43
Saltykov-Shchedrin, Mikhail, 122
Sarsenbayev, Altynbek, 115
scientific socialism, 111
Second Chechen War, 85, 89
security services, 110
self-determination, 107
semibankirshchina, 94
separatism, 56, 88–92
Seven Boyars, 94
Shaimiev, Mintimer, 92, 145n12
Sheinis, Viktor, 35
Shevardnadze, Eduard, 110
Silayev, Ivan, 36
Skuratov, Yuri, 84

Sobchak, Anatoly, 84
socialism, xvi
social mobility, 139–43
Solovei, Tatyana, 3, 26n36
Solovei, Valery, 3, 26n36
Somoza dynasty, 78n37
Sorokin, Vladimir, 106
sovereign democracy, xxi–xxii, 107
Soviet system, characteristics of, 116
Soviet Union. *See* Union of Soviet
    Socialist Republics (USSR)
special operations, 101–4
Special Purpose Mobile Unit
    (OMON), 138–39, 138–39n5
special services, 101–4
spiral, metaphor of, 169
SPS (Union of Right Forces), 86
stability, ideology of, 105
stability-stagnation, 142
Stalin, Joseph, 125n11
State Committee on the State of
    Emergency, 38–39
State Duma, 64
State Emergency Committee, 50
state-monopoly capital, 96
Stepashin, Sergei, 83
Stolypin, Pyotr, 17
strata, traditionalist *versus* new, 153
succession, 76–88
Supreme Soviet, 50
Surkov, Vladislav, 110
Syria, 78n37

T
Tajikistan, xviiin6, 6n5, 7n10,
    112n74, 115

Tatar-Mongol conquest, 16
Tatarsian, 56n16
technology, opportunities regarding,
    132n20
television, control of, 97. *See also*
    mass media
Ter-Petrosyan, Levon, 22n32,
    112n74
Third Duma, 99, 100
threats, elimination of, 45
Time of Troubles (Russia), 17–18, 61,
    94
totalitarianism, 1, 54n13
Transcaucasian republics, 156–57n6
Transfer of power, 77, 78
Transformation, 5–10, 91, 104–5
Transition
    to capitalism, 160
    consequences of, 41–44
    to dictatorship, 43n62
    difficulties within, xvi
    examples of, xix
    from imitation democracy to
        actual democracy, 147–49
    to liberal democracy, 160
    models of, 5
    necessity of, 156
    overview of, xv–xvi
    paradox within, 11–12
    political destabilization of, 107
    reform powers within, 50
    within Russia, 14–22
Tretyakov, Vitaly, 85
Tulip Revolution, xviiin6, 155n4,
    163
Turkey, 15n26, 157n6

Türkmenbaşy Saparmurat Niyazov, 12
Turkmenistan, xviin3, 6n5, 7–8, 78,
   78–79n38
The Twelve Chairs, 32, 32n48
2020 constitutional amendment,
   164–65

U
Udugov, Movladi, 97
Ukraine
   colour revolution within, 110
   defining of, 6n5
   imitation democracy failure
     within, 113
   invasion of, 159, 165
   Kuchma within, 112n74
   party structures within, 20n31
   peaceful transition of power
     within, xvii–xviii
   political history within, 16, 163
   public opinion within, 36
Union of Right Forces (SPS), 86
United Russia (ER), 98–101, 115
United Socialist Soviet Republic
   (USSR)
   collapse of, 168
   development of, 46
   dismantling of, 38, 39–40
   fall of, 1, 111
   federative character of, 4
   as greater Russia, 25n34
   liquidation effects within, 41–44
   NATO and, 108
   political function of, xix
   power struggle within, 49
   Russian secession from, 26n36

   as socialist, xxii
   Soviet missiles within, 1
   symbolism of, 106
   Transformation path of, 5–10
   Transition of, xix
   violence within, 4
Unity movement, 86, 99
Ust-Orda Buryat Autonomous
   Okrug, 90n48
Uzbek Communist Party, 145n11
Uzbekistan, 6n5, 49n4, 129n15

V
Vasily IV, 94
vassal principalities, 55n13
Venezuela, 111
Vishnevsky, Boris, 69–70
Vladivostok, Russia, 139n6

W
West
   cultural orientation toward,
     14–15
   democratic model of, xxin10,
     15n26, 17, 18–19n29, 31, 104,
     109–10
   emigration to, 24
   neglect of Russia by, 109–10
   Russian confrontations/tensions
     with, 108–17, 165
   Russian dependence on, 43
White House, 60–62

Y
Yabloko, 86
Yakovlev, Aleksandr, 3

Yanukovych, 165
Yavlinsky, Grigory, 72n32, 73n33,
   74, 87
Yeltsin, Boris
   accusations to, 54
   authoritarianism attempt by, 57
   bureaucratic social mobility
      under, 141
   campaign of, 73–74
   characteristics of, 85, 124
   conflicts of, 33n51, 34, 50
   decree powers of, 51
   democrats and, 33–34
   dictatorship and, 43n62
   election of, 34–35, 37–38, 59,
      66–68, 70–76, 119, 134
   golden cage of, 118
   ideology of, 32–33
   illness of, 68–69, 79
   influence of, 160
   leadership of, 9, 22, 42, 52n8, 70,
      89–90, 99, 125, 161, 168
   lies of, 68–69n30
   oligarchs under, 94
   opposition to, 71–72
   popularity of, 73, 122
   power surrender of, 43
   pressures to, 53
   quote of, 12, 27, 33n50, 33n51, 35,
      37n57, 39, 40, 40n60, 50,
      53–54n11, 56, 56n15, 60, 67, 81,
      83, 85, 86, 95, 102n62, 108
   resignation of, 86
   special services and, 102–3
   succession and, 79–83
   support for, xvii, 57, 58, 60, 61–62,
      73, 97
   as tsar, 66
   unpopularity of, 68
Yugoslavia, 4
Yukos, 95–96

Z
Zhakiyanov, Galymzhan, 96n56,
   115
Zhirinovskey, Vladimir, 8n13, 63,
   71, 72, 75, 87
Zhirinovsky bloc, 86
Zyuganov, Gennady, 8–9n17, 66–67,
   74, 75, 75n36, 87, 120